Advance Praise for
In the Beginning Was the Spirit

"Long recognized worldwide for his innovative and daring insights on the connections between Christian theology and other humanistic disciplines, O'Murchu displays once again his creative imagination and breathtaking ability to range over disparate academic fields to elaborate an innovative pneumatology. He helps us understand how the Holy Spirit dwells in the heart of the whole human history. O'Murchu's work will inspire and sustain the spiritual journey of people in all walks of life and in all parts of the globe." — **Peter Phan**

Peter Phan holds the Ignacio Ellacuría Chair of Catholic Social Thought at Georgetown University. He is author of Christianity with an Asian Face *and* Being Religious Interreligiously.

"*In the Beginning Was the Spirit* is an expansive and imaginative vision of a spirit-filled world, one that will challenge Christians to reflect on the possibility of the presence and activity of the Holy Spirit outside the boundaries of the church while simultaneously inviting non-Christians to consider how the cosmic spirit might also be uniquely related to Jesus of Nazareth." — **Amos Yong**

Amos Yong is Professor of Theology at Regent University School of Theology in Virginia Beach, Virginia, and author of The Spirit Poured Out on All Flesh *and* The Spirit of Creation.

"In this fascinating and wide-ranging exploration of the theme of 'the Great Spirit' in science, religion and spirituality, O'Murchu is not afraid to ask challenging questions to theology about its narrow treatment of the Holy Spirit. His open-minded approach suggests new avenues of enquiry which will enrich reflection on the power behind the universe." — **Kirsteen Kim**

Kirsteen Kim is Professor of Theology and World Christianity at Leeds Trinity University College, Leeds, and author of The Holy Spirit in the World *and* Joining In with the Spirit.

"Drawing on rich resources and surveying the Spirit from around the globe, O'Murchu presents a creative understanding of the Spirit and provides new insight about the Spirit's infinite dimension. As new ways of imagining the Spirit are scrutinized, it is evident that this book becomes a daring, inspiring, innovative, and challenging book for our time." — **Grace Ji-Sun Kim**

Grace Ji-Sun Kim is Associate Professor of Doctrinal Theology at the Moravian Theological Seminary in Bethlehem, Pennsylvania, and author of The Holy Spirit, Chi, and the Other.

"A remarkable achievement! Beautifully written with brio, passion, and analytic precision, this book focuses on the work of the Spirit that is refreshingly interdisciplinary, ecumenical, and global in scope. Sensitive to the interplay between the Holy Spirit of Christian witness and the Great Spirit of the world's religions, and carefully nuanced about the prospects for dialogue between postmodern cosmologies in science and time-honored creation stories, *In the Beginning Was the Spirit* is a magisterial proposal for a new appreciation of the power of the Spirit to renew all life on this beautiful and fragile planet. Very highly recommended!" — **Marc Wallace**

Marc Wallace is Associate Professor in the Department of Religion at Swarthmore College, Pennsylvania, and author of Finding God in the Singing River: Christianity, Spirit, Nature.

"For the past decade Diarmuid O'Murchu has been a daring explorer of our dynamic, interconnected and evolving universe. Here, he examines the Spirit as life-giving energy that transcends the boundaries of religious doctrine and undergirds the creativity of the cosmos itself. This book is a bold and innovative look at the role of the Spirit in creation. Intelligent, vibrant and full of insight, O'Murchu probes the cosmic depths of primal religions and sees the rich life of the Spirit at the heart of the universe. For those who want to expand their faith in an evolutionary universe, O'Murchu's book is dazzling and illuminative." — **Ilia Delio**

Ilia Delio, OSF, is Senior Research Fellow at Woodstock Theological Center, Georgetown University, and author of Christ in Evolution *and* The Emergent Christ: Exploring the Meaning of Catholic in an Evolutionary Universe.

"*In the Beginning Was the Spirit* complements well Diarmuid O'Murchu's earlier works *Quantum Theology* and *Evolutionary Faith*. This book not only stretches the horizons of Christian pneumatology by providing a wide-ranging treatment of twentieth century scientists' theories on cosmic processes, but it also surveys many diverse ways in which the religions of the world—from the indigenous American tribes to the peoples of Asia— point in differing ways to the 'Great Spirit' as a life-force that animates and energizes an evolving creation. Each chapter is punctuated by provocative questions, making this a book that invites both personal reflection and discussion with one's fellow spiritual travelers." — **Anne Clifford**

Anne Clifford, Ph.D., holds the Monsignor James Supple Chair of Catholic Studies at Iowa State University. She is author of Introducing Feminist Theology: A Liberation Perspective.

In the Beginning
Was the Spirit

In the Beginning
Was the Spirit

Science, Religion, and Indigenous Spirituality

Diarmuid O'Murchu, MSC

ORBIS BOOKS
Maryknoll, New York 10545

Founded in 1970, Orbis Books endeavors to publish works that enlighten the mind, nourish the spirit, and challenge the conscience. The publishing arm of the Maryknoll Fathers and Brothers, Orbis seeks to explore the global dimensions of the Christian faith and mission, to invite dialogue with diverse cultures and religious traditions, and to serve the cause of reconciliation and peace. The books published reflect the views of their authors and do not represent the official position of the Maryknoll Society. To learn more about Maryknoll and Orbis Books, please visit our website at http://www.maryknollsociety.org.

Library of Congress Cataloging-in-Publication Data

O'Murchu, Diarmuid.
  In the beginning was the Spirit : science, religion, and indigenous spirituality / Diarmuid O'Murchu.
      p. cm.
  Includes bibliographical references (p.   ) and index.
  ISBN 978-1-57075-995-6 (pbk.); ISBN 978-1-60833-229-8 (ebook)
  1. God.   2. Indigenous peoples—Religion.   3. Spirituality.
4. Religion and science.   5. Holy Spirit.   I. Title.
  BL473.O34 2012
  231'.3—dc23
                                                    2012007388

Contents

Acknowledgments ix

Introduction 1

Chapter 1   Method in My Madness   3
Trust Experience / 5
Multidisciplinary Strategy / 8
The Spirit That Blows . . . / 10
Creation as Primary Revelation / 12

Chapter 2   In the Beginning . . .   17
The Bang That Radiated / 18
Religious Origins / 22
Genesis Revisited / 23
Origins Fascinate / 27
The Inspired Mind / 28
The Enlivening Spirit / 29

Chapter 3   Out of the Vacuum   31
The Energetic Vacuum / 32
Vibrational Strings / 35
Meaning from Within / 37

Chapter 4   Energizing the Energy   43
Scientific Insight / 45
The Capacity for Self-Organization / 48
Is There a Theological Raison d'Être? / 50
The Supernatural in Creation / 57
Gifts of the Spirit / 60

Chapter 5   And There Was Life   63
Origin of Life / 65
Life in Action / 68

Life as System / 70
Life as a Cosmic Process / 71
The Spirit of Life / 72

Chapter 6   The Relational Web   75
              The Entangled Universe / 76
              Vibrational Relationships / 78
              Theological Implications / 80
              At the Nexus of Relating / 81
              The Relational Spirit / 84

Chapter 7   The Great Spirit: Aboriginal Wisdom   85
              Beyond Religion / 86
              Native American Religions / 87
              Australian Aborigines / 93
              Native American Spirituality / 96

Chapter 8   The Spirit of Africa   99
              Spirit: Ancient and New / 100
              African Animism / 103
              African Spirits / 105
              A Complex Landscape / 113
              *Is There a Great Spirit in
                 African Spirituality?* / 116

Chapter 9   The Asian Pantheon   119
              The Great Religions of Asia / 121
              Ancient Chinese Beliefs / 126
              Indigenous Religions of Asia / 130
              Shamanism and the Great Spirit / 133
              The Subverted Spirit / 135

Chapter 10   The Great Spirit in Christianity   137
              Upgrading the Holy Spirit / 138
              Trinity as an Archetypal Statement / 140
              Enter the Church / 141
              The Orthodox Wisdom / 143
              Spirit Christology / 144
              Wisdom from the East / 147

Re-visioning the Creator / 149
And What about Jesus? / 152
The Trinity Seen Anew / 153

Chapter 11   The Erotic Spirit in Creation   155
The Erotic Spirit / 157
Spirit of the Wild / 159
Sophia's Erotic Creation / 161
The Spirit of Nonduality / 163
The Befriending Spirit / 166
Invoking the Paraclete / 167

Chapter 12   A New Pentecost?   171
Historical Background / 172
True to Christian Origins / 174
Key Beliefs Today / 175
Impact on Conventional Churches / 177
Revivalist in What Sense? / 179

Chapter 13   Personal Obstruction   183
Defined by the Web of Life / 184
Innately Relational / 185
Spirit and Person / 186
Enter the Transpersonal / 188
The Transpersonal Spirit / 192

Chapter 14   The Spirit That Blows   195
Horizons of Greater Transparency / 196
*First Horizon: The Indigenous Notion
   of the Great Spirit* / 197
Second Horizon: The Spirit in Creation / 198
Third Horizon: The Spirit in Personhood / 199
Fourth Horizon: The Spirit in Religion / 200
*Fifth Horizon: From Third to First
   in the Trinity* / 200
*Sixth Horizon: Even Jesus Is Empowered
   by the Spirit* / 201
Seventh Horizon: Sacramental Empowerment / 202
Eighth Horizon: The Spirit That Lures / 203

Holy Restlessness / 204
The Final Word / 206

Appendix 1 Spiritualism and the Great Spirit							207

Appendix 2   Does St. Paul Have Anything to
             Offer on the Great Spirit?							209

Appendix 3 Carl Jung and the Holy Spirit							211

Notes														213

Bibliography												223

Index														233

Acknowledgments

MANY OF THE PEOPLE who have inspired this book belong to the Spirit world. In the 1990s I was first introduced to indigenous spirituality in Australia when working with different congregations of Sisters. I have had many conversations with Australian aborigines, and experienced a number of their sacred earth-based rituals. In 2001 the Marist Brothers introduced me to the Maori people of New Zealand and their wonderful resource center in Rotorua. Meanwhile, thanks particularly to the United Church of Canada, I encountered various first-nations peoples throughout Canada, and frequently was the beneficiary of indigenous welcome and hospitality.

Many of these encounters happened long before I decided to write this book. Sadly I do not recall specific names or groups that I would like to thank in a more personal way, but I wish to record my deep gratitude to all the inspiration and wisdom I received. Brief though those encounters were, they left an indelible impression on my psyche, and the Great Spirit kept pursuing me until I eventually committed pen to paper and gave birth to this book.

I have consulted with several people who have had direct contact with the indigenous cultures I describe in these pages, and specifically I am grateful to Seon Keun Ho (Korea), Robert Kaggwa (Uganda), Wellington Mutimurefu (Zimbabwe), and Sue Kidwell (United States) for checking my resources. I am deeply indebted to the following theologians who read the manuscript and offered advice and endorsements: Ilia Delio, Grace Ji-Sun Kim, Kirsteen Kim, Peter Phan, Marc Wallace, and Amos Yong.

Michael Leach of Orbis Books excelled once more in support and invaluable advice, while Bob Land graced me with his sharp eye for editorial detail. Last, my provincial, Joe McGee, MSC, graciously blessed the endeavor with his support and approval.

In the power of the Spirit I have been inspired by all those named above, and by several people whose names I cannot recall. To each and to all I am immensely grateful.

Introduction

For the Spirit reaches the depths of everything, even the depths of God.

— ST. PAUL (1 COR. 2:10)

The pressure of the Spirit from within is a universal phenomenon.

— JUDY CANNATO

ONE OF THE FIRST books I read about the Holy Spirit was John V. Taylor's *The Go-Between God* (1972). It left me with an indelible impression, but one that took several years to mature into the kind of adult faith underpinning the present work. It also left me with some disturbing dislocating feelings—not sure what I believed anymore, yet knowing in my inner depth that I was being held in the grasp of a foundational truth that would not, and could not, be severed. Now visiting the book some thirty years after first reading it, those feelings reawaken when I read:

> To think deeply about the Holy Spirit is a bewildering, tearing exercise, for whatever he touches, he turns it inside out. He gives himself in our most interior and private experiences and then shows that what we thought was our monopoly belongs to everybody. . . . For the Spirit, what is here is everywhere, yet would be nowhere were it not here. (Taylor 1972, 179)

That invitation to expansiveness inspires the present work. It is an attempt to outgrow doctrines and beliefs that have become congealed over time and need to be reframed in the freshness and vitality of

1

a new wineskin. If anyone deserves this refreshing newness surely it must be the Holy Spirit, famed for the freedom to blow where it wills and renew not merely humans but the face of the living earth itself.

This is a book about the *Great Spirit*, an outrageous attempt at a synthesis between first-nations spirituality, physics, biology, consciousness studies, theology, world religions, and various social sciences (especially psychology, paleontology, and anthropology). It is a multidisciplinary project, seeking truth through interdisciplinary dialogue. I claim no specialization other than my experience of working as a social scientist for almost thirty years. That experience leaves me in no doubt that interdisciplinary discernment is the surest pathway to deeper truth and meaning.

Who is the book aimed at? Those who, like myself, continue to seek depth—and to seek it in such a way that we bring on board all those who live by the questions. Welcome to this egalitarian endeavor. I hope it sets your heart on fire!

Chapter 1

Method in My Madness

A knowledge of the existence of something we cannot penetrate, of the manifestation of the profoundest reason and most radiant beauty, which are only accessible to our reason in their most elementary forms—it is this knowledge and this emotion that constitute the truly religious attitude: and in this, and in this alone, I am a deeply religious man.

— ALBERT EINSTEIN

Whenever I learn a little more of the processes of creation I am amazed afresh at the unbelievable daring of the Creator Spirit who seems to gamble all the past gains on a new initiative, inciting his creatures to such crazy adventure and risk.

— JOHN V. TAYLOR

IN MY CHRISTIAN UPBRINGING I first learned that God the Father created the world. I never questioned the fact, although creating it out of nothing was a puzzle I never resolved. Next comes Jesus; He is the one who came to save us, and he accomplished it through his death and resurrection. I found that easy enough to accept; in fact, I was well into my adult years before I began to wonder why did we need saving if it was God himself who had created us in the first place. Why a special intervention by God? And why all the blood and sacrifice?

Then there was a third aspect to God: the Holy Spirit. We were told it was a "person," but it sounded like a very different kind of person from the Father and the Son. Years later, as a theology student,

I could make no sense whatsoever of the Father and Son begetting the Holy Spirit, or that the Holy Spirit somehow encapsulated the love between Father and Son. And the popular depiction of the Holy Spirit as a dove only made things more confusing. The sacrament of Confirmation was supposed to mark a special conferring of the Holy Spirit; personally I felt no different after it.

As my faith began to mature through my midlife years, I figured out that the Trinity was not a dogma to be taken literally, but a primordial truth of universal symbolic significance. It was a human attempt to describe a core value (or set of values) of the God we Christians believe in—namely, *relationality*. Whatever else the notion of God denotes, it is first and foremost about a deep capacity for relating—a central feature of the Godhead itself, and an expression of God's desire for all forms of life in the universe. As I understand it, that insight has now become widespread as a theological discernment of the mystery (and reality) of the Trinity.

Convincing though that explanation was, this entity called the Holy Spirit still felt nebulous, vague, and somewhat amorphous. Sometime in the 1990s, threads began to connect. The new physics highlighted the central role of energy as the basis of all created reality. Energy could never be destroyed; it was always transformed into other energy forms. What was that inner power energizing the energy? Scientists could not answer the question, and I readily noted that some became distinctly uncomfortable—in fact, overtly agitated—when I asked the question. A few suggested that it was not an appropriate question to ask. Why not? Nobody ever attempted a response.

Except myself! Perhaps, the Holy Spirit of God energizes the energy! The longer I rested with that intuition the more sense it began to make. Then connections began to flow like a pregnant stream of consciousness. I had always been intrigued by the spirituality of aboriginal/first-nations peoples, and I had a limited acquaintance with Australian Aborigines and the Maori people of New Zealand in 2001–2002. Their faith begins with what they call the Great Spirit. That is their original source, and from that source everything in creation emanates; the Great Spirit is the energetic wellspring of pregnant possibilities.

It feels like a long journey from the birdlike imagery of the third person of the Trinity to the awesome earthy imagery of the world's indigenous peoples. And it certainly does not feel like a culmination. To the contrary, it has a resonance of beginning all over again, aptly articulated in the oft-quoted words of the poet T. S. Eliot:

> We shall not cease from exploration
> And the end of all our exploring
> Is to return to the beginning
> And know the territory for the first time.

Trust Experience

The scientific method prioritizes reason and rationality above everything else. Only that which can be tried and tested through rigorous rational analysis is to be believed. Theology places much emphasis on objective verification also, citing revelation based on scripture as an inherited corpus of indisputable truth. Although religion and science often fiercely oppose each other, beneath the cerebral dichotomy is a strange collusion; on closer examination both bodies of knowledge hold a great deal in common. The God of theology is an all-powerful patriarchal projection; the absolute reliability of scientific fact arises from the same patriarchal source.

When one reads the life stories of the outstanding scientists, one quickly begins to see another side to their remarkable genius. They trusted their hunches, they honored intuitions, and they extensively followed their creative imaginations. Without these prerational abilities, they probably would never have been able to enrich humanity with the marvel of their discoveries.

On closer examination, it strikes me that all of humanity's great breakthroughs arise from the ability to closely observe, monitor, and discern the richness of human experience—and that, too, is my methodological starting point. I broadly follow the philosopher-theologian Bernard Lonergan, whose four-stage methodology holds a deep resonance for me: *experience–understanding–judging–deciding* (Lonergan 1957).

Experience is often confused with subjectivism, even with solipsism. It is generally assumed that experience prioritizes feeling, emotion, and intuition to the detriment of rationality and logic. The dualism between head and heart also short-circuits possibilities. For me, *experience* is a multidimensional phenomenon involving body and mind, perception and feeling, reason and emotion; that which I am experiencing at any one moment is always being processed through innumerable networks that impinge upon my experience, including planetary and cosmic influences.

Despite the diversity that constitutes experience, an underlying unity seems to hold it all together. If this were not the case, experience would overwhelm, and even destroy us. That inner sense of the unity that holds diversity as one also seems to be a central feature of the Great Spirit explored throughout the pages of this book. Despite the divergent multiplicity we observe all around us, their lies deep underneath something akin to a life force forever realigning and enforcing deeper pattern and coherence. This process seems to defy human rationality, yet intuitively we sense that something is happening. The nature and significance of that underlying reality become more transparent as we explore the notion of the Great Spirit.

Everyone seeks to interpret and understand their experience. Our Western education, with strong emphasis on rationality, has poorly equipped us for this undertaking.

Understanding involves a quality of immediacy to perception, feeling, and insight that only become comprehensive when I bring to it all my sensory experience as a body-mind-spirit organism. Sometimes it is my body, rather than my mind or spirit, that serves as the vehicle through which I am processing experience; "listen to the body" is a cherished guideline in several schools of contemporary psychotherapy.

In the evolving culture of postmodernism, our experience and understanding are both informed by complex influences unknown to earlier generations. Not merely are we saturated with the explosion of information but our sense of basic identity—our embodied selves—has become transpersonal, with planetary and cosmic awakenings unknown in previous times. I bring a great deal more resourcefulness to the task of interpreting my experience than were available in former times, which has advantages and disadvantages.

We often feel bombarded by information that many feel unable to assimilate and use constructively. The problem, it seems to me, is not in the accumulation of information—an evolutionary fact that cannot be reversed and that is likely to be to human advantage in the long term. The problem, rather, is that we are ill prepared for handling such information, and our educational systems lag behind seriously in addressing this dilemma. Consequently, the third step—*judging*—tends to be done hurriedly, haphazardly, and hastily, seeking precise outcomes of a type that belong to an earlier, mechanistic, reductionistic consciousness.

Judgment here refers to key values needed for an empowering culture. The prevailing values of the earlier modern period—power, control, rationality, objectivity, fairness (John Rawls), competitive skill, anthropocentrism—are still useful but rapidly yielding pride of place to other values such as: empowerment, trust-the-process, relationality, justice (not the same as fairness), cooperation, and planetary and cosmic well-being. Here, the human being is called to serve a larger, embracing wisdom of cosmic and planetary proportion, not the "one-dimensional man" (Marcuse 1964) begotten of patriarchal culture who flourished during industrial civilization.

And last, *deciding*: because of the relational matrix within which all postmodern experience is couched, fruitful and empowering decision-making tends to be collectively activated (communal) rather than individually based. We see evidence for this in the explosive rise of networks in the modern world (see Hawken 2007). Correspondingly, it is becoming transparent on a global scale that major institutions (governmental, cultural, and religious) are becoming increasingly ineffectual. Transnational corporations, not national governments, are the powerhouses of modern economics, trade, and commerce. Several mainline governments today function largely through cross-party working committees.

Sadly, this methodology, with its strong process approach and relational dynamic, is largely unknown to the major religions of the modern world. Religionists argue that it is central to the foundational truths, which may well be the case, but clearly it is not what people experience, nor what is portrayed in public practice. Power and control, domination and violence, outdated rites and rituals—all are quite common in the religious cultures of our time.

Multidisciplinary Strategy

The bibliography at the end of this book provides the diverse range of source materials upon which I base this volume's insights. True to my social-science background I adopt a multidisciplinary analysis, reflected in a reading list that embraces science, theology, psychology, anthropology, mythology, and the wisdom of first-nations people. My experience assures me that nothing in our modern world can be understood merely through the lens of one dominant body of wisdom. To engage our complex world in a meaningful way requires familiarity not just with one but with several, related disciplines.

The same approach holds for the notion of the Great Spirit. In the storytelling traditions of indigenous peoples, one detects a multiplicity of internal and external influences. Our Western arrogance, sometimes reinforced by monotheistic religion, tends to underestimate and misjudge the richness embedded in indigenous experience. We need a multidisciplinary wisdom to understand and appreciate, not merely the verbal narrative and its accompanying rituals, but the preverbal conviction that underlies what is being articulated. This perspective is eminently important when it comes to indigenous spirituality.

At the outset I want to be honest and transparent with readers of this book. I am not an academic, and I have never worked in an academic institution. I cherish the wisdom bequeathed by academics, despite the fact that, occasionally, they can be dismissive of people like me who do not belong to the inner realm of the academy. I am an intellectual, not an academic. I belong to a vast sector of humanity that reads, studies, reflects critically, and shares wisdom, although they do not buy into the imperial and imposed knowledge of academic hegemony. An estimated 70 percent of human beings use their intellectual acumen conscientiously, although they have no formal academic qualifications. Generally speaking they are poorly recognized (especially in the West) and often dismissed in a biased and unjust way.

As a nonacademic intellectual, my methodology is different on a number of crucial points.

- I tend to opt for holistic rather than reductionistic analysis. At all times I strive to follow the scientific principle that "the whole is greater than the sum of the parts."

- I am suspicious of reason—and the rational approach—when used to the exclusion of intuition, imagination, emotion, feeling, and spontaneous insight.
- I regard dualisms as constructs of the human mind that have long outlived their usefulness.
- I believe deeply in the evolutionary nature of life at every level. For me, the word "evolution" denotes three basic movements detectable throughout the entire spectrum of cosmic-planetary existence: *growth—change—development.*[1]
- There are no absolutes in an evolutionary universe; everything is unfolding, emerging, becoming.
- The patriarchal way of dealing with reality still holds sway in our world, seeking absolute control from the top down, and presumed to be validated in heaven. It is beginning to fragment, and millions of people—myself included—have lost faith in its meaning and effectiveness.
- The parameters set by civilization (over the past five thousand years) strike me as being not merely shortsighted and reductionistic, but grossly irresponsible in the constructs of reality to which they give birth.
- I believe the age of the universe to be at least 13.7 billion years, Planet Earth to be at least 3.8 billion years, organic life to be at least 2 billion years, and human existence on the earth to be in the region of 7 million years. These expansive dates need to become the normative basis on which we engage with everything in daily life.
- I believe human wisdom is considerably older than the normative standards set by our dominant culture. The information explosion reclaims knowledge and information from those who seek to guard it exclusively, and for the sole purpose of patriarchal power. Millions of people are now thinking and perceiving laterally rather than in linear fashion.
- I believe spirituality (belief in the empowerment of spirit influence) predates formal religions by several thousand years.
- I am a lifelong learner, reframing wisdom and insight as new circumstances demand. Dogmas—whether in science or religion—strike me as being major distractions and confusing obstacles in an evolutionary universe.

Despite the fact that millions in the modern world operate out of these guiding principles—subconsciously rather than consciously— the dominant culture still considers such people to be misled, confused, and somehow irresponsible. They tend to be labeled as *postmodern*, implying that they have betrayed the conventional norms of modernism and therefore should be regarded as deviant, heretical, and not deserving of serious attention. The fact that such people might be countercultural and emblematic of the evolving future receives scant attention in most of the formal institutions of the contemporary world.

Pause for a Moment

Throughout the book, I am inviting the reader to quiet moments—to pause and give attention to your feelings and responses to what you have just been reading. All the religions and indigenous belief systems emphasize the interiority needed to discern more clearly what the Spirit of God may be inviting us to. In stillness, and silence, we can sense the movement of the Spirit. It may leave us with feelings that inspire or disturb us, and occasionally we may need to check out with a soul friend the deeper meaning we are asked to embrace. So, for this first reflective pause, I invite the reader to revisit my description (above) of a nonacademic intellectual. To what extent does it resonate with your experience of contemporary life? What are some ingredients of your intellectual vision?

The Spirit That Blows . . .

When it comes to the subject material of the present work—the Great Spirit—all the above features influence the analysis I present. To begin with, I trust the foundational wisdom of indigenous peoples, while acknowledging that like all human perception, such wisdom, at times, can be misplaced, misinformed, and inaccurate. I embrace the core insight that the Great Spirit inhabits the whole of creation and has done so from time immemorial. I also detect a deep truth in the perception that the Great Spirit represents what theology and religions call the Divine Life, although not necessarily a personal life force.

First-nations peoples do not speculate on the nature—or even the function—of the Great Spirit. They experience the Spirit as ultra-real, and mediated primarily through the surrounding creation that they consider to be alive, every bit as much as humans are alive. The Great Spirit transcends human identity, yet embraces everything authentically human. The Great Spirit is more foundational to spiritual/religious meaning than the Christian notion of the Trinity, or indeed the theistic constructs of any of the great religions. This foundational understanding of the divine as Spirit force has been variously named—from Hegel's intriguing notion of Absolute Spirit to that of the Originating Source, predating even the Creator God, according to Robert C. Neville (1991).

In their understanding of the Great Spirit, several indigenous peoples begin not with some theoretical foundation but with the living experience that arises from their close affiliation with the earth itself, which I consider to be a crucial starting point, one that affects my methodology throughout this book. Although immanent in creation, indigenous peoples do not envisage the Great Spirit as confined to creation; for them the dualistic distinction between inner and outer makes no sense, nor are they particularly interested in the scholarly distinctions between the notions of pantheism and panentheism.

The indigenous intuition of Spirit power is captivated in these inspiring words from scientist-cum-theologian Philip Clayton (2008, 153, 248): "Spirit is set free from any metaphysical parameters and allowed to roam freely, immersing itself fully in the self-creating enterprise which is its natural birthright. . . . Spirit is the creative, artistic impulse that rises on outstretched wings to soar above the objectifying forces of law-like explanation and prediction."

Throughout this book, therefore, I work with the notion that the evolving creation is the primary given data of our experience. Creation in both its cosmic and planetary expressions evolved and flourished for billions of years before humans evolved. We are not in charge, and I do not subscribe to the anthropic principle that life in the universe prevails so that one day it would lead to the intelligent life form that humans exhibit (Barrow and Tipler 1988). Rather, I follow several insights from contemporary science indicating that creation itself is imbued with an underlying resilient wisdom that stretches and outwits human wisdom. Human intelligence in all its elements is derived from the superior intelligence of the evolving creation itself. I explore this material in the first three chapters of the book.

I also support the insight that life—however we define it—is seeded within the evolving emergent process of the cosmic-planetary story. Our human way of being alive is a derived version of a more foundational organicity. For first-nation peoples in various parts of Planet Earth, that tangible sense of aliveness is foundational evidence for the existence of the Great Spirit; they also intuit that it is the Great Spirit that energizes the aliveness and sustains its dynamic nature, although they do not speculate on how that happens.

For the Christian reader, fearful that I might be undermining belief in the conventional understanding of the Holy Spirit, I want to offer a paradoxical reassurance, aptly articulated by the theologian, Peter C. Hodgson (2004, 139): "The Spirit transcends Christ and appears in a diversity of religious figures and traditions, which also contribute to the delineation and enrichment of spirituality. Thus we cannot say exhaustively what Spirit is; Spirit is both concretely figured and open to new possibilities." The Christian notion of the Holy Spirit strikes me as being a particular metaphysical articulation of a reality far more profound and all-pervasive. Therefore, in challenging the inherited wisdom, and seeking to transcend it, my hope is that I am laying foundations for a more robust and creative pneumatology. How these insights can be incorporated into Christian theology is a task for mainline theologians to negotiate and further refine.

Creation as Primary Revelation

In the *Summa* of Thomas Aquinas (*Summa Contra Gentiles* II.2.3) we read, "The order of the universe is the ultimate and noblest perfection of things." In a popular paraphrase it reads, "If we don't understand creation correctly, we can't hope to understand God correctly." Philosophy tries, using primarily the powers of human reason, to make rational sense of the reality that surrounds us. It is a distinctively anthropocentric enterprise working with a largely unexamined assumption that human wisdom is superior to everything else in creation, often postulating that the materiality of creation is the foundational truth of the universe and that the entire cosmic process is in fact a closed system. Mainstream science supports this view, and ironically so does formal theology.

Theology differs to the degree that the superior wisdom is attributed to God and not to humans. However, God is construed in anthropocentric terms. It is assumed that the power of human rationality is foundationally the dynamic within which the divine mind works, albeit at a more sophisticated level. Consequently, theology belongs almost exclusively to a learned elite tradition developed in the West, with a central role for the God-made man (Jesus), largely ignoring the wisdom that belongs to well over 70 percent of the human race. Strangely, most people seem unable to see the glaring idolatry and religious imperialism upon which the entire endeavor is construed.

Not surprising, therefore, within the Christian tradition itself, although the existence of the Holy Spirit was doctrinally formulated at the Council of Nicaea (325 CE), the concept has been a kind of theological backwater for most of Christian history. The Spirit comes third in the Trinity, and despite all the rhetoric for the equality of the three Trinitarian persons, third effectively denotes "last" on the three-tiered hierarchical structure. Another major obstacle is the metaphysical category of *person*, which enhances what the early church wished to declare about Jesus, but which seriously undermines the generic role of the Spirit as a transpersonal cosmic life force, the foundational meaning surfacing in the indigenous belief in the Great Spirit.

Like the Australian aborigines I follow a "songline" throughout the pages of this book: "The heavens are singing the glory of God." The music of the spheres echoes divine creativity; I want to contemplate the creativity in the hope of understanding it better, so that in turn such insight can make me a better person in how I participate in that creative process. The evolving creation is a symphony forever being composed, with the Holy Spirit serving as the primary catalyst in the symphonic endeavor. I am not interested in trying to figure out who or what the Holy Spirit is; instead I want to learn how I can best collaborate with this pervasive cosmic and earthly creativity. I am striving to better understand the divine life force at work in the world, primarily through the sacredness of the created order itself.

Taking creation therefore as the primary revelation and embodiment of the Great Spirit, I adopt an approach whereby I refrain from philosophical or religious speculation about that mysterious reality we call *God* or the *Divine One*. Much of the speculation done in the name of philosophy and theology strikes me as being dangerously close to idolatry: humans playing God. As a social scientist I prefer not to speculate about God. I feel a close affiliation with the Buddhist stance: "Let God be God, and let humans work at making the world a more God-like place by getting rid of meaningless suffering." Most of the meaningless suffering seems based on a kind of ignorance regarding the foundational spiritual meaning of creation itself.

Modern science particularly helps us to comprehend the complexity, paradox,[2] and mysterious nature of the cosmos to which we belong, along with the home planet we inhabit (cf. Primack and Abrams 2006; Dowd 2009; Gribbin 2009). I draw extensively on this research, which time and again awakens for me a sense of awe, wonder, and reverence for the elegance and complexity that characterizes the creative universe. I warm to Gordon Kaufman's proposal that we think of God primarily as a force for creativity, manifested first and foremost in the living creation itself (Kaufman 2004). Creation is our primary "revelation"—the oldest, most enduring, and most reliable source for everything we know, including our intuitions into the meaning of divine life.

In the opening chapters particularly I invite the reader to embrace a kind of mystical meditation on the expansive and intricate nature of universal life as divulged through the insights of modern science. In this exploration, time and again, I detect something akin to Rudolf Otto's notion of the numinous, at once terrifying and fascinating, holding one in its grip in a way that defies all rationality. In such moments I feel connected with the Great Spirit, that which inspires amid the plethora of diversity. This experience has endured throughout my lifetime, yet it still overwhelms and enthralls me.

Like many authors I have written my opening chapter after completing the rest of the book. At the end of this endeavor, the words of T. S. Eliot echo ever more coherently: It feels like being back at the beginning and knowing the territory for the first time. It certainly feels like a new understanding of the theological concept of the Holy Spirit—with several implications for theology and spirituality, implications that I hope are further explored by the scholarly minds that have inspired me and many others on our spiritual search.

⌇

Pause for a Moment

For the majority of people the notion of spirit denotes something to do with inner personal life, grounded in religious meaning, with transparency to a personal God perceived to be the source of that meaning. That is the starting point most readers bring to this book. The notion of the Great Spirit involves a great deal more. The personal expands into the transpersonal; religion is transformed by the primordial impact of what we now call spirituality, and most daunting of all—thanks to recent discoveries in the sciences—we detect divine mystery deeply embedded not merely in some heavenly realm beyond but right here within the material creation itself. Even in our postmodern times, these are still huge shifts of understanding for many people. Perhaps the biggest transition is in our new ways of understanding the creation that surrounds us, which indigenous people claim to be their primary source of connection with the Great Spirit. My exploration, therefore, begins with creation, adopting several groundbreaking insights from modern science and cosmology.

⌇

Chapter 2

In the Beginning . . .

The Spirit is all about flow.

— CATHERINE KELLER

There can be no recovery of vital belief in the Holy Spirit and, consequently, no true theology of mission, unless we are prepared to have dealings with the great deeps of an elemental energy.

— JOHN V. TAYLOR

OF ALL THE CREATURES who inhabit Planet Earth, humans seem unique in their ability to think about origins, how things begin and finish, how everything came into being, and especially the origin of the universe itself.

We begin with the question: What is the source of this curiosity? The intelligence to ask the question comes from the human brain—we assume! That would have been the standard scientific response for much of the twentieth century, until scholars began to distinguishing between brain and mind (see Clarke 2010). Then human intelligibility took something of a quantum leap.

The brain is still quite an enigma for human researchers. It certainly cannot be reduced to a human kind of computer, although many of its better-understood functions are computational and functional in nature. Brain activity is also involved in emotions, feelings, intuitions, and imagination, but precisely in what manner is far from clear.

Then we come to the mind. At one time we thought *brain* and *mind* were one and the same thing, but no longer. Mind cannot be confined to brain activity; it is bigger and more expansive. It cannot be identified with any one set of bodily processes. Mind exists within the human body, but also beyond it. These concepts represent virgin territory into which science has scarcely yet ventured.

So what is motivating the questing, seeking self: brain or mind? An intelligent guess suggests both, and I run with that insight in the reflections that follow.

The Bang That Radiated

According to the prevailing scientific wisdom, our universe came into being about 13.7 billion years ago. Before that time nothing existed; total nihilism prevailed. There was a sudden explosion, some describe it as a massive fireball, in which all matter, energy, space, and time came into being. For the first few moments after the big bang, the universe resembled a blisteringly hot fireball akin to a nuclear explosion.

But whereas the heat and light of a nuclear fireball dissipate into the atmosphere hours or days after the explosion, this was not true of the original fireball. It had nowhere to go other than the nascent universe itself; the "afterglow" of the big bang was bottled up in the universe forever. The afterglow came to be known as cosmic microwave background radiation, discovered in 1965 by Arno Penzias and Robert Wilson, two young astronomers working at Bell Labs at Holmdel, New Jersey. The cosmic background radiation is the oldest "fossil" in creation, and the most compelling evidence for the big bang theory.

Describing the radiation, Marcus Chown (2006, 147) writes,

> The cosmic background radiation is actually one of the most striking features of the universe. When we look up at the night sky, its most obvious feature is that it is mostly black. However, if our eyes were sensitive to microwave light rather than visible light, we would see something very different. Far from being black, the entire sky, from horizon to horizon, would be white, like the inside of a light bulb. Even billions of years after the event, all of space is still glowing softly with relic heat of the Big Bang fireball.

All of which gives substance to Michael Dowd's suggestion that instead of "big bang," we should rename the moment as "the great radiance" (Dowd 2009).

Current theories state that after one-thousandth of a second of the so-called big bang, the universe had cooled sufficiently (to 100 billion degrees centigrade) for elementary particles—electrons, protons, and neutrons—to form. Three minutes later, when the temperature had dropped to 900 million degrees centigrade, neutrons and protons combined to form stable atomic nuclei, initially those of hydrogen and helium. The cosmic dance of interrelating and procreating was well under way.

The origin of the universe is still, however, a heated topic of debate and controversy, with the theory of inflation disrupting the logical neatness of the big bang. "Inflation" became a cosmological buzzword in the 1990s (more in Davies 2006; Gribbin 2009). Something like the notion of inflation was needed to resolve two key problems arising from the standard big bang explanation. The first of these is the *horizon problem*—the puzzle that the universe looks the same on opposite sides of the sky (opposite horizons), even though there has not been time since the big bang for light (or anything else) to travel across the universe and back. So how do the opposite horizons "know" how to keep in step with each other? The second puzzle is called the *flatness problem*. This is the puzzle that the space-time of the universe is very nearly flat, which means that the universe sits just on the dividing line between eternal expansion and eventual recollapse.

Inflation is a general term for models of the very early universe for which we postulate a sudden bursting forth of energy popularly known as the big bang, followed a split second later by a short period—10^{-36} of one second—of extremely rapid, accelerating expansion. Symbolically the expansion can be envisaged as increasing from a region far smaller than a proton to something the size of a grapefruit (or even bigger). After the inflation period, the widely accelerating expansion gave way to the slow and steady development that followed for billions of years thereafter. This effectively means that it was the influence of the inflation period that effected what transpires thereafter rather than the big bang itself.[3]

So we have the widely known big bang theory, and the lesser-known (but no less important) theory of cosmic inflation. Primack and Abrams (2006, 190ff.) highlight a third approach to the scientific understanding of cosmic origins, namely the notion of *eternal inflation*. They postulate that inflation is a state of existence that is eternal. Once it starts it goes on forever, although it does stop in tiny pockets which become big bangs that evolve into universes, one of which is our own.

Other bubbles are constantly forming in eternal inflation. The big bang helps to explain the universe we inhabit, but it may well be only one of several universes simultaneously coexisting. Currently, the theory of a *multiverse* holds that there is at least as much scientific credibility as the notion of just a single universe (more in Gribbin 2009). That there is more than one universe, and that universes are continuously being created, is widely acknowledged as mainstream science, although precise proof for any of these theories is still to be obtained.

Throughout the twentieth century, the big bang theory posed a great challenge to all formal religions by stretching the beginning and duration of the known universe into time spans and spatial dimensions that religion could scarcely comprehend. The big bang theory also quickly undermined the simplistic notion of an engineer-type God instigating and directing the whole process from some distant heaven. Increasingly, the cosmos itself seemed a complex self-directing enterprise, propelled by an internal dynamism, that seems to defy all explanations of external intervention (and manipulation)—even by a divine creator.

In this league of new insights and discoveries, I offer a final example, that of the pioneering work of the British physicist Neil Turok, postulating an *infinite open universe*, developed more recently into the Hawking-Turok Instanton Theory (Steinhardt and Turok 2007). That we inhabit a multiverse without beginning or end is one visionary horizon stretching our imaginations to limits we scarcely can fathom or endure, but to be told that the whole thing is of infinite duration (cf. Deutsch 2011) is a challenge we cannot hope to handle without deep mystical insight.

More than anything else the new time horizons suggest that we are dealing with something more than mere rational science. That earth-shattering events can unfold in minuscule time scales is now standard science, but also an aperture to deeper wisdom that religion has scarcely recognized. In the 1930s, scientists began to examine the conditions that prevailed when the universe was three minutes old. In the 1950s, accelerators enabled us to detect energies that operated when the universe was a few hundred-millionths of a second old. By the end of the 1980s, particle physicists were probing energies that existed when the universe was about one-tenth of a thousand-billionth of a second old (10^{-13}). And as we enter the twenty-first century, aided by the new Large Hadron Collider (LHC) at the European Organization for Nuclear Research (CERN), near Geneva, we expect to be able to verify conditions when the universe was only $5x10^{-15}$ of a second old. All of this activity must surely confirm that we have transcended the rational mind in all its inherited dimensions. We are beyond the human as conventionally understood. I don't wish to suggest that we are in the realm of the divine, but we are certainly into esoteric and mystical spheres, probably engaging subliminal and archetypal truths the rational mind on its own is never likely to comprehend.

At the other end of the spectrum, we engage with billions of galaxies, forming over billions of years, in a multiverse of staggering complexity and profundity. Devoid of awe and wonder, we cannot hope to make sense of it all, never mind negotiate our way within it with a sense of empowering engagement. Imagination and the capacity for discernment become our primary survival skills.[4]

Pause for a Moment

Why do science and cosmology awaken religious sentiment for so many people in our time? Might science be a surer way to divine truth than religion, as the physicist Paul Davies intimated several years ago? Do you experience something of this spiritual awakening when engaging with scientific insight and wisdom? I recall the first time I read Stephen Hawking's classic work, A Brief History of Time (1988). Most of it I did not understand, and neither did my friends, yet we all shared a sense of being in touch with something very profound, which time and again has led me to ask the following: Beneath the doctrines of our religions, might there not be archetypal truths that modern science is illuminating afresh?

Religious Origins

Religion, too, is fascinated with origins, and for much of our recent history as a human species, we believed religious truth to be the ultimate verification of every aspect of life. Every religion has a beginning story. The Christian version comprises the opening chapters in the book of Genesis (in the OT) in which the creator God begets "the heavens and the earth" (Gen. 1:1). From there on, it is the Spirit of God, breathing over the formless void, who seems to be the force behind the recurring words: "Let there be. . . ." Quite quickly, the story moves toward the apex of human creation, thus reflecting a strong anthropocentric consciousness already prevalent when the book of Genesis was first written, around thirty-four hundred years ago.

That anthropocentric priority dominates the rest of the Christian Bible, with Jesus emerging as the deepest and primary identity of God, proclaimed in John's version of the beginning as the organizing definitive Logos (John 1:1), embodied first and foremost in the historical Jesus. At this stage it looks like the "letting be" of the Holy Spirit has been eclipsed if not largely subverted.

All the major religions, and several ancient myths, contain stories of cosmic origins. Many of these narratives would have been told over and over, and several of these ancient tales embody details being revisited by scientific research in our time. Scholars have applied various schemes to classify creation myths found throughout human cultures. Eliade (1963) and his student Charles H. Long identified five outstanding features that reoccur in most myths of origin:

1. *Creation ex nihilo* (from nothing), but evolving into existence through the thought, sound, word, dream, or bodily secretions of a divine being.
2. *Earth diver creation*, in which a diver, usually a bird or amphibian sent by a creator, plunges to the seabed through a primordial ocean to bring up sand or mud that develops into a terrestrial world.
3. *Emergence myths* in which progenitors pass through a series of worlds and metamorphoses until reaching the present world.
4. *Creation by the dismemberment of a primordial being*, sometimes two competing deities, a violent process in which the victorious

one becomes the primary creative force from that point forward.[5]

5. *Creation by the splitting or ordering of a primordial unity* such as the cracking of a cosmic egg or a process of begetting order out of chaos.

In most if not all the inherited myths, the earth is the center of the universe. The world (earth) tends to be the first aspect of creation, with the sun, the moon, and the stars following later. In fact, the sun, moon, and stars are often mythological, humanlike characters who first lived on earth but who, after a series of adventures or misfortunes, ended up in the sky to find their ultimate resting place as heavenly bodies.

Nearly all the ancient myths move quickly to the creation and dominance of the human. The origin of humans tends to fall into three main categories: (a) they have always existed on earth, (b) they did not always exist but were created in some way, and (c) they previously existed, but in another world, and had somehow to be brought to this one. Once humans have been created, anthropocentric preoccupation dominates the originating narrative.

It is noteworthy, however, that animals feature strongly in all such myths, as they do in the cave drawings of Ice Age art. The strong affiliation between the animal and the human probably reflects the agricultural background that provides the backdrop to many myths of origin. However, we also seem to be encountering a primeval recognition that animals and humans share something of the same living spirit, hinting at a shamanic interpretation (as in Lewis-Williams 2002), a Spirit force infused in all life but more tangible in the animal-human symbiosis.

Genesis Revisited

According to the book of Genesis, God created the world. Prior to that creation absolute nothingness prevailed, other than the Supreme God himself, all sufficient and all powerful. The "nothingness" that existed prior to the act of creation has long been recognized not as a statement on the nature of creation, but rather a perquisite for the absolute nature of God's power, before and after whom nothing does or could exist.

Many people are unaware of the fact that the Hebrew text of Genesis lends itself to another rendering, opening up other possibilities on how we might understand the original act of creation. Writing in 1983 the scripture scholar Everett Fox highlighted the alternative reading for the opening verse of the book of Genesis (1:1):

> At the beginning of God's creating of the heavens and the earth,
> when the earth was wild and waste (*tohu va-vohu*),
> darkness over the face of the Ocean,
> breath of God hovering over the face of the waters,
> God said: Let there be light. (Fox 1983, 11)

The New Revised Standard Version of the Bible adopts a similar translation, indicating that God did not create the world *from nothing*, but worked on the chaos—the unfolding raw material—that was already there. That which already existed contained within it the seeds of further development. It was a no-thingness, with a potential to be shaped and molded into more creative structuring. The divine influence is calling forth the potential (order) through which the creative material can further evolve.

Several important insights come to the fore:

• Creativity is already at work. Is this what Plato had in mind (in *Timaeus*) in postulating the "wherein" (*khora*) or "receptivity" (*hypodoche*), constituting a third kind of being, neither form (idea) nor material happening (concrete actual event), but instead a formless, nonmaterial, all-receptive mother of being? At this juncture let us recall that both A. N. Whitehead (1960) and Gordon D. Kaufman (2004) consider *creativity* to be the core ingredient of the divine life force. Rather than attributing the original creation to a miraculous once-off invention, perhaps it can be reconceived as the fruit of a more foundational creativity, without beginning or end. Along these lines, process theologian Roland Faber (2008, 156), envisages the original act of creation: "In the first phase, God is present as the future of the potential event that will yet arise; once that event actually 'becomes,' it has already always been there."

• We must not assume that this God "who has always been there" is the patriarchal Father-creator of Christianity nor his male equivalent in several other religions. Rather, this foundational creativity may be conceived as *divine eros* luring life into greater being (and becoming). Roland Faber identifies the eros with Plato's *khora* (wherein), and describes its articulation as that of the work of Logos-Sophia, the original inspiring force behind and within everything in creation. For Faber, *sophia* (Greek for *wisdom*) describes God's primordial nature, the ideal vision of all possible worlds, "the primordial implementation of precisely that creativity through which God also makes the world possible, . . . designating living unfathomableness, . . . the infinite sea of potentialities, the divine origin of the 'wherein' (khora)" (Faber 2008, 229ff.; also 250–54).

• At this juncture, let's embrace Catherine Keller's perceptive insight that *creatio ex nihilo* may need to be reconceived as *creatio ex profundis* (Keller 2003). As already indicated, the *ex nihilo* position is more of an attempt at affirming God's absolute power over creation from the very beginning—God's unilateral power, rather than God's inspired creativity, which is, perhaps, the issue at stake. *Ex profundis* signifies the primordial depths, the impregnating eros, the divine lure that predates the material creation by time spans we dare not try to measure. Infinity is the operative scale, and mystical insight alone is likely to plummet the depths of what we are asked to embrace.

• The lure of Sophia-Logos is distinctive in its space-time orientation: it belongs to the future rather than the past. "Sophia-Logos is immanent in the world as Eros, who within the tension between order and novelty 'lures' towards intensity and harmony. . . . She is always present as future, as 'trace,' which is already present at the locus of origination of every event, even before the event becomes" (Faber 2008, 230–31; more at 82–88). Noteworthy, too, are the observation of Galileo, Newton, Einstein, and others that the laws of physics could be regarded as thoughts in the mind of God, and their elegant mathematical form as a manifestation of God's plan for the evolution of universal life (cf. Davies 2006, 7).

• An apophatic mystical stance may be the most responsible in our attempts to discern the God who is there at the "beginning." Postulating a male patriarchal creator increasingly can be seen as a gross patriarchal projection. We can readily expect that humans would attribute an exalted status to the one who creates, but we seem to have grossly neglected that which precedes the Creator, empowering the Creator in the first place to do the work of creation. The one who fulfills that primordial role seems to be none other than that enduring life force known to Christian theology as the Holy Spirit.[6]

• This intuitive, ancient, and dynamic sense of divine involvement in creation is what indigenous people capture in their belief in the Great Spirit. Timeless and formless, the Spirit is nonetheless intimately real, communicable, and tangible in every movement of creation—constructive and destructive alike. It was there in the beginning, but also before and beyond all human sense of origins.

All myths of origin exhibit religious sentiment. The divine initiative permeates throughout. Not merely does God (or the gods) create at the beginning, but the divine being also sustains, nourishes, and enhances creation throughout its entire evolutionary trajectory. Process theologians may be sensing a deeper truth in suggesting that the originating work of the Spirit is always based on a lure from the future: "The gracious God is the Eros leading into a new future. In the conversion of processes, Eros opens up or inaugurates the world process from an absolute future" (Faber 2008, 223; Haught 2010). In most cases, we go on to construe God as a super human being, and this anthropocentric idealization consistently undermines and sidelines the role of the creative Spirit.

Inevitably, God then tends to be perceived as an anthropocentric projection: God is the human being enlarged and inflated. Faithful to Aristotle's depiction of the ideal rational male, God has to be male as well. Moreover, he is depicted as the One who rules and governs from on high. He exerts dominance and control as good men are expected to do. This is the God that the scientist Stephen Hawking had in mind many years ago when he declared, "Your God is too small for me." The God of formal religion is too anthropocentric and "ecclesiastical" to be relevant for new scientific vision. As Paul Davies hinted in his 1979 work, *God and the New Physics*, and Michael Dowd (2009) asserts in more recent times, science rather than religion is recovering the mystical and spiritual depths of the creation that surrounds us. Religion for the greater part still seems wedded to the idea that the human comes first, and everything else in creation is there for human use and benefit.

～

Pause for a Moment

I am suggesting that our inherited science and theology have been adopting a humans-first approach that seriously undermines both the grandeur of God and the elegance of creation itself. The grandeur of creation—which science and cosmology are beginning to illuminate—bequeaths to us an understanding of the Divine in which the power of Living Spirit seems to be foundational. First-nations people have long understood this insight. Has the time come to embrace it—and affirm it—more widely? How do you feel about this challenge? What are its implications for your own sense of faith and belief?

～

Origins Fascinate

When religion fails to captivate the mystical imagination, life opens up other creative outlets, and despite the material details and technicalities of science, apertures into the great mystery open up and illuminate the landscape in empowering and inspiring ways. Perhaps this is a good example of the Spirit that blows where it wills! And as it blows, the human mind becomes captivated by that sense of mystery and meaning, the very basis not merely of survival but of the natality—coming to birth—that endows universal life at every level.

Brain, inspired by mind, seeks to fathom the depths, which suggests that mind is transparent to depth and is not at home in shallowness. Mind seems to be coterminous with consciousness, and therefore the desire to know is also related to depth. In scientific terms, depth denotes the search for ultimate explanations, what Stephen Hawking metaphorically calls the mind of God (Hawking 1988). The ultimacy in question is functional and pragmatic, and it must be capable of enduring rigorous, objective testing. In scientific terms we are seeking the ultimate building blocks of nature. Today, that very pursuit seems to be transporting us into more transcendental territory: the ultimate foundation of nature itself.

Even scientists themselves know there is more to creation than mere materialism, and more to the search for origins than the identification of subtle elements, whether atoms, cells, or qualia. The construction of the CERN accelerator is postulated not upon finding new discrete physical objects, but in detecting in the debris the existence of entities that will probably never become visible even with our most sophisticated microscopes. Even the pursuit of objectivity betrays a deeper truth, forever elusive (it seems) but captivating for the human mind.

Hathaway and Boff (2009, 313–14) root our desire for depth in the power of the Holy Spirit. A sense of ultimacy haunts the human spirit, a restlessness without which we seem unable to come to a place of rest. This deep search cannot be explained in mere rational terms. It requires a hermeneutical horizon that defies human analysis.

The Inspired Mind

So, what inspires the mind in this deep search? The very word "inspires," from the Latin *in-spiritus*, plunges us right in. We encounter Spirit force in our thinking, imagining, intuiting, searching, and seeking. Those who acknowledge this Spirit force, and who seek to understand it in greater depth (whether scientifically or religiously), probe the human psyche for clues. They feel it is a unique human endowment unlikely to be unraveled outside the human context.

But outside we need to venture—and even science itself is already pushing us in this direction. The theologian Catherine Keller, herself well versed in the insights of modern science, names this virgin territory as *creatio ex profundis*. She is confronting the traditional doctrine of *creation ex nihilo* (creation from nothing), a dogma on which mainstream religion and mainstream science broadly agree. The very origin of creation itself, she claims, is not shrouded in oblivion, but in profound mystery, a captivating sense of awe and meaning that grips the human imagination.

"Profundity" is a word rarely used in daily language. We, rational creatures, like to talk about that which we can manage and control, and when that is not possible, we are often happy to leave reality unexplained—hence the idea of *ex nihilo*. Opting for the profound feels scary and not a responsible option for a generation well indoctrinated in the necessity for scientific rigor, objectivity, and rational outcomes. The scientific methodologies have indeed led to remarkable breakthroughs, yet millions know intuitively that a great deal remains to be discovered.

In the present work, I name the something more, the ancient profundity, as *primordial spirit power*, a creative resilience, without beginning or end—a foundational, energetic wisdom that cannot be quantified by any known human science or religion, but an invasive "presence" that pursued the human imagination for eons long before either science or religion evolved.

This primordial force is described in the book of Genesis as the spirit that hovered over the original chaos of creation, weaving it into form and structure in an evolving process spanning billions of years. Two correctives seem necessary to this description: first, *the profundity is in the chaos*, not something that only emerges after the chaos is sorted out, and, second, *the spirit awakens from within the chaos*, rather than some transcendent force operating from outside.

It seems important to highlight these correctives. A fundamental unity characterizes the entire creation, and has done so from time immemorial. What modern writers describe as the seamless web of life defies all our analyses, scientific and religious. Of particular concern is our human tendency to split reality into convenient dualisms, such as outside-inside, above-below, ordered-disordered, material-spiritual. Neat and orderly it would appear, but in truth grossly deceptive!

The original breathing Spirit outpaces all our human analysis and transcends every attempt to subject it to our intellectual and human categories. I am not endorsing any kind of determinism, nor do I envisage humans to be totally at the mercy of forces, transcendent or alien. I am striving to name afresh the dread of Albert Einstein around the God who plays dice with the universe. That playful, creative God is on to something far more complex than the arbitrary outcomes of dice-throwing.

The Enlivening Spirit

Inhabiting a complex, evolving (emergent), and often unpredictable universe leaves us with two foundational possibilities: become *beneficiaries of destiny* or *victims of blind fate*. Scientists believe that matter and antimatter evolved in the early universe in a complex dance on the delicate periphery of life and death. In what seems to humans like a game of winners and losers, and to many scientists a random capricious creation, life consists of both-and rather than the dualistic either-or, precisely because in the end the will-to-life wins out, and has been winning out ever since then.

Our fascination with beginnings is a fascination with life itself—with that unconquerable resilience that cannot be subdued. Within, we carry seeds sprouting into immortality, which in our arrogant anthropocentrism have often landed us in deep trouble. Our immortal yearnings belong originally to the creative web of life, and therein we first encounter the living Spirit that breathes in all things and gives everything vitality and the urge to become, to flourish, and to grow.

Spirit is the inspiring source and power of the *creatio ex profundis*. It is at one time a force close and intimate, yet awesome, complex, and cosmic. Strangely, indigenous peoples all over Planet Earth seem more receptive to this profound truth than many "civilized" peoples, conditioned by rationalism and the excesses of cerebral thought. Rightly, the indigenous peoples call it the *Great Spirit*—not great in terms of power and dominance, but in the profundity of the depths to which it belongs, and from which it generates possibilities too many to numerate and too complex to analyze.

Only the contemplative, mystical gaze can hope to plumb such depths, and today, science rather than religion leads the way. So, let's continue the scientific exploration, striving to remain open and transparent to the illumination that comes from deep within.

Chapter 3

Out of the Vacuum

The quantum vacuum generates the holographic field that is the memory of the universe.

— ERVIN LASZLO

The dialogue between theology and science is not a dialogue at all; it is a drama of the human Spirit.

— ALEXEI NESTERUK

THOSE PROFOUND DEPTHS FROM which everything came to be is known to modern science as the *creative vacuum*. Out of emptiness comes the fullness of everything we know—a metaphor long known to religious mystics of all traditions. From nothingness comes everything. From the domain of no-things comes all the observable data in universal life.

Let's begin with our own human experience. Mountains hold a sense of awe and mystery for most humans. Archetypally, we seem to be drawn to the heights and to the wonders we behold as we contemplate them all around us. It can be both exhilarating and daunting. One thing is inescapable, although not always consciously observed: most of what we see from heights is empty space. Why so much of it? And what purpose does it serve in the grand scheme of things?

On the cosmic scale, science evidences an intriguing paradox. We need large amounts of space for the galactic and planetary structures to evolve and develop, and despite what we yet have to discover about all the missing matter in the universe, we know it will still be minuscule compared to the expansiveness of open space that characterizes the creation to which we belong.

31

On the vast cosmic scale, emptiness dominates the scene. Perhaps not surprisingly we encounter a similar truth in the realm of the really small, the world of atoms and cells that is invisible to the human eye. An atom consists of a tiny nucleus (a proton) surrounded by over 99 percent empty space. Although the nucleus of a hydrogen atom consists of three quarks, they need to be envisaged as "points," or according to string theory, vibrations of energy. At the atomic level, solidity plays a minor role.

The same holds true for a molecule, the basic unit of chemical interaction in all living systems. A molecule is defined as an electrically neutral group of at least two atoms in a definite arrangement held together by very strong chemical bonds. Cells, the basic units in biology, comprise interactive molecules. However, the wisdom and power of the cell is captivated more succinctly in Deepak Chopra's insightful description: *a cell is memory with membrane wrapped round it* (Chopra 1989, 87). Once again, creative emptiness engages the human imagination, and I guess it takes something akin to the "pneumatological imagination" (Yong 2005, 28) to truly engage the fertile emptiness.

The Energetic Vacuum

Energy is all that is, from subatomic particles to the movement of galaxies, from the patterns of our thoughts to the manifestation of the human body in material form. Energy vibrates, rotates, has polarity, and is never at rest. What to the human eye looks like total emptiness is actually the power of energy as an overflowing fullness. Words are inadequate to describe the wholeness, which might be called the *total energy gestalt*. To experience it, one has to dissolve the barrier between observer and observed, and literally become the whole thing—the classic mystical experience of the blessed few!

The vacuum is a sea of fluctuations of tremendous electrical field activity described in modern physics as zero-point energy. Zero-point energy intimately interacts with everything, from the elementary particles comprising all of matter to the essence of our minds and consciousness. Zero-point energy is the lowest possible level known to science, studied mainly within the sphere of quantum mechanics. Zero-point energy is sometimes used as a synonym for the contents of the vacuum, an amount of energy associated with the vacuum of empty space. When the term is used in this way, sometimes it is referred to as the *quantum vacuum zero-point energy*, otherwise known as the Higgs field, after its inventor, the British physicist Peter Higgs (more in Laszlo 1998, 180ff.).[7]

The Higgs field contains a staggering density of energy. The late John Wheeler suggested a measurement of 10^{94} g/cm^3, amounting to more than all the matter in the known universe. A group of Russian scientists (details in Laszlo 1998, 232) exploring the nature and function of the vacuum postulate the existence of torsion waves, information carriers impacting upon all objects in the universe—from particles to galaxies to the neurons in our brains—with a movement in the rate of 10^9 C, 1 billion times the speed of light.

These minute spinning structures travel through the vacuum, and they interact with each other. When two or more of these torsion waves meet, they form an interference pattern that integrates the strands of information on the particles that created them. In this way the vacuum records and carries information on atoms, molecules, macromolecules, cells, organisms, and even populations. There is no evident limit to the information that the interfering vacuum torsion waves can conserve and convey. They can, in fact, carry information on the state of the entire universe.

Ervin Laszlo (2004) describes the vacuum as an interconnecting Akashic field, with a potential for cosmic interrelatedness far beyond the descriptive potential of either formal science or religion. In Hinduism, *Akasha* means the basis and essence of all things in the material world—the smallest material element created from the astral domain. As an underlying field of influence it is the seedbed of all potentiality, forever eager to explode into form. Within this all embracing field force, consciousness seems to play a crucial role, a cosmic transcendent force that quantum theory dances around without yet having the wherewithal to name its pregnant potential; of all the scholars I have consulted on this daring new horizon (of consciousness), the reflections of the Dutch cardiologist-cum-scientist Pim Van Lommel (2010) seem most persuasive and compelling. Consciousness may well be the most responsible and creative way to the connective tissue of universal life, reminiscent of the wisdom and intelligence we associate with that underlying divine empowerment that theology calls the Holy Spirit of God.[8]

All of this helps us appreciate the counterintuitive truth that the vacuum state, or the quantum vacuum, is anything but "empty." It thrives on overload, but at an ellusive, and even mysterious level, still being investigated by modern science. According to quantum mechanics, the vacuum state is not truly empty but instead contains fleeting electromagnetic waves and particles that continually pop into and out of existence. Brian Swimme (1996, 91–93) provides a vivid illustration in his reflections on the "cupped hands." He writes,

> Cup your hands together, and imagine what you are holding there. First in quantum terms would be the molecules of air—the molecules of nitrogen, oxygen, carbon dioxide, and other trace gases. There would be many more than a billion trillion. If we imagine removing every one of these atoms we would be left holding extremely small particles such as neutrinos from the sun. In addition there would be radiation energy in the form of invisible light, such as photons from the original flaring forth of the universe. In other words, to get down to nothingness we would have to remove not only all the subatomic particles; we would also have to remove each and every one of these invisible particles of light.
>
> But now imagine we have somehow done this, so that in your cupped hands there are no molecules left, and no particles, and no photons of light. All matter and radiation have been removed. No things would be left, no objects, no stuff, no items that could be counted or measured. What would remain would be what we modern peoples refer to as the "vacuum" or "emptiness" or "pure space."
>
> Now for the news: careful investigation of this vacuum by quantum physicists reveals the strange appearance of elementary particles in this emptiness. Even where there are no atoms, and no elementary particles, and no protons, and no photons, suddenly elementary particles will emerge. The particles simply foam into existence. . . . The particles emerge from the "vacuum." They do not sneak in from some hiding place when we are not looking. Nor are they bits of light

energy that have transformed into protons. These elementary particles crop up out of the vacuum, itself—this is the simple and awesome discovery. I am asking you to contemplate a universe where, somehow, being itself arises out of a field of "fecund emptiness."

The basic idea is as follows: The vacuum or nothing-with-special-dimensions is actually a real energy field, or state of subtle material substance, out of which all perceivable matter is formed and within which are found, in even finer levels of manifestation, the energy fields from which arise even our personal thoughts, feelings, and instincts.

~

Pause for a Moment

This is meant to be a book about the Holy Spirit—why all the scientific material? For almost one hundred years, scientists themselves have been baffled by the insights of quantum mechanics. The true nature of reality is far more complex, subtle, and illusive than we care to admit. Beyond our capacity for human observation, and the rigorous research of science, lies a more mysterious but real world. Religion has known this for several millennia, but religion itself has failed to honor the mysterious depths. Those depths, I propose, have now become the subject material for new theological discovery, and particularly for that aspect of sacred mystery we call the Holy Spirit. Let's allow ourselves to engage more deeply, and allow our spirits to be captivated by this mystical adventure.

~

Vibrational Strings

Subatomic particles are seen by modern physics more as smears of existential probability with wavelike and vibrational properties rather than viewed as solid blobs resembling billiard balls. "Very clearly," writes John Davidson, "the particles are coming out of 'nothing,' out of the vacuum. There is nowhere else for them to arise.

So 'nothing' must be 'something.' . . . From our understanding of the vacuum matrix we can see how all manifestation is a pattern, a dance, an affect given specific 'reality,' and linked to our consciousness through our sensory perception" (Davidson 1989, 30, 43).

Dance is a useful metaphor for highlighting the mobile nature of the creation in which we participate. Nothing is static or stable, and the movement is frequently characterized as if choreographed by a skillful pattern-maker. We see this illustrated in those ornate graphics known as *fractals* (more at http://en.wikipedia.org/wiki/Fractal), with the aid of which we can now read the intricacies and irregularities so common in nature (jagged coast lines) and in human beings (irregular heartbeats).

The sense of pattern, however, goes much deeper. For much of the twentieth century, physicists tried to describe and illustrate the wave-particle duality. We have long known that there is more to the makeup of our world than the conventional image of billiard-ball entities bouncing off each other. Wavelike patterns are more appealing and also more congruent to explain the complex nature of what we observe. Of particular interest to the research of this book is the notion of strings, which was first envisaged in the 1970s and which has gained scholarly momentum and greater approval since the 1990s.

Instead of envisaging the elements of creation as minute entities called *particles*, string theory suggests that creation is made up of vibrations of energy, similar to the resonances obtained when playing a musical instrument such as a guitar (more in Green 2000; see also http://en.wikipedia.org/wiki/String_theory). Creation is constituted by musiclike sound, manifesting as strings. These strings are so small that even when looked at very closely they may resemble points. Each basic particle is created by the strings vibrating in different patterns. What makes this theory particularly attractive to scientists is that gravitons (the ingredients of gravity) can also be mathematically described, a feat not possible in other approaches. What makes the theory difficult to substantiate scientifically is the fact that it requires ten dimensions, and not merely the standard four (three spatial factors and one of time), the other six being compacted and therefore not easily analyzed.

Excitement is scarcely containable on this esoteric subject. To date, the scientists have come up with six different string theories (supergravity being the sixth—requiring an eleven-dimensional configuration). Best known is M-theory, devised in 1995 by American physicist Edward Witten. This theory combines the five different string theories (along with a previously abandoned attempt to unify general relativity and quantum mechanics called 11D-Supergravity) into one theory. In M-theory, we meet the notion of the *brane,* related to the word *membrane.* This terminology is used to unravel the deeper secrets within the mathematics in which the extra space dimensions in a membrane are considered to consist of two branes; a string is called a one-brane, and a point is called a zero-brane. M-theory states that strings of energy could grow into larger membranes or branes even up to the size of the universe.

What does it all mean? Among other things it highlights the mystical pursuit that never ceases to drive the human spirit. Two observations are pertinent here that are explored further throughout this book:

1. We already know about the innate curiosity of the human mind; I want to further suggest that it is essentially *spiritual* in nature, and has been awakened in each of us by that inner life force called the Great Spirit (or Holy Spirit in the Christian religion).
2. More controversially, we seek deeper understanding of the creation we inhabit because the universe itself is inhabited by an inexhaustible life force that awakens our curiosity in the first place, and forever lures us to look deeply within, for therein are the depths that assure us that the mystery we inhabit is fundamentally sacred and benign.

Meaning from Within

Scientists like clarity, precision, and rigorous objectivity. As far as they are concerned, dealing with imponderables is best left to philosophers or others who dabble in esoteric matters. Nonetheless, we do encounter great thinkers whose human grounding in mystery still remains intact. We get valuable glimpses from the journals, letters, and private notes of the great Albert Einstein. In relation to the quantum vacuum, here is a gem from the renowned German physicist Max Planck (allegedly from a lecture he gave in 1944):

As a man who has devoted his whole life to the most clear-headed science, the study of matter, I can tell you, as a result of my research about the atoms, this much: There is no matter as such. All matter originates and exists only by virtue of a force which brings the particles of an atom to vibration and holds the most minute solar system of the atom together. . . . We must assume behind this force that existence of a conscious and intelligent Mind. This Mind is the matrix of all matter. (Quoted by Braden 2009, 334–35)

No matter as such! Only the creative emptiness! And the creativity is sustained by some kind of consciousness, intelligence, or Mind! Dare we name it: *Spirit power*! Our reflections on the nature and workings of the creative vacuum lead to a number of significant insights:

1. There exists in the entire creation a kind of "within-ness" that cannot be quantified or measured, and seems to defy all attempts at human analysis or explanation. Mysterious, yet inescapably real.
2. The meaning of creation and its complex functioning comes first and foremost from within, not from without (in terms of human comprehension or objective verification).
3. The force-from-within is restless, mobile, and pregnant with possibility for external expression at a whole range of levels, including material form.
4. The sense of generativity seems unassailable—and as modern physics suggests, infinite (cf. Laszlo 2004, 30), noting that the infinity in question is not about life hereafter, nor a particular characteristic of the divine, but an enduring quality of our open-ended universe.
5. There seems to be a sense of direction to what emanates from the creative vacuum, what science refers to as the *arrow of time*—not to be confused with the notion of intelligent design.[9] The direction seems to be toward greater and more abundant creativity, complexity, and enrichment—with a great deal of chaos and experiment included.
6. The force from within begets structure (e.g., particles, atoms, and the material forms of creation), but on closer examination,

it first engenders a capacity for relating (relationships), without which structure is unlikely to evolve.

7. Max Planck postulates a Mind behind (or within) the whole process; Van Lommel (2010) calls it *consciousness*. I name it as the Great Spirit (what the Christian religion calls Holy Spirit). It is fundamentally transpersonal, not personal or impersonal, a distinction clarified later in this book.

That the universe came into being *ex nihilo* (from nothing), whether via a big bang or some inflationary expansion, is still the favored theory of many scientists. However, the jury is still out, and the longer they stay "out" the more compelling and credible are the words of John Davidson (1989, 131), which I'd like to use as a focus for gathering in the main insights of this chapter:

The secret of the subatomic world must lie in the mystic construction of the creation from within-out, a holographically woven tapestry of polarity, pattern and relationship, reflected in the nature of its inward structure and dimensionality.

Consequently, it is not so much about a creation from nothing (*ex nihilo*) as an emergence from profound depths, Catherine Keller's named *ex profundis* (also Robinette 2011, esp. 525–32). Deep down is an intelligence, a source of meaning and possibility that defies all our rational theories, and indeed all our theological dogmas as well. It is difficult to avoid the conclusion that this is the Great Spirit so long cherished by the world's indigenous peoples, ancient and modern alike.

Theologian Philip Clayton understands the Holy Spirit as an emergent life force of cosmic significance, and he adopts the notion of panentheism to describe the immanent presence of the Spirit throughout the evolving process of creation (2008, 88ff., 133ff.). His central insight is encapsulated in these words:

The Spirit who emerges corresponds to the Spirit who was present from the beginning, and this Spirit's actions—both its initial creation and its continual lure—help bring about the world and its inhabitants as we know them. In so far as

this emergent theology remains panentheistic, it holds that
the physical world was already permeated by, and contained
within, the Spirit of God long before cosmic evolution gave
rise to life and mind. Gone, in this view, are the Spirit-body
dualities and those claims for immutability that stem from
the world of Greek metaphysics, which once served as the
philosophical authority for theology's fundamental categories.
(Clayton 2008, 111)

The original depths—Keller's *ex profundis*—are endowed with
an emergent orientation, with becoming and flourishing inscribed in
its dynamic flow. It sounds like creation could do nothing other than
flourish, blossom forth, and grow in complexity. This insight also
poses new questions for the notion of an original divine Creator:
Do we need such a postulate? Is there not already enough evidence
in the meaning-laden process of evolution itself? All of this may be
more compelling and persuasive than our elaborate dogmas of an
outstanding patriarchal male, often employed to justify and validate
the patriarchal will to dominance.

In a universe that may be without beginning or end (see the work
of Brian Green, Stephen Hawking, and Roger Penrose), is it not
more responsible and responsive for humanity to be more attentive
to the emergent process, striving to discern in a more creative and
enlightened way what the Great Spirit is doing in creation and
what we also should be about as responsible cocreators? Philip
Heffner (1993, 27) captivates our central and enduring task in these
challenging words:

Human beings are God's created co-creators whose purpose
is to be the agency, acting in freedom, to birth the future that
is most wholesome for the nature that has birthed us, the
nature that is not only our own genetic heritage, but also the
entire human community, and the evolutionary and ecological
reality in which we belong. Exercising this agency is said to be
God's will for humans.

For Christians particularly, the impersonal nature of this life force
is a major problem. As I indicate in later chapters, Christians (and

others) need a radical reevaluation of what we understand by the term *person*. It is constructed on several unexamined assumptions, made all the more intractable by the dualistic split between the personal and the impersonal.

The Great Spirit is not a person as understood conventionally in our daily human experience. But let's not rush to the conclusion that it therefore must be some type of impersonal force that poses a threat to our life and its meaning. Paradoxically, new insights from modern science help to illuminate the complexity and depth of this ancient idea, and the deeper we go into what Westerners dismiss as an impersonal force, the more we encounter a living presence, defying all our neat conceptual categories. Let's plunge more deeply into the depths!

~

Pause for a Moment

Are you getting the gist of my exploration? I began with that sense of profundity that prevails in the beginning of creation itself; scientists and theologians seem to be comprehending this primordial sacredness with new wisdom and insight. I then proceeded to unravel what science now calls the creative emptiness (the vacuum), seething with pregnant possibility. Over the next two chapters we explore the energy that is foundational to the creative vacuum and to all that it produces. As we shall see shortly, the energy is not random, but unfolds in patterns and relationships, indicating a guiding wisdom that indigenous peoples call the Great Spirit. There is a rational and compelling logic to this process, yet it requires the contemplative gaze to access its greater depths.

~

Chapter 4

Energizing the Energy

The Creator Spirit, as ground, sustaining power, and goal of the evolving world, acts by empowering the process from within. God makes the world, in other words, by empowering the world to make itself.

— ELIZABETH JOHNSON

Through the energies and potentialities of the Spirit, the Creator is himself present in his creation.

— JÜRGEN MOLTMANN

IN THE BEGINNING WAS the vacuum, and the vacuum was filled with energy. Energy was—and is—the primordial stuff from which all else was to evolve. And it continues to flourish, and will do so infinitely, it seems!

That is exactly the resounding call echoing from the opening words of the Christian Bible: in the beginning was the Word, translated in Greek as the *Logos*, but in Hebrew as *Dabhar*. All over the ancient Orient, in Assyria and Babylon as well as in Egypt, the word—especially the Word of God—was not merely an expression of thought; it was a mighty and vigorous force. The Hebrew conception of the divine word was deemed to be dynamic in character and possessed a tremendous power. Dabhar signifies divine prolific energy. All of creation contains the living wisdom of *Dabhar* with the creative energy inebriating every dimension of life, time, and space.

Several commentators have already drawn attention to the Hebrew word for Spirit, yet only a few explore the link between *Dabhar* and *Ruach* (e.g., Moltmann 1992, 41; Kim 2011, 42). The feminine *ruach* occurs 389 times in the Hebrew Old Testament, rendered *pneuma* in Greek (neuter) and *spiritus* in Latin (masculine). More than anything else *ruach* denotes *invisible force*; as coming from God, it is the invisible origin of life. For Geiko Muller-Fahrenholz (1995, 9), *ruach* is the breath, inspiration, and soul of the world, "the motherly energy of God, the inexhaustible and creative power that is exceedingly tender in the soft breezes and wondrously fierce in the tempest's blast." For John V. Taylor (1972, 61), *ruach* denotes the eternal lying in wait in every moment. It is experienced as inspiration, rather than revelation. "Spirit is that which lies between," avers Taylor (1972, 8), "making both separateness and conjunction real. It generates a certain quality of *charged intensity*" (emphasis added).

Ruach and the biblical concept of *ruach elohim* (the breath of God) tend to be popularly described in terms of life-giving potential, prioritizing everything that prizes life over death. The Spirit gives life, reinforcing the dominant Christian idea that death is an evil to expunge. Theologian Shelly Rambo (2010), partly inspired by the work of Catherine Keller (2003; 2008), forthrightly challenges this dualistic construct, proposing that the breath of Jesus from the cross (John 19:30) signifies a passing on of the living Spirit in the midst of death and chaos whereby people are empowered to grapple with the confusion and complexities of all that is transpiring in a dislocating space. The *dabhar* with which creation originates, the *ruach* (breath) arising from the creative depths, is not merely about order and harmony but also embraces chanciness, complexity, and process, concepts all included in Rambo's proposal of the "Middle Spirit." Describing the Middle Spirit in terms of the *ruach* (breath), Rambo writes,

> The breath of witness is not an active and creative presence of life but a movement in the deep and inarticulated middle. This figure is translated as a breath-spirit, whose essence is not defined except through movement. . . . The Spirit, instead of securing, navigates a third way in more tenuous terrain; in this way-making, the Spirit initiates a new language, a poetics. . . . The Spirit continually seeks form rather than securing it. (Rambo 2010, 124–25)[10]

The Spirit breathes order into creation, but also energizes possibility amid the untidy, and often chaotic, processes of evolutionary becoming. *Dabhar* and *ruach* seem to arise from, and cocreate within, the same foundational energy that has intrigued mystics and scientists over several eons. Energy is a richly endowed concept in many of the great Eastern philosophies. The Chinese *Chi*, the Japanese *Ki*, and the Sanskrit *Prana* are understood to arise from a cosmic energy flow, a vital force that courses throughout the entire universe. In the Asian context, energy indicates life, dynamism, and creativity, and serves as a unitive force: "*Chi* is a vital dynamic, an original power that permeates the entire universe and leads to an ultimate unity," writes theologian Grace Ji-Sun Kim (2009, 121). It envelops the personal, social, and cosmic realms. At one and the same time it is physical, psychological, and spiritual (also in Kim 2011, 9–33).[11]

In humans, the home of energy is the belly, *hara* in Japanese, *tanden* in Japanese, *dan-jeon* in Korean, and *dantian* in Chinese and Thai. The focal point for accessing this energy is that of the second chakra in Western esoteric wisdom, with its key focus a few centimeters below the navel. Sometimes the hara is described as a sea of energy, and in several Asian spiritualities this is the location of divine energy, the source of creativity, and the principal locus for religious experience.

Eastern Orthodox Christianity strongly endorses this spiritual view of energy (see Reid 1997). These words are attributed to John of Damascus: "Since the deifying gift of the Spirit is an energy of God, and since the divine names derive from the energies, God is called 'God' on the basis of this deifying energy" (quoted in Reid 1997, 2). Not merely does God energize creation, but the quote seems to suggest that the Godhead itself is energized by that life force known as the Holy Spirit.[12] Ancient Asian spirituality is replete with this notion of Spirit energy, a topic I further explore in chapter 9.

Scientific Insight

Science has always been reticent about the meaning of energy. Scientists define energy as the ability to do work. Modern civilization is possible because we have learned how to change energy from one form to another and to use it to do work for us and to live more comfortably. Energy forms are deemed to be either potential or kinetic. Potential energy comes in forms that are stored, including chemical, electrical, gravitational, mechanical, and nuclear forms. Kinetic energy—like heat, light, motion, and sound—enables us to do active work.

Energy is regarded as a functional property that makes things happen (see the useful overview in Smith 2008, 17ff.). Science shows little interest in tracing the origin or source of energy, deeming such pursuit to be a distracting metaphysical endeavor. Quantum physics, however, cannot avoid such investigation, not that it is going to produce neat conceptual answers, but because the very question itself becomes a quantum fluctuation that invites deeper intuition and alternative ways of viewing reality.

Ever since the development of field theory in the late 1800s, it is difficult to see how scientists could have been so averse to asking the deeper questions of meaning. *Fields* are constellations of energy, with assuredly functional properties and influences, but also endowed with potentialities that simple rational logic or mathematical formulas cannot explain. Fields thrive on relationships, always pushing forward toward enlarged horizons. The principle that *the whole is greater than the sum of the parts* is precisely what makes field theory so engaging and yet so difficult to predict or analyze in detail.

In describing field theory I find it useful to review what we know about the field influences operative in the human body. A great deal of wisdom—and practical know-how—has been gleaned from the work of healers all over the world (see http://www.holisticmed. com/ and http.www.valerievhunt.com/). Unfortunately, mainstream science and conventional medicine tend to be scathing in their dismissal and denunciation of this alternative wisdom.

The human body is surrounded by layers of energy of an electro-magnetic nature (this is true of all life organisms). The layer closest to the human skin is what is known as the *aura*. Healers work extensively with this field in seeking to rebalance the equilibrium for health and wholeness in the human personality. Some people have the gift of being able to see the human aura, and some technologies have been developed (e.g., the Kirlian camera) with which people claim they can see and analyze what is going on within the field.

Phantom pain provides strong evidence for the existence of field influence. A physical limb has been removed, yet the sensation of pain endures, and when the painful space is rubbed or stroked people often obtain relief as if it was the physical limb itself that was being massaged. Those who work in hospice care often observe changed patterns in breathing and other body motions shortly before a person dies; some wonder if this change might be activated by the departure of the field, leaving the physical body to cease functioning shortly thereafter.

Although some of these ideas are tentative and speculative, they are highly suggestive. In many cases they are reinforced by the discoveries of science itself, particularly of Asian influence. We know that energy is never destroyed, but always transformed into other forms. Energy forever recycles (and we don't need to invoke the notion of reincarnation to make sense of that fact). When the energy that constitutes my alive self leaves my body in death (or shortly before), it reunites with the great energy fields of creation from which it originated in the first place. Energy is never wasted; it is always in a process of transformation.

Moreover, the energy that characterizes the created universe is not a random process. It flows in patterns that constellate into configurations that impact upon specific outcomes, whether cosmic, planetary, or personal. Although invisible to human observation (as are gravity and electromagnetism), we know that fields are real and exert quantifiable influence. Philosophically (and, I would like to add, theologically), fields remind us that the entire universe is fueled by an energy source that evolves in patterns, aimed at creative expression of one type or another. What energizes the energy becomes the obvious question.

~

Pause for a Moment

What energizes the energy? It seems a very intelligent question to ask, yet scientists don't like the question. They feel it would lead to metaphysical speculation. Perhaps that is a useful step to the deeper reflection that the question evokes. The average reader will have guessed my own answer by now:

the energizing source is probably something akin to what the indigenous peoples call the Great Spirit. One does not have to be a religious believer to reach that conclusion. My suggestion is that science itself is pointing us in this direction. What do you think?

~

The Capacity for Self-Organization

Clearly the energy is characterized by an innate ability to self-organize. Self-organization seems to be a feature of all living systems—from the cell to the universe. This new breakthrough emerged initially in the 1970s mainly through the concept of *autopoiesis*, originally introduced by Chilean biologists Humberto Maturana and Francisco Varela in 1972. As well as being affected by external factors in a cause-and-effect modality, living systems manifest internal processes that cannot be observed merely at the level of cause and effect, nor can they be rationally explained in a rigorously objective way. Mary Midgley (2010, 105) describes self-organization as the mysterious generation of patterns from within. Living systems are characterized by something akin to an internalized wisdom (consciousness) that enables the system to move in the direction of growth, development, and complexity.

Several commentators equate autopoiesis with the notion of self-organization—an equivalence that Maturana and Varela stringently opposed. We need to distinguish structure from organization. Organization determines the identity of a system, whereas structure designates how its parts are physically articulated. Organization identifies a system and corresponds to its general configuration. Structure shows the way that parts interconnect. The moment in which a system loses its organization corresponds to the limit of its tolerance to structural changes.

The internal wisdom, therefore, embodies two notions: the unfolding processes upon which a life form thrives and flourishes, and the various mediations (organizational factors) through which the processes are mediated. As popularly used (cf. Kauffman 1993), the notion of self-organization embraces both ideas, alerting us the need to heed internal wisdom while applying external supports to maintain and nourish a living system.

While Maturana and Varela viewed autopoiesis as a closed, self-contained system, other researchers extend their insights to view the interactive process between biological systems and their surrounding environments, highlighting how important an environment is to the maintenance and development of a system, and more intriguing, how a system like a cell seeks out environments best suited to its own development.

The groundbreaking research of biologist Bruce Lipton (2005) may serve as a useful example. The Human Genome Project was supposed to verify the model that genes create life and to show us the more than 150,000 genes that are involved, but the project finished with only 23,000 genes, indicating that several aspects of human behavior arise from other influences. So, if genes are not the final arbiters, determining behavior—Dawkins's notion of the selfish gene—what role do they actually play, and what/who now occupies the higher ground?

The newly developing science of epigenetics claims that genes do not control our life; our perceptions, emotions, beliefs, and attitudes actually rewrite our genetic code (see Lipton 2005). Through our perceptions, we can modify every gene in our body and create thirty thousand variations from every gene just by the way we respond to life. In short, we are leaving behind a reality of victimization (by our genes) and moving into the awareness that our mind—our consciousness, the immaterial realm—influences our experience and creative potential. We are coparticipants in the organizing wisdom of our embodied selves when we choose to honor a wisdom greater than our rational minds, yet inherent to our evolutionary well-being.

Linking these insights with the role of the Holy Spirit, theologian Gunter Altner reminds us, "The reality of the Spirit manifests itself in the self-structuring processes of matter, energy, and information" (quoted in Bergmann 2006, 253). The statement seems to suggest that the Spirit is the principle for conferring order on what is emerging. However, it is never a static or mechanical process but one characterized by movement, change, growth, and development. Thus, the manifestation (revelation) of the Spirit is itself always in process. More important, it is an internal process that human investigation can never fully access. The more we learn about what is happening deep within, even more remains to be understood and comprehended.

The immune system of the human body serves as another useful example. Human immunity defends the body from attack by invaders recognized as foreign. This extraordinarily complex system relies on an elaborate and dynamic communications network that exists among the many different kinds of immune system cells that patrol the body—particularly white blood cells (the leukocytes). At the heart of the system is the ability to recognize and respond to substances called *antigens*, whether they are infectious agents or part of the body (self-antigens). If we did not have an immune system, we would never get over the flu or even a minor cold and would end up dying due to the simplest of illnesses.

The capacity for self-organization may be compared to an innate intelligence characterizing everything in creation, for which contemporary consciousness studies provide the most compelling articulation (as in Van Lommel 2010). In itself, this is not an argument for intelligent design, because the wisdom I allude to also embraces several deleterious forces—such as earthquakes—that overtly seem quite destructive, but internally are essential to the viability and flourishing of the earth. There prevails a deep and extensive intelligence—Niels Henrick Gregersen (2006, 24) describes it as "the grace of self-organization"—but it is a wisdom characterized by paradox, as can be evidenced in the cycle of birth-death-rebirth all over creation, cosmic and planetary alike. This will-to-life—and the creative energy that supports and catalyzes it—seems to witness to that life force we call the Great Spirit.

Is There a Theological Raison d'Être?

Writing in 1972 Anglican bishop John V. Taylor made this astute observation: "As a believer in the Creator Spirit, I would say that deep within the fabric of the universe, the Spirit is present as the Go-Between who confronts each isolated spontaneous particle with the beckoning reality of the larger whole and so compels it to relate to others in a particular way; and that it is he who at every stage lures the inert organisms forward by giving an inner awareness and recognition of the unattained" (Taylor 1972, 31). As suggested by

Hathaway and Boff (2009, 313ff.), the Spirit is primarily about *depth,* a more foundational apprehension for which modern science offers more compelling evidence than a great deal of spiritual or theological tradition.

The interface with science advanced further in the 1980s, when the German theologian Wolfhart Pannenberg (1976; also *Systematic Theology* 2:79–83) began to explore links between science and Spirit, dovetailing leading theories in physics with the Christian notion of the Holy Spirit. Having acquainted himself with field theory in physics, he began by asking if we might not consider the Holy Spirit to be something akin to a cosmic field force, which like the fields of gravity and electromagnetism pervades the entire universe.

Wolfhart Pannenberg regards the Spirit "as the marvelous depth of life out of which all life originates" (1976, 106). Pannenberg understands the Spirit as active in the self-transcendence of life, and he has used the field theories developed by Michael Faraday (1791–1867) and his successors to understand the Spirit's activity in the world. According to Pannenberg, these field theories "claim a priority of the whole over the parts. This is of theological significance because God has to be conceived as the unifying ground of the whole universe if God is to be conceived as creator and redeemer of the world. The field concept could be used in theology to make the effective presence of God in every single phenomenon intelligible" (Pannenberg 1988, 12).

For Pannenberg, the Spirit is the environmental network or "field" in which and from which creatures live. By virtue of the fact that they are alive, creatures participate in God through the Spirit. The Spirit is the "force" that lifts creatures above their environment and orients them toward the future. Thus, the Spirit as force field is the most comprehensive and powerful field from which all creatures derive the purpose and function of their existence.

That purpose—according to Wolfhart Pannenberg, and particularly Jürgen Moltmann—is to consistently affirm life. Wherever there is passion for life, there the Spirit of God is operating: life over against death, liberation over against oppression, justice over against injustice, and so on. To live by the Spirit is to affirm life unambiguously. Additionally, the Spirit can also use the dynamics of vulnerability—as in sickness, pain, and trauma—to awaken solidarity and hope in those life experiences that do not yield easily to comprehension and meaning, vividly illustrated in the seminal work of Shelly Rambo (2010).

Since the 1980s science has advanced in leaps and bounds (see Green 2011; Smolin 1997), suggesting that it might be more pertinent to view the Holy Spirit as the field that underpins the various fields known to science and adopted by the indigenous wisdom of several Asian traditions. The Spirit is not just another field force, but might well be envisaged as the force that energizes and animates all the fields upon which creation thrives and functions. Although not stated in such explicit terms, current thinking in pneumatology (Pinnock 1996; Karkkainen 2002; 2009) and several process theologians, including Joseph Bracken (1991) and Roland Faber (2008), embrace this same insight.

The German scholar Wolfgang Vondey (2009; 2010) is among the leading theologians carrying forward Pannenberg's pregnant insight. He provides an informative analysis of the significance of Spirit force in the thinking of Isaac Newton and Albert Einstein. For Newton, God is eternal in relation to time, but ubiquitous in relation to space. The everywhere-ness of God may be compared to a subtle spirit pervading the entire natural world. Newton uses the notion of the ether to describe the dense energy sustaining everything in creation, and that ether is the vehicle for the activity of the living Spirit. (For more, see Dobbs 1991, 101–2.) Newton considered God to be the ultimate cause of everything that exists. God the Creator seems to be one who acts from a distance, something akin to a great engineer. The Spirit, on the other hand, is more immediate and intimate, a universally present vitality. Vondey (2010, 82) synthesizes Newton's pneumatology into five key points:

1. Spirit is a necessary component for a philosophy of nature.
2. Spirit is an intermediate agent of the transcendent God in creation.
3. Spirit is a universal principle present in all natural phenomena.
4. Spirit is an internal medium of infinite duration (time) and extension (space).
5. Spirit is a cohesive and conforming force in nature.

Einstein's understanding of the spirit at work in nature is quite different. Einstein's special theory of relativity stripped the ether of its fundamental mechanical quality; it became an unnecessary hypothesis. For Einstein, Spirit (*Geist*) is the rationality at work in the cosmic order, endowing the laws of nature with meaning and order, and bestowing an overall sense of unity and coherence in the workings of nature. Again, Vondey (2000, 83) provides a five-point synthesis:

1. Spirit is a necessary component in the scientific endeavor.
2. Spirit is the rational order of the universe.
3. Spirit is a universal principle present in all natural phenomena.
4. Spirit is the symmetry of the space-time continuum.
5. Spirit has no physical material reality.

As a Christian theologian, Vondey is pleased to see both eminent scientists acknowledging and addressing the force of divine Spirit at work in nature and in creation; he bemoans the fact that neither Newton nor Einstein make any link with the personal, embodied identity of the Spirit as upheld by conventional Christian faith. On Vondey's part, the desire to protect the more personal interpretation of the Holy Spirit may in fact be inhibiting access to the transpersonal understanding of the Holy Spirit that is explored in subsequent chapters of this book.

More significant than the theories of Newton and Einstein is the evolution of quantum physics in the early twentieth century. Like Einstein's theory of relativity, *quantum physics* reveals the universe to be a single gigantic field of energy in which matter is just a slowed-down form of energy. The postulated indeterminacy, however, challenges much of the rationality inherent to science and theology.

Scant attention has been paid to the theological potential of quantum theory, and more specifically to the role of the Holy Spirit in the mysterious worldview arising from quantum mechanics. The 2000 autumn edition of *Zygon: Journal of Religion and Science* (vol. 35, 489–560), provides a useful overview of the contemporary synthesis of quantum mechanics and theology. The oft-cited names devoted to this research include William Pollard, Robert J. Russell, Nancey Murphy, John Polkinghorne, and Keith Ward. In all cases the divine action of God (rather than the Holy Spirit) is under consideration, and in most cases God tends to be portrayed as in academic Christian theology, frequently a patriarchal figurehead for whom power and control are deemed to be important.

This portrayal of God (more accurately the patriarchal attributions and assumptions) immediately begets conflict with the worldview of quantum mechanics in which everything is essentially indeterminate; things seem to flourish through an irresistible creativity. That being the case, no reconciliation is possible with the God we deem to be in charge and in control of everything that transpires in creation—a God who becomes an interventionist no matter how much we try to escape that fact. Consequently, Nancey Murphy (1997) proposes a resolution whereby God works with and within the indeterminacy of events, but in the end has a controlling hand in what transpires, selecting desired outcomes. For Keith Ward (2000), God creates a world that is fundamentally an open process "a gappy universe" whereby God can act in freedom within it, and gear it in the direction of what God desires. In both these cases, we seem to be dealing with a strangely manipulative, mechanistic kind of God, very different from the indigenous understanding of the Great Spirit.

Nicholas Saunders (2003, 535–537) attempts a final synthesis outlining four possibilities for quantum-based divine action:

1. God alters the wave function between measurements (in the case of Schrödinger's cat, instead of an outcome of dead-alive, there would ensue a three-way possibility of dead—alive—desired).
2. God makes God's own measurements on a given system.
3. God alters the probability of obtaining a particular result.
4. God controls the outcome of measurement, thus ignoring or bypassing the indeterminacy that quantum mechanics predicts.

For various reasons, Saunders rejects positions 1, 2, and 3, and sees 4 as the only coherent possibility. As suggested above, scholars striving to build a bridge between science and religion—a project that has been in place for many decades and has attained a significant level of dialogue and agreement—tend to adopt a distinctive patriarchal view of God: dominating from on high, controlling outcomes, intervening at will, manipulating reality to (God's) advantage. For several decades now, this view of God has been losing credibility and meaning. It strikes me that several of the key researchers in this field have kept up with their science *but not with their theology*. They adopt a strangely archaic understanding of God and divinity, although one has to concede that several Christian denominations and churches in the modern world still hold to this understanding.

We are on more fertile territory in exploring links with the indigenous notion of the Great Spirit. This is much more a God that is immersed in the evolving, emergent nature of life, a God whose presence is persuasive and empowering rather than manipulative and controlling. It is also a God whose very becoming is enfolded into the evolution of creation itself. This is the position of process theology, sometimes described as *panentheism*, although frequently condemned as pantheism. In this synthesis, God is not envisaged as a person but rather as a transpersonal life force that can never be reduced to the physical creation (essentially because creation is not physical anyhow), yet percolates and informs every aspect of its growth and development. In this case, revelation is not a foundational set of revealed rational truths, but rather constitutes those understandings of God and life that become clearer as creation evolves and flourishes. Thus we come to Thomas Berry's assertion (2009) that creation is the primary revelation of God for us.

These reflections invite us to connect with the work of Ken Wilber (1984, 16), who writes about the "the most notorious and (and unavoidable) paradox of Spirit," whereby the Spirit is completely transcendent to the world and yet completely immanent in it. Because of the complexities of this paradox, Wilber suggests that we should avoid any attempt to forge links between quantum theory and theology, and forthrightly denounces those who pursue such a task. I am saddened by this conclusion, from somebody of such brilliant intellect, because it seems to suggest that we humans should only engage with mystery within the framework of our human rationality.

Instead I wish to suggest that it is precisely this paradox that evokes the intuitive suspicion that quantum physics has much to contribute to a relevant pneumatology for our time. If we stay long enough with the paradox (adopting a contemplative gaze), I suspect the paradox can yield some significant insights. The quantum worldview is appealing as much for what is insinuated as for what it overtly articulates. It alerts us to what is hidden and how powerful the hidden variables are in the entire workings of universal life; Ernest L. Simmons (2006) draws a parallel with what he describes as the primordial hiddenness of the Holy Spirit in creation.

More recently, the Korean theologian Young Bin Moon (2010) describes this divine hiddenness, adopting insights from information technology and systems theory. She proposes a contemplative exploration using these five guidelines:

1. *God is an observing system sui generis*: the ever-watchful eye of God whose very beholding of creation is itself a form of creativity that defies and transcends human reason; Kaufman (2004) articulates a similar conviction.
2. *Self-referential communication is divine operation*: from the very within-ness of the Holy One comes the external manifestation of an unceasing, unending, evolving creation.
3. *Unsurpassable complexity is divine mystery*, and appreciation of complexity is essential to our comprehension of the depth and meaning of everything in life.
4. *Supratemporal autopoiesis of meaning is divine processing*: divine cocreativity always transcends cause-and-effect agency. Empowerment comes from within, and not from without in any sense.
5. *Agape is the symbolic medium of divine communication*. In the simple language of the Christian gospel, reiterated in the teachings of every major religion, God is love. However, the translation of that ideal, via symbolic expression, is a formidable undertaking.

The in-between Spirit is the great connector, while also being the subtle life force whose irresistible impregnation no force in creation can halt. The pioneers of quantum mechanics had no doubt that several transpersonal forces were at work in the universe. They seemed to be standing on the brink of a mystery almost too incomprehensible to embrace. And after almost one hundred years of rigorous and profound research, the mystical hunch has not been undermined or eroded; to the contrary, it seems to have gained momentum and added credibility.

⌒

Pause for a Moment

Before reading the next section, consider for a moment the fear of many fundamentalists (in all religions) of identifying God too closely with creation. Why are we so keen to keep God at a distance? Why must God be superior to the material creation? Might it not be the tenacious grip that dualistic splitting still holds on us? The sacred and secular must not be seen to be too closely aligned. Why not? Isn't God the source of both?

⌒

The Supernatural in Creation

I want to add some qualifications around my proposal that the Holy Spirit is the one that energizes the energy constituting everything in creation. First, in no way is this a covert suggestion either to impose or extrapolate spiritual meaning regarding creation itself (as in *spiritualism*; see Appendix 1); in other words, I am not trying to spiritualize something commonly regarded as secular or materialistic. Second, I am not adopting any God-of-the-gaps strategy, trying to create a this-worldly niche into which the divine sky-God can be inserted. Third, I am not supporting any theories of divine intervention; rather I am suggesting the Spirit belongs intimately to creation from time immemorial. Fourth, I am not trying a formulate a new theodicy; rather, I am striving to discern what the divine might signify by attending closely to Spirit power at work in creation. Last, the goal of my endeavor is one of unearthing a foundational integration that has prevailed in creation and, in my opinion, always will. It transcends all dualisms, and should not be dismissed as a form of pantheism.

As an approach, it carries one major theological adjustment. Instead of trying to discern how God in himself (the supernatural

God from outside) works in the world, I suggest we need to discern more deeply the dynamics at work in creation itself. These dynamics reveal to us not merely how the divine operates in creation but provide us with vital clues to the meaning of divinity itself and its impact on our daily lives. In all his major works, the theologian Gordon D. Kaufman endorses this perspective:

> Instead of continuing to image God as The Creator, a kind of person-like reality who has brought everything into being, I have for some years been developing and elaborating a conception of God as simply the creativity that has brought forth the world and all its contents. . . . God is an activity rather than a person. (Kaufman 2004, xi, 48)

Interestingly the theoretical biologist and complex systems researcher Stuart A. Kauffman endorses a very similar stance when he writes,

> We do not need that supernatural God. The creativity in nature is God enough. . . . God is our name for the creativity in nature. Indeed, this potent symbol can help orient us in our lives. Using the word God to mean the creativity in nature can help bring us to the care and reverence that creativity deserves. (Kaufmann 2008, 142, 284)

Instead of so much philosophical speculation underpinning our theodicy in the past, I am proposing a more discerning disposition, whereby we speculate less about the nature of God, and instead seek to be responsive to the revelation of the Holy Mystery that surrounds us in the landscape of creation's own sacredness. I believe that the mystery of God and the mystery of the human would actually be enriched in this process. This view is also endorsed by Gloria L. Schaab (2007, 138) when she writes,

> Within the vivified, dynamic, and emergent self-creativity of the cosmos, God is revealed as continuously creative and an immanent source of cosmic creativity in, with, and under the self-creativity of the cosmos itself. Moreover, this

cosmic self-creativity is not to be understood as a separate movement or energy apart from or alongside the creativity of God as immanent and continuous Creator but truly as God-self immanently present and active in and through the self-creativity of the cosmos.

Several years ago, the priest/paleontologist Pierre Teilhard de Chardin seems to have reached a similar conclusion when he wrote these words:

Besides the phenomena of heat, light and the rest studied by physics, there is, just as real and natural, the phenomenon of spirit ... [which] has rightly attracted human attention more than any other. We are coincidental with it. We feel it from within. It is the very thread of which the other phenomena are woven for us. It is the thing we know best in the world since we are itself, and it is for us everything. (Teilhard de Chardin 1969, 93)

What is being described here involves, among other things, a significant shift in our metaphorical understanding of God. We liberally apply the notion of power to God, depicting one who rules, governs, and controls. All too easily this metaphor feeds into a dualistic split between the all-powerful God and the powerless human being. Codependent theories of redemption and salvation readily ensue, often leading to notions of flawed humans inhabiting a flawed creation. We end up with a violent God who violates the sacredness and mutuality of everything in creation. It is a dead-end theology.

The metaphorical shift from power to energy moves us toward deeper levels of understanding and engagement, as illustrated by contemporary theologians like Peter C. Hodgson (1994), Marc I. Wallace (2002; 2005) and Kirsteen Kim (2007). We encounter not a controlling, judgmental God, but an inviting inspiring sense of Holy Mystery that permeates and animates everything that exists. This vision also challenges our own anthropocentrism. We are not the center of the universe, and we certainly are not in charge or in control. Our role is one of mutual participation, relating creatively with our relational God, whose primary presence and purpose are embedded and embodied in the living energy of the universe itself. That relational energy/presence is what theology names as the Holy Spirit of God.

Gifts of the Spirit

In conventional Christianity the seven gifts of the Holy Spirit are *wisdom, understanding, counsel, fortitude* (or *courage*), *knowledge, piety,* and *fear of the Lord* (based on Gal. 5:22–23). These are widely perceived as human virtues, indicative of how humans should live as Spirit-inspired people. Christians were traditionally in tune with the Holy Spirit to the extent that they remained aloof from the material creation with all its distractions and temptations.

How vastly different, and awe inspiring, is the reformulation of the Spirit's seven gifts provided by Miriam Therese Winter (2009, 122–56). Drawing on the insights of quantum physics, and the central significance of energy in the quantum worldview (described briefly above), she suggests that we rename the seven gifts as follows: *relativity, uncertainty, probability, complementarity, nonlocality, synchronicity,* and *change.* These are the dynamics through which the open-ended creation flourishes, through which the wave-particle duality weaves eternal possibilities, through which the mutual interconnectedness of universal life is expressed and proclaimed. These creative impulses are forever awakening in the empowerment of the living Spirit.

~

Pause for a Moment

Sit quietly with the two lists outlined above. Initially, one may feel very personal and the other impersonal. Allow your inner wisdom to transcend the dualistic split, and see if you can connect with a deeper inspiration, the pulsating cosmic embrace of the Great Spirit. Thus you begin to enter the realm of the transpersonal.

~

The giftedness of the Spirit is first and foremost an endowment of the whole creation. Therein the divine emerging empowerment has been at work from time immemorial. The more recent notion of a multiverse—rather than a universe—reinforces this sense of infinitude; see the fine exposition in John Gribbin (2009). Infinite in a way that truly stretches the human imagination (cf. Deutsch 2011), and contrary to the fear expressed by many religionists, the notion of a multiverse does not diminish the integrity of personhood but expands and deepens this sense of cosmic infinity.

Every person is a quantum creation always poised at the threshold of new possibilities. Life is a process, not a product. The process is born out of those energetic dynamics that characterize the entire web of life. Intimately linked with that web, we humans begin to know our rightful place. It is not a prerogative based on power or domination, but based on a risky creative endeavor of ever growing into the larger horizons the Spirit weaves amid the coevolutionary growth of universal life. Therein, we encounter who we really are: creatures forever in the generic process of becoming.

This encounter has two dimensions of enormous importance that we explore in the next two chapters. Beyond the preoccupation with power and domination is the horizon of relationship and mutuality. We are creatures of quantum entanglement, an interactive, interconnected identity that we must never betray. But before exploring that new dynamic interconnectivity, let's look at life itself, a concept often reduced to mere biology or physiology, ignoring once more the enlarged horizon to which Spirit empowerment unceasingly invites us.

Chapter 5

And There Was Life

*Life was bound to arise under the prevailing conditions. . . .
Life and mind emerge not as the results of freakish accidents,
but as natural manifestations of matter, written into the fabric
of the universe. I view this universe . . . made in such a way
as to generate life and mind, bound to give birth to thinking
beings.*

— CHRISTIAN DE DUVE

*Spirit is at the heart of all that is, was, and will be, and is in
some way one with our own being and becoming.*

— MIRIAM THERESE WINTER

A S WE MOVE FORWARD let's carry with us the captivating phrase
of Brian Swimme—"the fecund emptiness"—or the equally
intriguing words of John Davidson: "Nothing is actually a real
energetic something." The very emptiness itself is programmed for
fertility, for possibility, and indeed for life itself. Biologically, we
define life as a *self-sustained chemical system capable of undergoing
Darwinian evolution.* Living things are systems that tend to respond
to changes in their environment, and inside themselves, in such a
way as to promote their own development and perpetuation.

Before offering any definition, all modern sciences alert us to
the fact that life is a complex process that cannot be reduced to
biology nor indeed to any single science (Davies 2006; Barrow
2011; Deamer 2011). Holmes Rolston III (2006) makes the
observation that when sodium and chlorine are brought together
under suitable circumstances, anywhere in the universe, the result

is salt; the capacity is inlaid in the atomic properties. On the other hand, when nitrogen, carbon, and hydrogen are brought together, the spontaneous result may be amino acids, providing the coding for hemoglobin molecules. The coding for salt is already in the sodium and chlorine; the know-how to make hemoglobin molecules is not secretly coded in the carbon, hydrogen, and nitrogen.

Rolston (2006, 199, 205) continues, "The essential characteristic of a biological molecule, contrasted with a merely physiochemical molecule, is that it contains vital information, an information producer-processor (the organism) that can transcribe, incarnate, metabolize, and reproduce itself. . . . Life is an accident waiting to happen, because it is blueprinted into the chemicals, rather as sodium and chlorine are preset to form salt, only much more startlingly so because of the rich implications for life and because of the openness and information transfer also present in the historical life process." With Stuart Kauffman (1993, xvi), we can add, "I believe that the origin of life was not an enormously improbable event, but law-like and governed by new principles of self-organization in complex webs of catalysts."

Information seems to play a key role in the emergence of life. In fact, for the theoretical physicist John A. Wheeler (1990), the physical universe is fundamentally informational; matter itself is derived from a transformation of information. Where does the information come from, and what precisely is its nature and its apparent ability to catalyze the conditions that lead to what we call life? Contemporary biologists are divided across a spectrum about whether this creative cybernetic evolutionary history is entirely contingent, probable, or even inevitable. The British scholar Simon Conway Morris (2003, 8, 20) claims that "life shows a kind of homing instinct." It defies neat definition or conceptual clarification. Are its ultimate origins somewhere in the deep recesses where creative potential can be discerned but not rationally explained? Might this also be home to that force we call the Great Spirit?

More enthralling and challenging for mainstream scholars is the idea that life is seeded throughout the entire spectrum of the material creation, and may well have initially evolved from within the creative vacuum itself. From that observation, let's not hastily conclude that life from the very beginning was geared to culminate in creatures like us humans (the anthropic principle). That which has evolved over several millennia, cocreating many organic expressions including humans, will continue to flourish long after we humans have outlived our usefulness. The Spirit continues to blow as it wills.

⟶

Pause for a Moment

I opened this chapter with a provocative quote from the Noble Prize–winner Christian de Duve, whose pioneering work on the meaning of life is widely known (de Duve 1996; 2002). Not all mainstream scholars would support this enlarged view, many expressing unease with its underlying philosophical implications. Knowingly or otherwise, de Duve goes beyond philosophy in declaring life to be a natural manifestation of matter. This is a short step from the theological assertion that life is also a supernatural manifestation of matter. Scholars devoted to the study of the life sciences have been hinting at this expansive view for several decades. I take the risk of making more explicit intuitive hunches that have been around for quite some time.

⟶

Once we premise the primacy of Spirit power at work in creation, the dualistic divide between natural and supernatural begins to fall apart. The emergence of life denotes a great deal more than matter energy evolving into another manifestation. Creation seems to have been seeded with a potential for life from the very beginning.

Origin of Life

Evidence suggests that life on earth has existed for about 3.7 billion years. While most of the scientific research seeks out a mechanism explaining the formation of a primordial single cell from which life originates, popular scientific writer John Barrow (2011) explains the evolution of life in the generic processes that already characterized creation in its nascent stages, complexifying in the formation of stars and galaxies—with planets such as Jupiter and Venus playing a central role—constructively seeding on Planet Earth, and eventually manifesting in the vast array of organic creatures known to us today. The will-to-life seems to be inscribed in the evolution of the cosmos itself.[13] Among the scientific community divergent views still prevail on how life originated. Currently, these are the leading theories:

• Life came to earth *from another planet*. In 1884 a Swedish scientist named Svante Arrhenius proposed a theory he called "Panspermia." He calculated the possibility that microorganisms could be blasted into space by volcanic eruptions and planetary air currents. He then proceeded to calculate that microorganisms would be pushed through space by pressure exerted by the sun's light rays. He reckoned that in a mere fourteen months, a microorganism could be pushed out of our solar system and would reach our nearest neighboring star, Alpha Centauri, which lies four light years from earth, in only nine thousand years. The central weakness of this proposal rests in the fact that we know of no life form that can survive the extreme temperature and radiation of outer space.

Along similar lines, the British astronomer Sir Fred Hoyle proposed that life ejected into space, mixing with space dust and eventually meteors, which protected the life and created an environment where the life could reproduce. But when meteors enter the earth's atmosphere, they are engulfed in a ball of flames. Only occasionally, in the case of large meteors, does something survive to strike the earth's surface.

Although these theories are credible, they do not solve the problem of how life originally began. The theory that is currently most accepted by the scientific community is that life formed on earth from nonorganic compounds and base elements, which formed organic compounds, amino acids, themselves known to be the building blocks of proteins and therefore only one step removed from the molecules of life.

• *The primordial-soup theory*, or the Miller-Urey experiment, further refined by Dr. Sidney Fox, shows how amino acids could cluster to form protocells. The conditions on the primitive earth may have favored chemical reactions that synthesized some amino acids and other organic compounds from inorganic precursors, laying the foundations that led to the emergence of organic life and its replication thereafter. The role of DNA, RNA, and various proteins in the development of organic life continues to be a debated issue, with the RNA-first hypothesis enjoying general support (see a useful review in Marshall 2011).

• *Life from the seabed* is the favored theory of biochemist Nick Lane (2009). Scientists have gone down to explore and study these deep ocean hydrothermal vents and were completely surprised to find the areas immediately around the vents teeming with abundant life. The temperature of the water coming out of the vents has been measured at the source, and it varies from just 68 degrees to as much as 600 degrees Fahrenheit. At sea level, water reaches the boiling point at 212 degrees Fahrenheit, but down in the deep ocean around hydrothermal vents where the water can reach well over the boiling point, the water coming out of the vents doesn't boil. What prevents the scalding hot seawater from boiling (turning into vapor) is the extreme hydrostatic pressure of all the overlying water. What surprised scientists was that there was an entire ecosystem, a community of diverse life forms, absolutely thriving in conditions that were previously thought to be inhospitable to any kind of life.

The diversity of life on earth today is a result of the dynamic interplay between genetic opportunity, metabolic capability, environmental challenges, and symbiosis. Life is a complex endeavor, understood to flourish through the dynamics of Darwinian adaptations, within a range of competitive and cooperative adjustments. It is widely agreed that the following elements are essential to organic life forms: energy (sunlight or chemical energy), water, temperature, atmosphere, gravity, nutrients, and ultraviolet solar radiation protection.

Additionally, all life forms require certain core chemical elements for biochemical functioning. This list of core life elements usually includes carbon, hydrogen, nitrogen, oxygen, phosphorus, and sulfur—the "Big Six" elemental macronutrients for all organisms. Together these constitute nucleic acids, proteins, and lipids, the bulk of living matter. Initially, the elements were carved out of the interactive behavior of evolving stars. Ironically it was—and is—through the death of stars that these same elements became integrated into the biochemical process we popularly call life. We must also remember the crucial role played by sunlight in the process of photosynthesis. This is the medium through which humans receive the vastly nourishing and sustaining potential of what we popularly call the universal life force.

Life in Action

"What makes life special," writes Paul Davies (2006, 253), "is not the stuff of which it is made, but the things it does." Life is a systemic process incorporating at least three central features. First, as already highlighted, biological organisms are the product of Darwinian evolution: the evolutionary principle of replication with variation and selection is undeniably fundamental. Second, although living organisms are subject to the same physical forces as all other material systems, they are able to harness those forces in a remarkably unique way.[14]

Third, life is an information process that can interpret and carry out genetic instructions. Physicist David Deutsch, known for his pioneering work on quantum computation, points out that a genome contains an internal representation of the world—a type of virtual reality—constructed over eons of evolution, incorporating the necessary contextual information for the associated organism to be well adapted to its environmental niche. He claims that life in its essential nature is about a physical embodiment of knowledge.

For Paul Davies, life is defined by "the things it does." And what does it do? It consistently processes information. For instance, "A living cell is a specific and peculiar state of matter with high information content. The genome of the smallest known bacterium contains millions of bits of information—information which is not encoded in the laws of physics" (Davies 2006, 263). By nature, information is mobile, illusive, and dynamic. It develops through complexity and an inherent tendency toward connection and communication. It is difficult to avoid the conclusion, abhorred by mainstream scientists, *that information seems to exhibit a preferred sense of direction* (Lombardo 2006; Stewart 2000).

A graph of increasing complexity is evidenced in the following developments: In biological organisms we note progressive increases in capacities for sentience (ears, eyes, noses, antennae); enhanced capacities for locomotion (muscles, fins, legs, wings); more elaborated capacities for manipulation (arms, hands, opposable thumbs); enriched complexity in neural networks with control centers—brains—surpassing mere genetic and enzymatic control; more sophisticated capacities for acquired learning (feedback loops, synapses, memory banks); and newly acquired skills for communication and language acquisition. Nothing seems more evident over the long eons than that complexity has increased. In the Precambrian there were microbes; in the Cambrian period, trilobites were the highest life form; the Pleistocene period produced persons.

Stephen Jay Gould spent much of his career "denying that progress characterizes the history of life as a whole, or even represents an orienting force in evolution at all" (1996, 3). We are, he claimed, the accidental result of an unplanned process, the fragile result of an enormous concatenation of improbabilities, not the predictable product of any definite process. For Gould, natural selection is a theory of *local* adaptation to changing environments. It proposes no perfecting principles, no guarantee of general improvement. Natural selection provides no reason to believe in innate progress in nature; none of the local adaptations are progressive in any cosmic sense. Not surprisingly Gould concludes, "Almost every interesting event of life's history falls into the realm of contingency" (1989, 290).

Many evolutionary biologists follow this line, loathing any suggestion of direction or purpose in evolution generally and in organic life in particular. Several concur with Michael Ruse's conclusion, "Evolution is going nowhere—and rather slowly at that" (1986, 203). Committed to the scientific pursuit of objective fact, discrete elements, and hierarchical structure, the very rigor of the scientific methodology short-circuits the complex information constituting the life process itself. More accurately, in seeking factual *information*, science itself fails to comprehend the complex nature of *knowledge* and grossly neglects the more nebulous domain of *wisdom*.

Organic life embodies all three: information, knowledge, and wisdom. Information is favored for its precision and accuracy. Knowledge has long been relegated to the more ephemeral realm of philosophy. And wisdom comes so close to religious speculation, it tends to be scorned in scientific circles. Ironically, that which comes last—and least—in the order of credibility may prove to be the key that unlocks the pursuit of life's meaning itself.

~

Pause for a Moment

Have you noticed the intensity with which biologists and others argue about the meaning of life? That which surrounds us in abundance seems to be a tantalizing puzzle, an academic annoyance, that will not succumb to our intense need for conceptual neatness and masterly control. Perhaps life is out of our control. Is this what the scientists are so scared of? If so, we need a different kind of wisdom that asks all the "why" questions without condescending to a compulsive need for precise analytical answers.

~

Life as System

Insights from living systems theory are adopted today to explain the nature of life, in a way that is more amenable to embracing insights from all three structures: information, knowledge, and wisdom. Such a general theory, arising out of the ecological and biological sciences, attempts to map general principles for how living systems work. Whereas mechanistic science (and biology) is determined by forces and trajectories, evolutionary processes function in terms of change, growth, and development, requiring a new science of complexity. Instead of examining phenomena by attempting to break things down into component parts, a general living systems theory explores phenomena in terms of dynamic patterns of the relationships of organisms with their environment. The scientific principle of the whole being greater than the sum of the parts plays a central role.

One popular application of this approach is the Gaia hypothesis, popularized by the British researcher James Lovelock, exploring the idea that life on earth functions as a single organism that actually defines and maintains environmental conditions necessary for its survival and flourishing. The earth's ability to self-organize and maximize its own resources to advance its growth and development is understood to be a central feature not merely of the earth itself but all living systems.

From this and other starting concepts, Robert Rosen (2005) developed a "relational theory of systems" that attempts to explain the special properties of life. Specifically, he identified the "non-fractionability of components in an organism" as the fundamental difference between living systems and "biological machines." As Harold J. Morowitz (2002) explains it, life is a property of an ecological system rather than a single organism or species. He argues that an ecosystemic definition of life is preferable to a strictly biochemical or physical one. Robert Ulanowicz (2009) also highlights mutualism as the key to understanding the systemic, order-generating behavior of life and ecosystems.

Life as a Cosmic Process

First and foremost, therefore, we need to abandon the popular perception that life is an organic process, confined to the domain of organic creatures. Religions tend to operate within a narrower frame of reference, whereby life is exclusively a divine prerogative (which in its essential nature science cannot decipher), mediated primarily, if not exclusively, by human beings. From the religious point of view, the aliveness of the nonhuman world (animals, etc.) is a secondary life form, frequently perceived to exist for the use and benefit of humans.

This form of reductionism seems dangerously anthropocentric, undermining not merely the spiritual empowerment of all life (being explored in this book) but relegating humans to a cosmic and planetary superiority that seems to be at the roots of many of the major problems confronting humanity today.

Already in this book, we have laid the foundations for life as a cosmic prerogative, mediated to humans through our earthiness, which itself is enlivened through its participation in the coevolution of all that exists. First and foremost we have the creative vacuum, the fertile emptiness redolent with creative possibilities. Next we have the irresistible quantum fluctuations, translating into what is popularly known as *energy*, and as we have seen, energy is not random, but moves within self-organizational forms known as fields.

More controversially, all energy seems to flow in patterns (sometimes chaotic), and the patterns seem to have a preferred sense of direction, tantalizingly close to what may be described as a sense of purpose. Third, from within this patterned energy process, we arrive at David Deamer's theory of interconnectedness (Deamer 2011): life comes forth to thrive and complexify through relationships (the subject of our next chapter).

However, fascination with this flow must not blind us to the cruel dynamics that also characterize—and catalyze—life's potentials. The *predator-prey phenomenon* is merely one expression of this paradox. Some organisms brutalize, destroy, and consume others, seemingly with little regard for the well-being of the other. Nature itself exhibits an unceasing combination of creativity and destructibility; indeed, a great deal of creativity seems to require a form of destruction before the novel forms can evolve and flourish. The beauty is more than complemented—many would say tarnished—by ugliness and a lot of precarious suffering. How this destructive element fits in with the notion of the Great Spirit is explored in chapter 11.

The Spirit of Life

The inherent destructibility of the natural world matches the human paradox that life often flourishes—and even thrives—in the midst of pain and suffering. Theologically, this paradox is nowhere more explicitly stated than in the Christian notion of new life emerging from the power of the cross. But this Christian iconography is much more complex than even theologians themselves have been able to illuminate. Shelly Rambo (2010) grapples courageously and insightfully with this baffling mystery, suggesting that the "Middle Spirit" infuses both life and death—more accurately life-through-death—with a resilience and empowerment foundational to all growth and development. The Spirit breathes life and meaning, not merely in the rational progressions through which we judge progress, but also from within the chaotic chanciness that often remains unpredictable, problematic, and precarious.

The priest/paleontologist Teilhard de Chardin disturbed a lot of fellow scientists in his day when he suggested that the elements of nature and the creativity within which they operate lie in the direction not of matter but of spirit (Teilhard de Chardin 1970, 387–403). The cosmic evolutionary process involves a great deal more than just a random series of mutations or fluctuations, awaiting a more advanced physical (material) theory to explain the functional dynamics.

A theory of everything (TOE), so keenly pursued throughout the twentieth century, may belong more to what Ken Wilber calls the Great Chain of Being rather than a discovery dependent on piecing together a vast cosmic jigsaw. The ultimate meaning, I suggest, rests in that indefinable and inexplicable will-to-life that has flourished and complexified ever since matter began to outwit antimatter in the creative chaos of the early evolving universe. That indefatigable vital resilience is evidence for a cosmic life force, radiant in the earliest throes of cosmic evolution, and ever since then impregnating the vast diversity that characterizes the realm of organic life forms.

I don't know of any one scientist who links the creative life impulse with the Great Spirit, or with the Christian notion of the Holy Spirit. (Up to this day only a mere handful of theologians make the connection.) It does intrigue me that the physicist Paul Davies, perhaps in an unintended moment of creative fantasy, suggests that behind and within the story of creation there seems to be "an unexplained starting-point," which he whimsically names as a *levitating super-turtle* (Davies 2006, 283). If this is a Freudian slip, it is one of the most intriguing I have ever encountered.

Might we be approaching a time when the theological dove and the scientific levitating super-turtle realize that they share a common symbolic ecology? Is this another hint of the Spirit that blows where it wills, and cannot be restrained either by the devotional symbol of religion or the creative fantasy of a modern scientist?

Chapter 6

The Relational Web

It is communion that makes things be; nothing exists without it, not even God.

— JOHN ZIZIOULAS

The community of creation, in which all created things exist with one another, for one another and in one another, is also the fellowship of the Holy Spirit.

— JÜRGEN MOLTMANN

IN EVERYDAY LANGUAGE, relationships are all about humans and how they relate to one another. Applying the concept to other creatures seems odd, and to many scientists feels like a form of romanticism alien to the spirit of rigorous science. Even within the human realm, as primatologist Frans de Waal (2005) indicates, studies on human violence and conflict seem far more appealing to the scientific community than a focus on altruism or creative relating.

Charlene Burns (2006) makes the bold suggestion that the altruism we observe in the natural world may be considered a manifestation of the energy of God at work in creation. The late Stephen J. Gould (1989; 1996) as well as E. O. Wilson (1993) frequently draw attention to this biophilia (love of life) we experience in nature but that is often overlooked in studies of the natural world. In the human realm, a similar shift has also been noted, highlighting the human propensity for altruism, cooperation, and the wider interdependence with the planetary web of life (Hrdy 2009; de Waal 2001; Rifkin 2009).

The relational horizon is expanding, not merely in our understanding of the human sphere, but in reference to the entire wider web of planetary and cosmic life. *Interdependence* is the word frequently used in a range of studies, arising from various applications of quantum physics and the new cosmology. Nothing makes sense in isolation. Everything needs everything else for its fuller realization. The relationships may not always be harmonious in the popular sense; many of nature's processes are distinctly paradoxical: destruction, violence, and death often serve new evolutionary breakthroughs. This paradoxical element, so essential to life at every level, also contributes to relational richness.

The Entangled Universe

The philosophical inheritance of classical Greece has been passed down to us through outstanding thinkers such as Socrates, Plato, and especially Aristotle. Central to this worldview is the notion that "the real is rational." Only that which can be formulated in, and substantiated by, rational argument is to be taken seriously. In this paradigm, rationality denotes individual, separate identity—for objects and persons alike.

Throughout the course of the twentieth century, the emphasis shifted significantly. "The real is relational" became the new compelling slogan. Science, it seems to me, is the primary catalyst for this new relational orientation. Almost one hundred years ago, Albert Einstein, in his special and general relativity theories, developed mathematical formulas telling us that matter and *energy* are equivalent, that space and time are inseparable, that the rate of the passage of time for a body in motion is relative to that body's rate of travel through space-time. In this way, Einstein was able to mathematically demonstrate that these apparently separate aspects of physical reality were all interconnected.

Then came quantum theory. Even Einstein found it hard to accept. At the level of the unimaginably tiny, at sizes below what physicists call the Planck limit, the material universe ceases being classically material. There, quantum flow replaces discrete, isolated objects, and what we call "matter" becomes a relational process rather than an objective material construct. The quanta that constitute matter and energy can no longer be accurately described as little balls bouncing off each other, nor as wave forms, nor (even) as always either "here" or "there," nor "now" or "then." Reality becomes virtual rather than rational.

Entanglement is a strange feature of quantum physics, the science of the very small (more in Aczel 2003; Clegg 2009; Verdral 2011). It is possible to link together two quantum particles—photons of light or atoms, for example—in a special way that makes them effectively two parts of the same entity. You can then separate them as far apart as you like, and a change in one is instantly reflected in the other (similar to the notion of *nonlocality*). This odd, faster-than-light link is a fundamental aspect of quantum science. Erwin Schrödinger, who came up with the name *entanglement*, called it "the characteristic trait of quantum mechanics," described more recently by Vlatko Verdral (2011, 20) as "the quintessential quantum effect."

Entanglement does not dispense with the notions of cause and effect, but it does underline the fact that quantum particles have a range of probabilities on the values of their properties rather than fixed values. And while it seems to contradict Einstein's special relativity—according to which nothing can travel faster than the speed of light—it is more likely that entanglement challenges our ideas of what distance and time really mean.

Consider this fascinating story from the medical missionary Sister, Miriam Therese Winter (2009, 143), describing a practice adopted by her colleagues in their mission hospital in Patna, India:

> "What is that?" I asked, pointing to a tray that held a number of very small vials. Annamah, who is one of our sisters, said that each of the vials held a follicle of hair taken from a former patient. These represented individuals who had completed their course of treatment and returned to their village homes. Periodically the hair was analyzed for any indication that their illness might have recurred. She said it was possible to assess the state of a person's health this way, even though the individual and the follicle of hair were no longer connected. That was my introduction to non-locality.

People have become much more aware of the interconnected dynamics of the natural world, thanks to several pressing issues of our time, like global warming and the depletion of natural resources.

It has taken something as acute as these looming crises to alert us to the profound ways in which everything in creation is interconnected and interdependent. The metaphorical image of the flapping of a butterfly's wings off the coast of San Francisco affecting the course of a tornado along the East China coastline is not merely some poetic fantasy. It is a rigorous scientific fact.

Quanta (such as quarks and photons) can become entangled with each other across distances in a way that makes them act like a single connected process, occupying different locations, without any "physical" link whatsoever. We now have to come to terms with electrons and photons, mesons and nucleons, which tease us with their elusive double lives as one moment defined by position, next by momentum, manifesting to one perceiver as particles, to another as waves, identified as mass, and simultaneously as energy—and all in response to each other and to the environment. Fundamental properties in physics are all about relationships, not isolated absolutes.

Vibrational Relationships

Science pursues prediction, but by finding explanation. The holy grail of scientific explanation is the conviction that physical reality is integrated, which is why science today prefers the explanations that tie together all of the evidence and fully integrates the related theories. Science's pursuit of the grand integration of explanation is really a faith stance. It comes out of the core conviction that everything can be explained in that way because reality ultimately is that way.

String theory (described in chapter 2), one of science's latest attempts to arrive at a comprehensive explanation of the material realm, offers an even more comprehensive relational description of matter and energy as something resembling higher-level geometry. Instead of discrete material particles, string theory suggests that the universe is made up of waves of energy, metaphorically resembling the musical vibrations resulting from strumming a guitar or playing a violin.

Starting with Einstein's insight that time and space, matter and energy, cannot be described independently of one another, we are rapidly moving to a more radically comprehensive view: nothing can be adequately described except in its relationship with the rest of reality. In the words of philosopher Gilles Deleuze, "Even the rational is relational."

A simple but intriguing example is a phenomenon known as *entrainment*. While working on the design of the pendulum clock in 1656, Dutch scientist Christian Huygens found that if he placed two unsynchronized clocks side by side on a wall, they would slowly synchronize to each other. In fact, the synchronization was so precise that not even mechanical intervention could calibrate them more accurately. The two clocks provide a simple example of a system responding to entrainment.

Entrainment is a principle of physics, defined as the synchronization of two or more rhythmic cycles. The principles of entrainment are universal, appearing in chemistry, neurology, biology, pharmacology, medicine, astronomy, and more. These principles enable us to decipher workings of the many complex systems known in the modern world, including the human brain, and several features of the natural world.

Cosmology, rather than formal science, embraces the new relational paradigm with even greater fervor, with the visionary work of Brian Swimme, Thomas Berry, and others coming to the fore (cf. Swimme and Berry 1992). Our sun is one of the 100 billion stars that the Milky Way swirls around itself, each of them spinning about in a bonded relationship with every other one. And the Milky Way remains bonded to all 100 billion galaxies of the cosmos, as, instant by instant, the universe creates itself as a bonded community.

Swimme and Berry (1992) identify three cosmological processes that highlight the relational dynamics through which everything in creation flourishes and grows in complexity. First is the *differentiation* that confers on everything a unique identity. This concept is captured in the phrase from the Christian Gospels: every hair on your head is numbered. While mainstream science then proceeds to quantify each rib of hair, following the principle that the whole equals the sum of the parts, Swimme and Berry opt for internalization rather than external analysis.

Their second stage is variously named as *interiority* or *autopoiesis*. Everything draws its meaning from within, and cannot be fully appreciated or understood merely by external evaluation. The wisdom of Spirit power consistently favors truth that comes from within, particularly the forces at work that facilitate and augment the capacity for self-organization (autopoiesis).

Only when time and attention are given to the inner dynamics, which become transparent through reflection, intuition, and inner wisdom, rather than through rational analysis, will we be in a position to embrace the third dimension, which Swimme and Berry name as *communion*. This is the relational entanglement outlined above. Interiority, therefore, is not a preparation for outbound action; rather it leads to greater depths within, where the dominance of the relational matrix becomes even more compelling. Insofar as we can detect a sense of direction to evolution, it is an expanding and embracing horizon forever seeking deeper and more intimate webs of interconnection.

Theological Implications

Entanglement is not merely about connection and communion. It includes the forces that require the interconnectivity. Moreover, entanglement always includes the paradoxical elements of birth-death-rebirth. It is essentially a process of complexification, as illustrated in this quote from Hathaway and Boff (2009, 329): "The Spirit permeates all as an entanglement of the universe with itself; as an awakening of consciousness, desire, and enthusiasm; as a cry of liberation, and as a force of communication and communion."

It is as if the universe cannot really fall apart, being held together by a glue that stretches all our imaginings in both analytic research and contemplative gaze: "It is communion that makes things be and become in an evolutionary universe. An emergent and inter-relational universe springs from within the divine communion. That same divine communion is creation's eschatological destiny" (Edwards 2004, 26). Within the created universe is a pulsation, a desiring, and a consciousness that is restless and resourceful beyond all our imaginings. Is this the "fierce Spirit" that empowers Gandhi's notion of *satyāgraha*?[15]

Gandhi applies the concept of satyāgraha mainly to personal nonresistance in the face of oppression and political violence. It is very much an anthropocentric adaptation of a concept with far more profound implications. Satyāgraha denotes an intensity of presence to what is transpiring while also denoting a resilience to endure the suffering necessary for empowering liberation, quite similar to Shelly Rambo's theology of remaining (2010, 102ff.). The first dimension can be seen to be rooted in what Christian theology calls the doctrine of the *Trinity*, and the second in what Swimme and Berry describe as the great paradox of *creation-and-destruction* (more on this below).

Regarding the first dimension, the doctrine of the Trinity is deemed to be foundational to Christian belief and has parallels in several of the great world religions. It was originally formulated in the fourth century, employing metaphysical constructs of problematic value for our time (e.g., the notion of person). In the closing decades of the twentieth century, theologians moved their attention to the metaphorical significance of the three-in-one, understanding it more as an archetypal statement of how all reality functions, including the Godhead, as a web of relationships. This relational significance of the Trinity is very much an issue in our time and is explored in greater detail in chapter 10.

On the human level, relationships are rarely simple and straight-forward. They tend to be complex and often unpredictable. Indeed, what makes life exciting and valuable is precisely the human ability to negotiate the intricacies of human relationships with wisdom, skill, and perseverance. Applying the same insight to relationships at the more cultural, planetary, and cosmic levels is still a novel idea not widely adopted. Here we often abdicate our relational responsibility, assuming that those more competent in religion, governance, and the social domain can sort things out for us. The culture of patriarchy often inculcates such destructive codependency; it has done irreparable damage to the web of life at the personal and cultural levels.

At the Nexus of Relating

The relationality named in this chapter transcends human compre-hension as well as the wisdom of conventional science and main-stream religion. The intimacy mediated in human love cannot be comprehensively measured or analyzed; by attempting to do so we undermine the mystique that we know enriches and sustains such intimacy, while never being able to describe fully what we observe—

hence the ubiquity of the notion of love in all the great religions, and its central role in spiritualities ancient and modern.

At the human level, foundations for such love can be deciphered in the transcendental anthropology for which the theologian Karl Rahner is well known. Speaking to a theological culture that favored the sin-laden view of human nature, a deficit that could only be remedied by divine graced intervention, Rahner (1978, 139) boldly declared, "God . . . has already communicated himself in his Holy Spirit always and everywhere and to every person as the innermost center of his existence." In this deeper inner affiliation with God's living Spirit, the human being intuitively knows the power of unconditional love, the unique basis for all forms of spiritual relationality.

The relationality described above—in its wider planetary and cosmic expression—evokes a wisdom that transcends the prevailing resources we adopt to understand the world we inhabit and the universe to which we belong. Our human minds are unable to grasp the enormity and complexity of what we experience, nor can we comprehend why these expanding horizons cause so much fascination in our time. We assume that the foundational deficiency has to do with limitations of human ability.

Human intelligence is certainly limited. However, our universe is clearly a highly complex organism, and today we understand its emerging and evolving nature with insights we have never known. As these insights become more available to more people, the mysterious nature of the universe itself becomes ever more alluring and overpowering. Something is at work in creation that intrigues and fascinates the human spirit.

⌐

Pause for a Moment

Can you recall times when you sensed or suspected that "something more" may be at work, especially in those noetic moments when nature surprised you—and you made a choice to stop and just be? In such moments we encounter a truth that no religion or philosophy can unravel or explain. Intuitively we know our senses have not been deceiving us, precisely because our response arose from a depth that transcends even our sensory awareness. In such moments, we know instinctively and intuitively that all is one, that relationship defines the very core of life itself.

⤳

More important, even people of no overt religious adherence are often awestruck at the elegance and intricacy of the created order. Something takes hold not merely of the human imagination, but seems to connect and resonate at a deeper inner level. Some spiritual writers of our time (e.g., Moore 1992; 1994) describe this deeper connection as the realm of soul or the experience of soulfulness. The word captures something of that profound fascination that can enthrall the human spirit, whereby we are drawn into the extraordinary sacredness of ordinary things. (In this context, the word "soul" has nothing to do with the conventional understanding— denoting that which enlivens the human body, and will leave the body at death.)

I want to suggest that this enthralling, mystic-type wisdom is another expression of the Great Spirit infused into the fabric of the created order itself, yielding what Amos Yong (2005, 267) calls "a pneumatological theology of creation." In this case, we are connecting with the Spirit that is the central force field whose empowerment of creation is done relationally rather than through discrete, individual entities—whether atoms or cells. Atoms are essentially relational forces that through their subatomic constituents—quarks and leptons—are programmed to relate, and their impact at more overt levels of creation only seems possible through their relational potency.

This situation is much more obvious at the cellular level, as has been documented by scholars such as King (2004), Lipton (2005), and Van Lommel (2010). Several years ago, Deepak Chopra (1989) made the bold claim that a cell is memory with membrane wrapped around it. According to this description, a cell is an organic process that thrives by building on the generic memory, the informational base of DNA/RNA, through which the cell functions in a healthy and dynamic way. The role of the membrane is very much a discovery of the twentieth century. The *membrane* is the porous "wall" through which nourishment is ingested (especially proteins) and waste is excreted. The cell functions and flourishes through its interdependent relationship with the surrounding environment. Without a healthy and supportive environment, the genetic programming on its own can achieve very little.[16]

The Relational Spirit

In 1 Corinthians 12:4–13, St. Paul describes the Christian community as endowed with a variety of gifts, generating a vast diversity that functions for the benefit of the whole, thanks to the one Spirit that holds all in unity. This is the "go-between" Spirit that John V. Taylor (1972) described. More aptly, today, we can describe it as the Spirit that functions primarily as a relational facilitator. In and through the Spirit's relational empowerment, the diverse gifts are invoked in a way that dovetails for the benefit of the entire group.

What Paul perceived at a human and ecclesial level, we can apply on a larger canvas, thanks to the insights of indigenous peoples on the role of the Great Spirit. This is the universal life force, the primordial inspired energy, through which everything comes into being, and which is sustained within the relational matrix of the entire creation. The Spirit unifies not by aligning physical forces as postulated by classical science but rather through the dynamic fluctuations we encounter in quantum physics.

When it comes to the Spirit's creativity, there is no room for a bland sameness, nor for the patriarchal desire for that kind of uniformity deemed necessary to exercise anthropocentric control. The Spirit is beyond our control, fluctuating, flowing, and impregnating in a relational cosmic dance that begets and empowers the organicity of all life. We are called to participate in that dance, a feat that is only possible when we begin to outgrow our individualistic isolation, and embrace the relational enterprise that confers on every creature its true and lasting identity.

Thus far, I have been exploring the Spirit's role in creation's becoming, employing mainly insights from science and cosmology. I adopt this approach in the hope of better understanding the intuitive insights of first-nations peoples in their understanding of the Great Spirit. Their first connective link is not with an inherited religion, with its creeds and dogmas, but rather with the living creation itself, and the meaning they glean through nature's processes and seasonal unfoldings. Let's hear from their legends, their wisdom, and their inspiring insights.

Chapter 7

The Great Spirit:
Aboriginal Wisdom

The Spirit is arising for us today from the underside of history.
— PETER C. HODGSON

*The ecological wisdom of many indigenous religions we have
come to admire these days is carried in a Spirit matrix.*
— SHARON V. BETCHER

EVEN A CURSORY GLANCE at the cultures of indigenous peoples
(sometimes called first-nations peoples—especially in Canada)
reveals one outstanding feature: *belief in the Great Spirit.* We
encounter this phenomenon in the aboriginal peoples of Australia
and New Zealand, in the first-nations peoples of the United States
and Canada, in the tribal groups throughout Africa, and in the native
peoples of several Asian countries. It is one of the most remarkable
common factors occurring in vastly diverse groups, and in all cases,
the foundational beliefs are quite similar: The Great Spirit is

- All-pervasive
- Transcendent, yet totally immersed in creation
- Evoking creative potentials in every dimension of creation
- Awesome and at times frightening, yet intimately close to
  every aspect of life
- Life affirming, but operative in both the process of creation
  and destruction

- Close to humans, yet essentially transpersonal in itself
- Capable of being experienced in all motions of nature (e.g., wind and fire), and not merely in human feeling, emotion, or sentiment
- Captured in religious concepts like the Christian notion of the Holy Spirit, yet predating and transcending all formal religion.

Beyond Religion

To the external observer, religious fervor abounds, yet belief in the Great Spirit means a great deal more than adopting a formal religion. In fact, we are not dealing with a structured religion centered around dogmas, codes of ethics, or ritual elements commonly found in the great religions. Belief in the Great Spirit requires ethical demands, and elaborate rituals are often in evidence, but dogma and doctrine hold little or no significance.

Belief in the Great Spirit is based more on lived experience than on mental assent to a set of beliefs. Spirit is understood to be an innate dimension of life at every level. One cannot escape from its impact and influence, but neither is it subject to human control or management. The existence of the Spirit is ultra-real, yet quite mysterious: a paradox that indigenous peoples readily embrace, apparently without struggle or confusion.

Obviously they trust this pervasive life force. They live in awe of its mystery, in fear of its demands, but most important of all, in deep trust of its benign and empowering ability. This is how the South American theologian and missionary Jose Comblin (1989, 161) describes the sense of faith associated with the Great Spirit:

> Now the Spirit has been acting in pagan peoples and in all religions since humanity began. The Spirit leads peoples and religions in directions we cannot know in advance. All we can do is observe the signs of the Spirit at work and go along with it. There is no way we can anticipate it. If the Spirit leads nations to Christ, we do not know what steps or ways it has actually taken; about this we are as ignorant as pagans. We, in fact, know less than them, since the signs of the Spirit were

given to them first and not to us. We have to learn from them how the Spirit has acted in their evolution.

Native Americans, for example, do not accept the idea of the soul as it is expressed by Christian doctrine. They see the world instead, and each person in it, as being animated not by soul but by Spirit. The wisdom of the Spirit is inherited from ancestors of several past generations. It informs all behavior, inducing love and respect for all living things, and enhancing a quality of change necessary for growth and development (Kidwell and Alia 2001; Tinker 2008).

Spirit is power—not supernatural power, but the power that informs every relationship that exists between one thing and another throughout the entire creation. Indigenous peoples do recognize a difference and a distinction between the spirit world and the one where ordinary and everyday events and people occur and live. The spirit world, however, is not otherworldly in the way that heaven and hell are thought to be in Christian faith. Rather, the spirit world is contained in this world, in the realm of everyday events, yet transcends the material and personal creation. It is a form of panentheism, rather than pantheism. Often, this fact is not fully articulated clearly in native belief systems and can be difficult to understand or explain to outsiders.

Native American Religions

Indigenous peoples still survive in several parts of the Americas and Canada. Although more widely recognized in recent years, and more favorably disposed to government assistance and protection, their numbers remain quite small, and their integration with the wider society raises several challenges that both sides struggle to negotiate and resolve (see Irwin 2000; Tinker 2004). These challenges include the inherited notion of the Great Spirit, which is scarcely recognized in formal theology; it fares a little better in the study of spirituality.

I briefly outline the belief systems of some of the better-known groups that fall under the title of Native American (many of these groups also exist in Canada). As with similar categories in Africa and Asia, we can never clearly differentiate the foundational set of beliefs from the impositions and alterations borrowed from formal religions, especially Christianity. Most allusions to a monotheistic line, particularly with a significant male at its pinnacle, have almost certainly been infiltrated with Judeo-Christian or Islamic influence. Nonetheless we do receive glimpses into central values and key beliefs, with the aid of which we can delineate a profile of the role of the Great Spirit in several of these ancient systems.

The Iroquois

According to Lewis H. Morgan, Iroquois religion is characterized by a monotheistic belief in an all-powerful creator known as the *Great Spirit*, or *Ha-wen-ne-yu*.[17] "The Iroquois believed in the constant superintending care of the Great Spirit," writes Morgan (1962, 146), yet Morgan portrays the Great Spirit as one who rules and administers the world through a class of inferior spiritual existences, by whom the Spirit is surrounded. These earth-based spirits were known as "invisible agents" or "Ho-no-che-no-keh." The power possessed by these spirits was given to them by the Great Spirit, and they were often considered to be the manifestations of his unlimited power.

Theoretically, Iroquois spirituality is not extensively studied, and several of its features are poorly understood. We access its richness mainly through ritual ceremonies practiced by the Iroquois tribes. Many of these are associated with seasonal periods throughout the year. The rituals were handed down through the generations and remained unchanged for centuries. The most significant festivals commonly occurred during agricultural seasons. Worship and thanks are given to the Great Spirit, which is perceived to be the source of all that is necessary for survival, the one perceived to be the primary life force protecting people from threat and danger.

The Oglala Lakota (Sioux)

In the Lakota tradition, the Great Spirit is known as *Wakan Tanka*, which some scholars translate as "the Great Mystery." According to Raymond J. Demallie, the Oglala Lakota (often referred to as the Dakota) culture was "characterized by its oneness, its unity" (1987, 27). There is no separation of the natural world from the world of the supernatural. This unity in nature is thought to be beyond the comprehension of humankind and could only be shared through the practice of rituals. This animating force pervades universal life at every level.

Wakan Tanka is an amorphous category most precisely defined by its incomprehensibility. The Dakota rituals are based on mystical experiences instead of systematic worship. Personal ecstatic experience, expressed in word or chant or movement, is central to the group's ritual practice. Ritual dance is the most extensive medium employed to express religious sentiment. The Dakota are encouraged to contribute to the understanding of Wakan Tanka through their own individual relationship with the spirit world.

One significant influence that Christianity has had on the Dakota belief system is the tendency to personify the Wakan Tanka (Demallie 1987, 28). Before contact with European settlers, Wakan Tanka was without distinction. The Dakota seem to have given anthropomorphic attributes to their creator, fashioned after the God images of the imposed Christian faith.

The Hopi

To the Hopi, the Great Spirit is the source of all wisdom, spiritual and practical. The cultural values of daily life, the rituals of worship, the procuring and sharing of food, and the arts of planting and harvesting are all attributed to the Spirit that provides and protects. Hopi tradition tells of sacred tablets that various deities imparted to the Hopi. Like most of Hopi mythology, accounts differ as to when the tablets were given and in precisely what manner. The tablets are a set of ivory stones with hieroglyphs cut into them, adopting strange figures, and they are thought to resemble sacred carvings of other indigenous traditions. For the Hopi, stones serve as sacred icons, providing a guiding sacred text and revealing instructions for living well, prophecies, and warnings.

Most Hopi accounts of creation center around *Tawa*, the Sun Spirit. *Tawa* is the Creator who formed the first world out of Tokpella, or Endless Space, as well as its original inhabitants. Hopi mothers still seek a blessing from the sun for their newborn children. However, other accounts have it that *Tawa*, or *Taiowa*, first created *Sotuknang*, whom he called his nephew. Taiowa then sent Sotuknang to create the nine universes according to his plan, and it was Sotuknang who created *Spider Woman*, or *Spider Grandmother*. Spider Woman served as a messenger for the Creator and interceded on behalf of the people. In some versions of the Hopi creation myth, she is the one who creates all life under the direction of Sotuknang. This is the first of several references to a possible feminization of the Great Spirit, a topic we encounter in subsequent chapters.

The Inuit

The Inuit practice a form of shamanism based on *animist* principles.[18] They believe that all things are imbued with a form of spirit, including humans, and that to some extent these spirits can be influenced or appeased, so that people are empowered in the face of challenge or opposition. The *angakkuq* of a community of Inuit is not the leader, but something closer to a healer or psychotherapist who tends wounds and offers advice, as well as invoking the spirits to assist people in their lives. His or her role is to see, interpret, and exhort the subtle and unseen. These leaders are not trained, but are assumed to be born with gifts to serve the community, an ability that the community recognizes as they approach adulthood.

Inuit religion is closely tied to a system of rituals integrated into the daily life of the people. According to a customary Inuit saying, the great peril of our existence lies in the fact that our diet consists entirely of souls (the spirits of other creatures). By believing that all things, including animals, have souls like those of humans, any hunt that failed to show appropriate respect and customary supplication would only give the liberated spirits cause to avenge themselves. Ritual plays a central role in how the people relate with the spirit world in daily life.

The Navajo

The traditional Navajo way contains no concept for religion as a sphere of activity separate from daily life.[19] Navajo religion has been described as "life itself, the land, and well-being." All living things— people, plants, animals, mountains, and the earth—are relatives.

Each being is infused with its own spirit, or inner form, that gives it life and purpose within an orderly and interconnected universe. The interrelatedness of all creation is recognized through daily prayer offerings and an elaborate system of ceremonies. The purpose of Navajo life is to maintain balance between the individual and the universe and to live in harmony with nature and the Creator. In order to achieve this goal, Navajos devote detailed attention to rituals and other religious practices.

The Navajo people believe that the Creator placed them on land between four sacred mountains: Blanca Peak in Colorado, Mount Taylor in New Mexico, the San Francisco Peaks in Arizona, and Hesperus Peak in Colorado. According to their own history, the Navajos have always lived between these mountains, and they believe that they have been instructed by the Creator never to leave their sacred homeland. For the Navajo peoples, land is ultra-sacred. Worship (ritual), therefore, tends to be associated with well-defined geographical sites, where true encounters with the Great Spirit can be facilitated and experienced.

The Inca

The pre-Inca and Inca had a pantheon of gods and goddesses, all connected somehow with life or nature. Most important were *Pacha Mama* and *Pacha Tata*, earth mother and father. Three other gods gained importance in the lives of these people: snake, puma, and condor. The *snake* represents intellect, knowledge, and the past. Of course, the Spanish destroyed most of what they came across, but they left the snake symbolism intact, because they saw it as proof that the Incas were evil devil-worshipers.

The *puma* represents courage and internal strength to engage with the challenges of daily life, and is foremost of importance in pre-Inca and Inca symbolism. For example, Lake Titicaca means "the meeting place of the pumas." The temple of the sun in Cuzco has a puma-tooth design. Pumas are central to Inca lore also because they signify life completely in the present—the moral ideal of the culture.

The *condor* represents what people should strive for: balance. The condor is also significant in discerning the meaning of the future, the possibility of life in another dimension—free, balanced, and soaring toward the heavens. Many other natural "deities" are in the Inca pantheon, but these few illustrate the importance of nature to their entire worldview.

The Osage

The Osage religion is pantheistic.[20] All life forms and changes in the universe are considered to be the product of a single mysterious life-giving force called *Wa-kon-tah*. Humans are merely one manifestation of Wa-kon-tah. Traditionally, clans have been totemic, in that the members of a particular clan were more closely associated or linked to some manifestation of Wa-kon-tah than others. The Osage never claimed to fully understand this force and how it worked. There were spirits, and through visions, humans communicated with them and gained their support. Some humans could turn themselves into animals. Power derived from supernatural knowledge was deemed to be neither good nor evil.

The peyote religion was brought to them in the 1890s. The Osage peyote church was based on Christianity and totally rejected traditional religious beliefs and practices. By the 1910s, traditional religious ceremonies were gone. Only a few Osage peyote churches exist today, and these are now affiliated with the Native American church.

The Maya

The traditional Mayan religion of western Honduras, Guatemala, Belize, and Mexico (Chiapas and Yucatán) is a southeastern variant of *Mesoamerican* religion. Like all contemporary Mesoamerican religions, it results from centuries of symbiosis with Roman Catholicism. When its pre-Spanish antecedents are taken into account, however, traditional Mayan religion already existed for more than two millennia as a recognizably distinct phenomenon.

The ancient Mayan concept of "deity" or "divinity" (*k'u* in Yucatec, *qabuvil* in ancient Quiché) is poorly understood, but can by no means be reduced to a mere personification of natural phenomena. Deities are intimately related with every aspect of daily life: agriculture, midwifery, trade, warfare, and hunting. The life cycle of maize, for instance, lies at the heart of Mayan belief, but the role of the *Mayan maize-god* transcends the sphere of agriculture to embrace basic aspects of civilized life in general (such as writing).

These tribes believe that every being—living and nonliving—has a creative spirit. They call this creative spirit the "Great Mystery." They believe that the "Four Directions" (east, west, north, and south) have to be well-balanced for good things to occur. The four directions symbolized by four brothers—and the center point, by a female, their sister—are represented using certain colors or animals.

The Blackfoot People

Also known as the *Niitsítapi* (the "Original People"), the Blackfoot are a tribe of Native Americans who currently live in Montana and Alberta, Canada. They lived north and west of the Great Lakes and came to participate in Plains Indian culture. "Old Man" is how the Blackfoot people refer to the Great Mystery. Old Man personally created all things and instructed the Blackfoot people on how to attain spiritual wisdom in daily life. Old Man is not a humanlike divinity similar to Jesus, nor a panentheistic deity as in Brahmanism. Rather, Old Man is simply acknowledged to exist in the sense of the Aristotelian "prime mover," and the traditional teachings are attributed to "him" as a source.

There are specific fables regarding Old Man, not codified as in a religion, but rather used to guide individuals and communities on a moment-by-moment basis. As noted with other groups above, love for the land—and reverence for all it embodies—is a central feature. Insofar as a sense of divine presence prevails, it is known first and foremost through the natural world, and is perceived to be a spiritual life force, with obvious similarities to the notion of the Great Spirit.

Australian Aborigines

Aborigines have occupied Australia for at least forty thousand years. They came originally from Southeast Asia, entering the continent from the north. Although Aborigines are classified as *Homo sapiens*, biological isolation has meant that, racially, they are not closely related to any other people. Because of their relative cultural isolation, Aborigines were forced to develop their own solutions to the problems of human adaptation in the unique and harsh Australian environment. The result was a stable and efficient way of life. Probably because of its effectiveness, the society was slow to change, especially technologically, giving a popular but false impression of a primitive people. The archaeological record reveals a number of innovations, among them the earliest known human cremations, some of the earliest rock art, and certainly the first boomerangs, ground axes, and grindstones in the world.

Central to Australian aboriginal spirituality is the double notion of Dreamtime and the Dreaming. First, the Dreaming refers to a sacred past era in which ancestral totemic spiritual beings formed the creation we know today. Two ancestral beings known as the *Ungambikula* awoke from the ancient dream and surfaced on earth, encountering unshaped bundles of organic matter. With their great stone knives, the Ungambikula carved heads, bodies, legs, and arms out of the bundles. They made the faces, and the hands and feet. At the end of the process, human beings were fashioned.

This work done, the ancestors went back to sleep. Some of them returned to underground homes, others became rocks and trees. The trails the ancestors walked in the Dreamtime are holy trails. Everywhere the ancestors went, they left sacred traces of their presence—a rock, a waterhole, a tree. The Dreamtime does not merely lie in the distant past; the Dreamtime is the eternal now, and the Dreaming is the practical living-out of the spirituality embodied in the Dreamtime.

The Dreaming establishes the structures of society, rules for social behavior, and the ceremonies performed to ensure continuity of life and land. It governs the laws of community, cultural lore, and how people are required to behave in their communities. The condition that is the Dreaming is met when people live according to the law, and participate in the rituals and ceremonies, richly adorned with song and dance (www.aboriginalculture.com.au/religion.shtml). The Dreaming is a complex network of knowledge, faith, and practices that derive from stories of creation. It pervades and informs all spiritual and physical aspects of an indigenous Australian's life.

They believe that every person essentially exists eternally in the Dreaming. This eternal part existed before the life of the individual begins, and continues to exist when the life of the individual ends. Both before and after life, this spirit-child is believed to exist in the Dreaming and is only initiated into life by being born through a mother.

In the Aboriginal worldview, every event leaves a record in the land. Everything in the natural world is a result of the actions of the archetypal, ancestral beings, whose actions created the world. Central to all the different spiritual beings (deities or spirits) is the Great Spirit, which inhabits all things, including the air we breathe. This Great Spirit was known by various names in different areas. In some cases, a number of different communities adhered to the same Great Spirit. Byamee, Wandjina, and Nargacork were some of the most commonly worshiped Great Spirits.

The Great Spirit is usually described as a male figure, a great father, with the earth correspondingly understood as the Great Mother. From the legends we learn that in the beginning, the mighty Creator was responsible for creating every aspect of the earth's environment. The mighty Creator organized the seasons, created the sun and moon, constructed the wildlife, and finally made men and women. It was believed that the Great Spirit lived eternally, watching and protecting his followers affectionately.

(Material on the Maori of New Zealand appears in chapter 9.)

Pause for a Moment

As you reflect on the material of this chapter, consider these words from the scripture scholar, John Dominic Crossan: "It is not that those ancient people told literal stories and we are now smart enough to take them symbolically, but that they told the stories symbolically and we are dumb enough to take them literally." Undeniably, we have advanced in knowledge and technology, but along the way we may have lost a sacred wisdom that would enable and empower us to engage life with greater grace and creativity. The split between the sacred and secular was largely unknown to our ancient ancestors. Perhaps once more we need to invoke the Great Spirit to redeem us from all the false divisions that bewilder and confuse us in the modern world.

Native American Spirituality

The following words are attributed Chief Seattle (1854), and while the source is not known with certainty, they provide a useful focus for understanding Native American spirituality: "Humankind has not woven the web of life. We are but one thread within it. Whatever we do to the web, we do to ourselves. All things are bound together. All things connect." The statement asserts the foundational belief that a wisdom within creation is foundational to all that exists. That is the wisdom of the Great Spirit.

The Spirit is not equivalent to the material or cosmic creation, yet the Spirit dwells deeply within all that exists—energizing, animating, and sustaining everything in the process of being and becoming. The metaphorical role of mothering comes readily to mind, as we see illustrated in the Ten Commandments known to several indigenous American groups:

- The Earth is our Mother, care for her.
- Honor all your relations.
- Open your heart and soul to the Great Spirit.
- All life is sacred; treat all beings with respect.
- Take from the Earth what is needed and nothing more.
- Do what needs to be done for the good of all.
- Give constant thanks to the Great Spirit for each new day.
- Speak the truth; but only of the good in others.
- Follow the rhythms of nature; rise and retire with the sun.
- Enjoy life's journey, but leave no tracks.

These guidelines are clearly addressed to humans, yet embody a different emphasis from what we often find in popular myths of origin, where the human prerogative comes to the fore. For the various groups described in this chapter, a sense of confusion is detectable between a primordial spirituality focused on the work of the Great Spirit in creation at large, and the more anthropocentric sense of structure that in all probability is an import from formal religion. In several cases cited above, the original creator is a dominant male figure, significantly different from the Earth Mother who heads the list of indigenous commandments.

We also detect in the literature describing the spiritual evolution of the above groups a preoccupation with structure, order, and control. Even in the notion of the Dreaming in Australian spirituality, the freedom and unpredictability of the dreaming process is quickly molded into beliefs that have assumed dogmatic significance over time. Indeed, for several indigenous groups of our time, a rather painful tension prevails in dealing with the incursions made by modern consumerist values. In theory they seek to counteract those influences, but in practice they often collude with them, and end up being absorbed by them.

In one form or another all the above groups acknowledge the key role of the Great Spirit. Having acknowledged it, they tend not to speculate on what it is or how it functions. It is not an anthropocentric entity of any type, yet embraces all that is authentically human and personal. Clearly, it is a very different understanding of God or divinity than what we encounter in mainstream religion. For indigenous people the Great Spirit is ultra-real, awesome yet intimate, tender yet fierce (as in storm and catastrophe), all-pervasive yet transcendent, capable of being known and experienced yet inexhaustible in its wisdom and creative potential. It transcends all dualisms and works cocreatively with every emergence of the evolving creation.

Elizabeth Johnson (2008, 124) captivates the primordial essence of the Great Spirit in these inspiring words:

> Since what people call God is not one being among other beings, not even a discreet Supreme Being, but mystery which transcends and enfolds all that is, like the horizon and yet circling all horizons, this human encounter with the presence and absence of the living God occurs through the mediation of history itself in its whole vast range of happenings. To this movement of the living God that can be traced in and through experience of the world, Christian speech traditionally gives the name Spirit.

Humans are not invited to serve and obey the Great Spirit. Patriarchal imagery is distinctive by its absence. We are invited to cocreate with the Spirit. The living enterprise is a partnership, embracing challenges and responsibilities that far outweigh those of formal religion, as illustrated by Canadian ecofeminist Sharon V. Betcher (2007). Ethically, it is not a case of getting it wrong or right, but of always being open to learn, change, and grow. That learning requires above all else contemplative attention to the earth we inhabit and the universe to which we belong. Through our belonging—how we appropriate and embrace it—we learn to live responsibly and creatively.

American feminist writer Charlene Spretnak often describes spirituality as the aspect of human existence that explores the subtle forces of energy in and around us and reveals to us profound interconnectedness (see Spretnak 1991). Groundedness in the Great Spirit is what spirituality is all about, connecting deeply with the sacred within and without, and striving to live in graced fidelity to God, the world, and all the other creatures who share the planet with us.

Chapter 8

The Spirit of Africa

There is no theology if it is not a liberating theology. The new theology will now have to be cosmo-biocentric in order to humanize both humanity and the planet from a perspective of eco-justice.

— JOSE MARIA VIGIL

The point of the Christian doctrine of the Spirit is that God's Holy Spirit can work in, with, and through all places, spaces, and scales of creation.

— SIGURD BERGMANN

AFRICA IS THE BIRTHPLACE of the human race. Africa is the collective homestead we have known and inhabited for an estimated 7 million years. Thanks to the intensive and sophisticated research of modern paleontology, and its exploration of human origins, we now have access to ancient developments depicting not merely the noble savage of the past, but generations of ancestors whose aspirations and achievements evoke wonder, amazement, and deep spiritual significance (cf. Gibbons 2007; O'Murchu 2008).

We have evidence for artistic expression dating back almost two hundred thousand years and a repertoire of ritual behaviors dating to some one hundred thousand years ago. When it comes to Africa, the enduring influence of Spirit power can no longer be dismissed under the labels of primitive savagery or pagan ignorance. Spirit-filled growth and transformation seem to have been at work from our primal origins. In the landscape of Africa, the Holy Spirit has been breathing in the human soul, not merely for thousands, but for millions of years.

Spirit: Ancient and New

Christian missionaries often remark that the Spirit leads people to Christ, a statement made with the underlying assumption that only toward the Christ of Christianity can the Spirit lead. For several millennia, however, the Spirit has led people to a sense of holy mystery, long before the Christian religion ever evolved. We need to be wary and much more discerning lest our Christian ideology (an imperialism) leads us away from deeper truth rather than toward it. Assuredly, the Spirit leads people in ways we can only discern with hindsight and in retrospect. It may or may not be toward the Christian Christ, but consistently it will be to energize and empower people toward a fuller and deeper sense of our sacred humanity, as well as a deeper recognition of the sacred at work in every sphere of God's creation.

Throughout the long eons of emergence in our African homestead, we encountered the empowering Spirit in several significant ways. Our cultural acquisitions—through art, music, ritual, and human ingenuity—characterize a species that acts wisely and creatively for most of our emerging history. This is a very different portrayal from the flawed, sinful creature popularized in conventional Christianity (and occasionally in other religions, too). As we access the deeper layers of our human evolutionary story, it is not original sin that we encounter but *original blessing*. We evidence a species cocreating constructively and responsibly—augmented, it seems, by one major influence: *a close affiliation with the natural world*. The land is the sacred nexus through which ancient Africans—and several other indigenous peoples—first encountered the vitality of the Great Spirit.

Thomas Berry (2006, 118) describes our ancient earth experience in these words:

> Humans in this earlier period of human development, experienced themselves as owning nothing, as receiving existence itself and life and consciousness as an unmerited gift from the universe, as having exuberant delight and unending gratitude as their first obligation. It was a personal universe, a world of intimacy

and beauty. A universe where every mode of being lived by a shared existence with all other modes of being. No being had meaning or reality or fulfillment apart from the great community of life. This primordial Earth community itself existed through the presence of the indwelling spirit whence came its sacred character.

When humans remain close to the earth and emulate the processes of nature in our daily lives, the indications are that we behave in a benign and constructive fashion, benefitting the living earth from which we derive all the benefits upon which we survive and thrive. For much of the twentieth century, anthropologists dismissed this "enmeshment with nature" as a primitive, infantile dependency, from which advances in rationality would release us. As we became more rational, allegedly we would transcend our earthbound dependency and thus become more fully human. Here we evidence a classic and tragic example of humans projecting onto past experience the so-called civilized norms of the present time, undermining our ancient sacredness, and depriving subsequent generations of a resource richly imbued with meaning and hope.

In recent millennia, widespread alienation characterizes our evolution, leading progressively to exploitation and violence, symptoms of a species that has lost its way because it has been disconnected from its primal moorings. We need to reconnect with this ancient wisdom, particularly with its African foundations, not by regressing into some fantasized idyllic past, but by reappropriating our grounding where we truly belong. Thomas Berry aptly describes the challenge (2009, 52):

> It is necessary to speak of these earlier traditions in order to identify the continuing need that humans have for placing human affairs within the integral structure and functioning of the universe. All these earlier traditions had two sacred obligations. One was to understand and revere the all-pervasive numinous presence throughout the universe. The other was to realize the essential continuity of all things within the universe and to abhor any isolation from the larger

community of existence. Both these commitments of earlier human societies have been abandoned, and we have, as a result, become lost and the world about us desolate. A break of immense significance has occurred.

The breakthrough—the call to repair the disruption from our primal rootedness—requires a profound shift in perception, understanding, and action. Central to that endeavor is a rediscovery and reappropriation of the creative Spirit that inhabited the living earth long before formal religion ever evolved. It is not a totally new learning. Intuitively and instinctively we know what it is about, and as a species we know it particularly from the long millennia we spent in Africa. That is where we first encountered the living force of the empowering Spirit, and that is where we first learned to cocreate with the evolutionary awakening of God, as the Spirit—time and again—hovered over our efforts to coexist lovingly and responsibly within the living earth itself (see more in Mayson 2010; Mbiti 1991).

⸝

Pause for a Moment

Were you already aware of the fact that Africa is the cradle of humanity, the first birthplace we all have known? And what Christians call Incarnation—God's radical immersion in human flesh—first took place in Africa. In 2008 I did a field trip to the Olduvai Gorge in Tanzania, led by a young African man. I asked him why African people seemed so ignorant of the great human story, endemic to their land. His response: "Because the missionaries denounced our indigenous wisdom as primitive paganism." Is there still a place for Christian mission to the two-thirds world? If you were designing a program for modern missionaries, what would be the key ingredients and the central strategy of the undertaking?

⸝

The oldest Pentecost known to the human race happened in Africa. Today, an authentic overview of the role of the Holy Spirit in the African context should not begin merely with early Christian developments in North Africa (monastic Egypt or Augustine's Algeria), nor with the Western missionary impetus of the eighteenth and nineteenth centuries, but rather with Africa's evolutionary story as revealed through modern paleontology. This ancient story is richly imbued with creativity and exploration, indicative of a searching heart and a seeking spirit. Once we overcome the colonial bias of savagery— noble or primitive—we discern in our ancient ancestors psychic and communal propensities arising from a deep spiritual source. This is the living Spirit of God breathing over the void, filled in this case by humans evolving over a time span of some 7 million years.

African Animism

Long before animism or totemism were coined as ways of describing the spiritual development of African peoples in prereligious times, spirituality was flourishing in Africa. It is noteworthy that the anthropologist Edward Tylor writes extensively about animism in Africa, but develops his key insights as a theory of *souls* rather than of *life forces*. His Western bias prevented him from seeing the deeper and wider significance of what was transpiring. We hear similar echoes in James Frazer's classic work, *The Golden Bough*: "To the savage the world in general is animate, and trees and plants are no exception to the rule. He thinks that they have souls like his own, and he treats them accordingly" (quoted in Harvey 2005, 146).

Graham Harvey (2005) provides a fine overview of animism, acknowledging its transpersonal and spiritual significance (see also http://www.animism.org.uk). Harvey defines *animism* as the attempt to live respectfully as members of the diverse community of living persons (only some of whom are human) that we call the world or cosmos. His use of the term "person" can be initially dislocating. Harvey wants to dislodge the exclusiveness of human rationality by claiming that the consciousness and creative energy that constitute human beings belong to all organic life throughout the planetary creation. We all receive this "living energy" from the larger cosmos, the creative source of all that exists.

Harvey does not invoke the notion of the Spirit as I do throughout the present work. His use of animism, however, is remarkably similar: *everything is animated, enlivened, or, energized by an underlying life force*. Living out of an animistic perspective, therefore, means a quest to find an appropriate manner of expressing respect, communicating mutuality, and engaging with the web of life in a way that enhances the well-being of all sentient beings.

In the African context, ancestor worship serves to highlight the culture of animism. Not all who have died are deemed to be ancestors. The term refers to named individuals and not merely to some amorphous and vague conglomerate of all the departed. To be an ancestor is to continue to be in relationship in a distinctive way. This may ensue in the perception that the ancestor inhabits a particular tree, plant, lake, or mountain, and very specifically will be perceived as embodied in one or more members of the next generation(s).

Here the sense of *ensoulment* is different from the Western notion of the soul. Animism transcends the dualistic emphasis that places soul over body, spirituality over physicality, mind over matter, culture over nature, intention over performance, and inner over outer. This sense of interconnectedness comes closest to the Christian notion that the Holy Spirit is a force for embodied unity throughout the entire creation. In the words of theologian Marc Wallace, "God is not a sky-God divorced from the material world. As once God became earthly at the beginning of creation, and as once God became human in the body of Jesus, so now God continually enfleshes Godself through the Spirit in the embodied re-ality of life on earth" (personal correspondence with author, January 4, 2012). In and through the living Spirit, the animistic sense of aliveness endures.

African animism is woven into the legends and myths of ancestral wisdom. Worship of the ancestors has long been a central feature of African spirituality (cf. Mbiti 1991; Kirwen 1994; Gehman 2005). Among other things, ancestor worship serves as a means of relating creatively with the spirit world, so that a benign and fruitful relationship can ensue. The fruitfulness is never merely between two individuals, but is better envisaged as a deeper quality of engagement with the organicity of the living universe. The ancestors continue to be truly alive, because everything in creation is endowed with a sense of aliveness. Even the living dead are connected with the web of life.

African Spirits

Much of this ancient belief system still flourishes among contemporary African peoples. Often misunderstood and maligned by researchers, and frequently denounced by Christian missionaries, it nonetheless continues to survive and thrive. Contemporary researchers such as Gerrie ter Haar (2009)—more aware of, and sensitive to, cultural conditioning—provide us with more perceptive insights. While not denying the recessive and destructive employment of ancient practices (by Africans and others), today we more readily clarify and differentiate the authentic from the superficial, that which belongs to deeper layers of meaning rather than that which has been corrupted by internal or external forces.

I outline a small sample of contemporary African spirituality, highlighting the vision of some of the better-known indigenous traditions. Being part of the modern world, these groups are heavily influenced by corroding forces of our time that threaten the integrity of their inherited wisdom. Sometimes the groups themselves react defensively, striving to hold on to tradition for the sake of tradition—a response that tends to undermine the wisdom they have to bestow while also truncating their own development and evolution. Adjusting authentically to the modern world is a big challenge for all indigenous cultures.

In the following analysis, as far as possible I try to honor the inherited wisdom, while also highlighting its usefulness for people of our time. My interest is predominantly in the area of spirit power and spirit influence, just one aspect of indigenous African spirituality, but as we shall see an underlying construct on which several other dimensions evolve and grow.

The Maasai

The Maasai are one of the oldest and best known of African tribes. They believe in one God, whom they call *Ngai*. Ngai is neither male nor female, but seems to have several different aspects. There are two main manifestations of Ngai: *Ngai Narok*, which is good, benevolent, and black; and *Ngai Na-nyokie*, which is angry and red, like the British. Ngai is the creator of everything.

In the beginning, Ngai (which also means sky) was one with the earth and owned all the cattle that lived on it. But one day the earth and sky separated, so that Ngai was no longer connected with humans. The cattle, though, needed the material sustenance of grass from the earth, so to prevent them dying, Ngai sent down the cattle to the Maasai by means of the aerial roots of the sacred wild fig tree, and told them to look after them. The Maasai do this to the present time, quite literally taking the story as an excuse to rob neighboring tribes of their own livestock. No surprise, then, to find that cattle play an important role in ritual occasions, such as initiation, marriage, and the passage of one life stage to the next, where the sacrifice of the animal is understood to bridge the gap between humans and God.

At birth, Ngai gives each person a guardian spirit to ward off danger and carry each one away at the moment of death. The evil are carried off to a desert, while the good unsurprisingly go to a land of rich pastures and many cattle. In this tribe, the notion of spirit is distinctly anthropocentric. Although spirit is perceived to be present everywhere in creation, the providing and protective care of the spirit for humans forms the basis of most Maasai mythology and ritual practice.

The Zulu Tribe

For many people, the Zulu are known far beyond their African homestead. Their military exploits led to the rise of a great kingdom that was feared for a long time over much of the African continent. The Zulu are the descendants of Nguni-speaking people. Their written history can be traced back to the fourteenth century.

Zulu religion includes belief in a creator god (Nkulunkulu), who is above interacting in day-to-day human affairs. It is possible to appeal to the spirit world only by invoking the ancestors (Ama Dlozi) through divination processes. As such, the diviner, who is almost always a woman, plays an important part in the daily lives of the Zulu. All bad things, including death, are believed to be the result of evil sorcery or offended spirits. No misfortune is ever seen as the result of natural causes.

Ancestral spirits are important in Zulu religious life. Offerings and sacrifices are made to the ancestors for protection, good health, and happiness. Ancestral spirits come back to the world in the form of dreams, illnesses, and sometimes snakes. The Zulu also believe in the use of magic. Anything beyond their understanding, such as bad luck and illness, is considered to be sent by an angry spirit. When this happens, the help of a diviner (soothsayer) or herbalist is sought. He or she will communicate with the ancestors or use natural herbs and prayers to get rid of the problem.

For the Zulu, spirit force is very real, and the ancestral mediation of spirit power is frequently invoked. Yet the fear of spirits is quite prevalent, and rituals seeking to control or expel the evil spirit seem more widespread than those used to invoke the spirit world positively or proactively.

The Kikuyu Tribe (Kenya)

The Kikuyu believes in one God, Ngai, the creator and giver of all things. He has no father, mother, or companion of any kind. Ngai cannot be seen by mortal eyes. He is a distant being and takes little interest in individuals in their daily walks of life. Yet he becomes hugely significant at life's crisis moments. At the birth, initiation, marriage, and death of every Kikuyu, communication is established with Ngai. The ceremonies for these four events leave no doubt as to the importance of the spiritual assistance that is essential to them.

In the traditional religion of the Kikuyu, the elders, or the older people within a clan, were considered to be the authority of God (Ngai). They used to offer to Ngai propitiatory sacrifices of animals, in chosen places that were considered sacred, usually near a fig tree or on the top of a hill or mountain. Even today there are large sacred trees where people sometimes gather for religious or political meetings or particular feasts. Mount Kenya, especially for the clans who live on its slopes, is considered the home of God.

In everyday life, there are no specific prayers or religious cere-monies. As long as people and things go well and prosper, the presumption is that God is pleased with the general behavior of the people and the welfare of the country. In this happy state there is no need for prayers. Indeed, they are inadvisable, for Ngai must not needlessly be bothered. Only when humans are in real need can they approach him without fear of disturbing him and incurring his wrath.

The Kikuyu faith system, like others throughout Africa, suggests strong Christian influence. The distant sky god essentially belongs to a mysterious, heavenly realm. While personal, this god rarely comes close to people. While in daily life people often sense the closeness of the living spirit of God, this awareness only features minimally the Kikuyu's more formal system of ritual and worship.

San Bushmen

The San peoples worship mighty Kaggen, the trickster-deity. He created many things and appears in numerous myths where he can be foolish or wise, tiresome or helpful. The San believe that there is a supreme god, lesser gods, and other supernatural beings as well, including the spirits of the dead. The San of the Kalahari believe that the supreme god is associated with life and the rising sun, and the lesser god with illness and death. The shamans—medicine people— have access to the lesser gods, who can help in getting rid of illness during ritual dance and trance behavior.

The San also pay homage to the spirits of the deceased. Most San believe that upon death, the soul goes back to the great god's house in the sky. The dead influence the lives of the living. For example, when a medicine man dies, the San would be concerned as to whether his spirit may return to haunt and endanger the living.

San beliefs center around the concept that everything is part of the same great web of nature, and all have an equal right to existence. Humans, as mere parts of the cosmos, have no special claims over the animals and the birds. Birth, death, gender, rain, and weather are all believed to have supernatural significance, with fortune, for good or ill, dictating how people experience these events.

To deal with life's fortunes, the shamans play a crucial role. By entering into a trance, which links them to the spiritual world, they are able to heal, drive away evil spirits and sickness, foretell the future, control the weather, ensure good hunting, and generally look after the well-being of the group.

The San seem to have a more developed sense of Spirit engagement, with the shaman playing a more empowering role, as distinct from the religious functionary in most tribes, who tends to be male and often endowed with exalted patriarchal power.

Yoruba (Southwestern Nigeria)

In the Yoruba creation myth, Olodumare (also called "Olorun") is the creator. Olodumare is so all encompassing that there can be no gender assigned. Olodumare is therefore most correctly referred to as "it." To the Yorubas, Olodumare is supreme and controls the destiny of all living beings. During human creation, Olodumare gave the *emi*, or breath of life, to humans.

According to oral tradition, the high god, Olodumare, asked Orishala to descend from the sky to create the first Earth; Orishala was delayed, and his younger brother, Oduduwa, accomplished the task. Shortly afterward, sixteen other *orisha* came down from heaven to create human beings and live on earth with them. The descendants of each of these deities are said to have spread Yoruba culture and religious principles throughout the rest of Yorubaland.

Traditional Yoruba religion is centered around a pantheon of ancestral deities called *orisha*. When a child is born, a diviner (*babalawo*) is consulted to determine which orisha the child should follow. As adults, the Yoruba often honor several of these deities. The orishas help to create and maintain order on earth.

Yoruba philosophy holds that all humans have the *ayanmo* (destiny, fate) to become one in spirit with Olodumare, the divine creator and source of all energy. The thoughts and actions of each person interact with all other living things, including the earth itself. Each person attempts to achieve transcendence and find one's destiny in the spiritual realm of those who do good and beneficial things. One's spiritual consciousness in the physical realm (known as *Ori-Inu*) must grow in order to consummate union with the divine.

Despite some patriarchal elements, Yoruba spirituality considers spirit power to be innate to all living beings, and through this power humans can link directly with the divine source of all life.[21]

Ibo (or Igbo)

Igbo people are among the largest and most influential ethnic groups in Nigeria (southeastern regions). Today most are Christian; over half are Roman Catholic. The ancient Igbo religion and traditions are known as *Odinani*. The Igbo are a profoundly religious people who believe in a benevolent creator, usually known as *Chukwu*, who created the visible universe (*uwa*). Opposing this force for good is *agbara*, the devil, to which all evil is attributed. In the realm of nature, spiritual influence is attributed mainly to spiritual forces, known as the *alusi*.

The alusi are minor deities, and they are forces for blessing or destruction, depending on circumstances. They punish social offenses and those who unwittingly infringe on their privileges. The role of the diviner is to interpret the wishes of the alusi, and the role of the priest is to placate them with sacrifices. Either a priest is chosen through hereditary lineage, or he is chosen by a particular god for his service, usually after passing through a number of mystical experiences. Each person also has a personalized providence, known as *chi*, which comes from *Chukwu* and returns to him at the time of death. This chi may be good or bad.

There is a strong Igbo belief that a person's ancestors keep constant watch over human behavior. The living show appreciation for the dead and pray to them for future well-being. Speaking badly of a spirit is against tribal law. Those ancestors who lived well, died in socially approved ways, and were given correct burial rites live in one of the worlds of the dead, which mirror the worlds of the living. They are periodically reincarnated among the living and are given the name *ndichie*—the returners. Those who died bad deaths or lacked correct burial rites cannot return to the world of the living or enter that of the dead. They wander homeless, expressing their grief by causing harm among the living.

Spirit influence is mediated through the ancestors, and interestingly the diviner rather than priest can directly access to the spirit world. (On the role of diviner, see Kirwen 1994.)

Bakongo

The Bakongo people (the Kongo) dwell along the Atlantic coast of Africa from Pointe-Noire, Congo (Brazzaville), to Luanda, Angola. To the east, their territory is limited by the Kwango River, and to the northeast by Malebo (Stanley) Pool, in the Congo River.

According to the traditional religion of the Bakongo, the creator of the universe, Nzambe, lives above a world of ancestor spirits. Many people believe that when a family member dies a normal death, he or she joins this spirit world (or village) of the ancestors, who look after the living and protect the descendants to whom they have left their lands. Spirits of those who die violent and untimely deaths are thought to be without rest until their deaths have been avenged. Using fetishes or charms called *nkisi,* sorcerers are hired to seek out and punish those who were responsible for the death.

In addition, healing practices and traditional religion go hand in hand. Traditional healers called *nganga* may be consulted for herbal treatments or to root out *kindoki,* the negative influence of witches who practice black magic. The role of the witch doctor in this and other African groups is extremely difficult to evaluate objectively. One suspects that the indigenous regard is more subtle and creative, and that much of the negative denunciation is related to Western missionary influence.

Once again, Spirit power is linked to the ancestral line, and although spirit force is fundamentally benign, the Bakongo seem to be concerned primarily with the influence of evil spirits, using the sorcerer as the main resource to dampen such negative affect and ward off its potentially dangerous influence; one wonders how much of this negative view arises from Western moralistic impact.

Bemba

Precolonial religious beliefs revolved around the worship of ancestral spirits *(imipashi)* and nature spirits *(ngulu)*. These spirits controlled uncultivated land and were responsible for the harvest. Chiefs and clan elders prayed and offered sacrifices to the spirits at shrines, which were miniature huts housing relics or natural sites such as waterfalls and springs. Such rituals occurred at important economic events such as the cutting of trees to prepare fields for agricultural use, or before hunting or fishing expeditions. Although rare, these rituals are still performed in parts of northern Zambia.

Chiefs, clan elders, and other ritual specialists pray and make sacrifices to the spirits. Precolonial prophets such as Bwembya claimed to derive their prophecies from the ancestral spirits of kings. Christian prophets such as Alice Lenshina claimed to hear the voices of God and Jesus. Witchcraft purification and detection are still performed by witch finders *(abashinganga)*, often on behalf of traditional chiefs and councilors.

Most Bemba are Christians; biblical stories and proverbs are popular among them. Church congregations led by elected church elders exist in most villages. In the Bemba culture, a degree of integration between indigenous belief and Christianity has taken place; the sense of the spirit world is strong, and in its positive affect works well alongside the Christian practice.

The Malinke

The Malinke (also known as the Mandinka) are one of the largest ethnic groups in West Africa, located mainly in the Gambia, Guinea, Mali, Sierra Leone, Côte d'Ivoire, Senegal, Burkina Faso, Liberia, Guinea Bissau, Niger, and Mauritania. In the 1860s, the Malinke were forced to convert to Islam. Today, over 99 percent of Mandinka in Africa are Muslim, and present understanding of their indigenous beliefs is not easily available as a result.

However, some significant features have been noted. Belief in Spirit power is widespread and adopted in a range of local customs and behavior. The life force that enlivens all reality is known as *nyama*. It controls nature, the stars, and the motions of the sea. Nyama is truly the sculptor of the universe. While nyama molds nature into its many forms, the *nyamakalaw* (handlers of nyama) can shape nyama into art. The nyamakalaw spend their entire lives perfecting special secret skills that are passed down from generation to generation. The "secret" wisdom percolates into several artistic expressions, as in bardic poetry, song, dance, elaborate rituals, and the extensive use of the Djembe drum, called the *Dyinbe* by the Malinke peoples.

In daily life, the creative energy of nyama is mediated through the land. The "spirits of the land" ensure the success of crops. The earliest farmers to have settled in a particular region were believed to have made a deal with the spirits to ensure the successful production of their crops. The Malinke of Mali believed that people of the present were able to keep in touch with the original settlers through spiritual contact with their ancestors, and thus with the spirits of the land. The village head, known traditionally as the *Mansa*, was perceived to be the guardian of the ancestors, and he served as both a religious and secular leader for the people.

Much of this ancient Spirit-informed wisdom prevails—partly subverted yet integrated—in the Muslim-dominated culture. For instance, local spiritual leaders known as *Marabouts* follow the Islamic religion using material from the Qur'an to channel and control the power of the spirit world. They are perceived to be experts at preventing and healing ailments or injuries inflicted by mortals or those who are believed to have been inflicted by evil spirits.

Not unlike the evolutionary spirituality unfolding in the West today, we witness among modern Malinkes a public religious profile (Muslim), and a more covert spiritual dynamism, too hastily dismissed as primitive and barbaric. Behind the public religious veneer there prevails something of the indomitable wisdom of the Great Spirit, with a durability and resilience that is not likely to be subdued.

A Complex Landscape

Several of the above groups have been influenced by Christianity, with varying degrees of syncretism detectable.[22] Labeled as pagan, primitive, and barbaric for much of the missionary epoch, throughout the nineteenth and twentieth centuries a process of inculturation had not yet evolved. Such mutual interaction is very much the product of the closing decades of the twentieth century and remains more of a conceptual than a practical goal. On the other hand, tribal religions that were infiltrated by Islam, such as the Afar peoples in the Horn of Africa, the Berber along the North African coast, and the Dinka in Southern Sudan, have largely lost their indigenous heritage to the indoctrinating influence of the invading religion.

African spirituality is a highly complex amalgam of beliefs, customs, and devotions. Scholars of African religions are keen to emphasize the nondualistic, unified nature of indigenous African spirituality (cf. ter Haar 2009; Mayson 2010). Everything is seen as one, permeated through and through with divine meaning. Binary distinctions of sacred-secular, earth-heaven, and body-soul have no place in African faith systems. All is sacred, an awareness that has seeped into every sphere and domain of life.

However, several African tribal religions exhibit a distinctive patriarchal influence, with deities such as Orisamla of the Yoruba tribe and the God, Olokun, in Benin, portrayed as exercising unilateral power. God is often characterized as exercising absolute control over the entire universe, and such divine governance in descending fashion through patriarchal deities.

In such cases, the Spirit is not a major divine influence in its own right, as in several other indigenous traditions. Rather the Spirit is a mediated force, with the ancestors serving as the primary mediators. This results in a strong anthropocentric influence; the worth and relevance of Spirit tends to be judged by its usefulness for humans, or as in most cases, the potential threat it holds, through sickness, misfortune, or the fatality of death itself.

In the African traditions, Spirit is deemed a problem to be managed, a force to be controlled, requiring the mediation and influence of shamans, diviners, sorcerers, or priests (occasionally). This problematic view may well be linked to missionary influence either from Christianity or Islam. One has to be cautious, however, in drawing conclusions, because little or no scholarly research has been done to help us differentiate what is authentically African and what has ensued from other cultural influences (cf. ter Haar 2009).

Where the patriarchal influence prevails, it is often accompanied by an elevated role for religious leaders such as clergy, with the Spirit-filled people treated as passive and largely unenlightened, thus forced into faith practices of popular religiosity that are neither enlightened nor empowering. With possible Christian influence, Western forms of theism come to be normalized, and for some Africans we see the Genesis narrative being repeated in depicting the omnipotence of

God, enabling him to create the first man and woman, while others consider God to be responsible for all things visible and invisible.

Ever since the beginning of the missionary movement from the West to Africa, African spirituality has been demonized and denounced. Allegations of sorcery, witchcraft, and demonology have been extensively employed. Only in recent times have some missionaries attempted to understand, first, what indigenous African spirituality is about, and second, to engage with it in ways more conducive to dialogue and mutual enrichment.[23] Aided by this new scholarly interest, we can enumerate with greater clarity and conviction how African spirituality is evolving within the African continent today. The following features are still prevalent and may have predated Christian or Islamic missionary influence:

• Until the Europeans came along, Africa knew no written scriptures. The indigenous spirituality was based on oral transmission, with legend and story as the central features.

• Living faith was expressed through ritual, often with ornate elaborate ceremonies—embracing extensive dancing, chanting, and symbolic gifting—and thanking, beseeching, or appeasing the spirits. Strictly speaking, African ritual was not worship as we understand it today; it marked a celebration of life, in conjunction with the spirit world, rather than worship of a deity on high.

• Devotion to the ancestors—as indicated above—has long flourished in African spirituality. The ancestors are perceived to be spirit beings and can influence life in the here and now for better or for worse. The destructive influence of a spirit can be tamed (appeased) or channeled through ritual, sometimes involving sacrifice of a bird or animal.[24]

• African spirituality is earth-centered and nature-focused. Some of the most inspiring communal rituals relate to the changes of the seasons, the fertility of the earth, the equinoxes, and so on. The earth is deemed to be alive, with the power of living spirit. All life springs into being from the aliveness embedded in the soil itself.

• Several texts on African religions refer to belief in a supreme being, or Creator, called by a myriad of names in various languages. It is impossible to establish if the notion of a supreme being is a Western imposition that became normative or if it is inherited from indigenous traditions. Many of the leading myths, while claiming to be innate to Africa itself, smack of colonial influence. The strong emphasis on hierarchy and patriarchy is unlikely to be of African origin.

• Because of the priority today of the patriarchal religious models, the spirit world is often depicted in an abstract and esoteric way, whereas the realm of the Gods is deemed to be more real, influential, and powerful. The spirit world is somewhat illusive, temperamental, and even devious, whereas the Gods behave more rationally and predictably. Those who claim to be familiar with the spirit world as mediums or spirit guides tend to be harshly judged, dismissed, and demonized—many echoes here of postcolonial import.

Is There a Great Spirit in African Spirituality?

The role of the Great Spirit in African religions seems a good deal more complex than elsewhere on the planet. The religious consciousness is a kind of muddied water in which the clarity of the primordial Spirit power is clouded by invasive patriarchal domination. The Great Spirit is frequently confused with the Divine Creator from on high, progressively translating into formal belief systems in which the assertion of faith in the supreme being seems to outweigh the experiential acquaintance with the Spirit that permeates all.

All of which makes it difficult, if not impossible, to discern the role of the Great Spirit in African spirituality either in the past or at the present time. In African religious literature, several allusions are made to the idea of a Great Spirit, but nearly always with a subdued or inferior significance. Negatively, several tribal peoples now view those inhabiting the spirit world as endowed with abstract powers, shadows, or vapors, which take on human shape; these are perceived to be immaterial and incorporeal beings.

The Yoruba and the Igbo believe in another curious category of spirits known to them, respectively, as *abiku* and *ogbanje*. These spirits were born to die. Similarly, there was and still is a belief that these are wandering spirits that specialize in the sadistic mischief of finding their way into women's wombs to be born in order to die.

In some African cultures, the Spirit seems to be reduced to a human artifact in which the Spirit itself seems split between good and evil, perceived to prevail in the human world. Thus the *ori* among the Yoruba and *chi* among the Igbo represent this ambivalent force, capable of bringing good or evil to humans.

Of singular importance for this study is the rapid rise of modern Pentecostalism in Africa today. Often pioneered by vivacious preachers of U.S. origin (or trained there), their preoccupation is to sell fundamental Christianity with little or no regard for the planetary and cosmic dimensions of indigenous faith. The influence of Spirit belongs primarily to worship, an individual endowment often predicated on the reception of Baptism in a particular church or denomination. When the Great Spirit, by whatever name, moves among the worshipers some may cry out in release from the accumulated tribulations of daily life. This emotional dimension may be cathartic and contribute to healing and well-being, but it all too quickly becomes a God of the gaps, creating an unhealthy codependence, disempowering people from being able to engage the wider vicissitudes of their daily life and existence.

Today the worship of Spirit in Africa (and elsewhere) has become ensnared in a culture (or cult) of divine deliverance; the ensuing proselytizing can easily beget an unhealthy codependency on the foreign evangelizers, creating confusion and ambivalence around the largely subverted wisdom of the inherited African tradition. The onetime benign sense of the Spirit world, long known to the African peoples, is progressively undermined and eroded by Western evangelical preachers, more preoccupied with their own religious ideology—and the power and wealth they accumulate from it—than with the cultural or spiritual well-being of the African people.

However, the Pentecostal influence in Africa—as elsewhere—deserves a more nuanced evaluation (as in Anderson 1991). As the Pentecostal movement itself seeks to confront its own fundamentalist shadow, it deserves a more discerning assessment, as a movement of our time that is growing rapidly and exerting extensive influence on the evolution of modern spirituality on a global scale. I review this movement in detail in Chapter 12.

Chapter 9

The Asian Pantheon

Asian religions seem to have a better track record in respecting Mystery.

— PAUL F. KNITTER

The Buddha's path did not focus on desire as an enemy to be conquered, but rather as an energy to be perceived correctly. . . . The recognition of the divine in the desire is less about moving towards an ideal than it is about acknowledging its immanence.

— MARK EPSTEIN

WHEN IT COMES TO spirituality and religion, Asia is the panoramic landscape of variety and elegance. But how can anybody hope to do justice to this highly diversified and complex scenario? Asia includes two highly diverse cultural units, China and India, each consisting of over 1 billion people. Added to this are a number of other distinctive cultural regions, such as Japan and Indonesia to the East, Pakistan and Iran to the West, and a vast range of islands that constitute modern Oceania.

The religious environment is also complex, diverse, and subject to syncretistic developments spanning at least five thousand years. Compared with the public face of the major Asian religions—Hinduism, Buddhism, Islam, Shinto, Confucianism, Taoism, Jainism, Sikhism, and Christianity—indigenous spirituality has received scant attention. In fact, we can glean more about Asian indigenous faith from studies done in Oceania (e.g., Polynesia, the Maori of New Zealand) than from research done within mainland Asia. When it

119

comes to the notion of the Great Spirit, the best we can hope for is extrapolation from enduring cultural influences, such as the notion of energy (*Chi*) in several Asian contexts and the central emphasis on meditation and interiority (more in Kim 2011).

After Africa, Asia seems to have been the next part of the planet to be inhabited by human beings, notably in China and in Indonesia. Two famous archaeological finds in China (a hominid skeleton at Jinniushan in the northeast in 1984, and a skull at Dali in the southwest in 1978) confirm the presence of humans from about 200,000 years ago, people who combine the anatomical traits of *Homo erectus* and *Homo sapiens*. On the island of Java (part of present-day Indonesia), paleontologists have unearthed three *Homo erectus* skulls from Sangiran and Mojokerto; they have been dated from 1.8 to 1.6 million years ago (Etler 1996).

Early *Homo sapiens* appear in the fossil record at numerous sites all over China, dating from what archaeologists term the Middle Paleolithic period (125,000 to 40,000 years ago), one of the better-known sites being Zhoukoudian, near Beijing. Illustrated in many of these finds is evidence of increased sophistication in stone-working and tool-making, comparable to the skill and creativity of *Homo sapiens* in Africa, Europe, and elsewhere (more in *Nature* 458 [March 12, 2009], 198–200).

Numerous ancient fossils of the species *Homo erectus* have been found on the Indonesian island of Java. The first, discovered at Trinil in 1891 by Eugene DuBois, has been recently redated to around 1.6 million years in age. Recent research in Indonesia focuses on a partial skeleton found on the island of Flores in 2004 belonging to the species *Homo floresiensis*. The discovery has been dated to 18,000 years ago and, because of its small, hobbit-like stature, is still the subject of intense scholarly debate.

What relevance have these discoveries to the subject material of this book? As I illustrated in a previous work (O'Murchu 2008), advances in paleontology (study of human origins) pose counter-intuitive challenges for many of our long-term assumptions and prejudices, whereby we perceive our ancient ancestors to have been barbaric, primitive, pagan, and largely incapable of anything resembling religious sentiment. Evidence gathered from ancient art forms, burial rites, and a range of prehistoric rituals indicate, to the contrary, that our ancestors often behaved in spiritually informed ways, with a degree of spiritual integration that our contemporaries have either lost or abandoned. Any analysis of spirituality in Asia must—in the name of justice—at least acknowledge this fact, despite the lack of concrete evidence to verify and substantiate its existence.

The Great Religions of Asia

Although the major religions of Asia are unlikely to embrace the spiritual unfolding of the Asian peoples going back into deep time, they offer us an initial aperture to mine the spiritual richness of the Asian continent.

Jainism

The oldest known of the extant religions is Jainism. Numerically quite small (4.2 million), and followed mainly in India, Jainism provides links with the notion of the Great Spirit that are not as obvious in some of the other major faiths. Historians date Jainism's foundation to sometime between the ninth and the sixth centuries BCE. Some have speculated that the religion may have its roots in much earlier times, reflecting native spirituality prior to the Indo-Aryan migration into India. In the Jain religion, every living being has a soul and every soul is potentially divine, with innate qualities of infinite knowledge, perception, power, and bliss. In fact, everything in creation is endowed with an inherited sacredness, hence the central importance of harming no other creature with whom we, humans, share the planet.

There is no supreme divine creator, owner, preserver, or destroyer. The universe is self-regulated; as outlined in chapter 4, science has only stumbled on that idea in relatively recent times. The universe, however, keeps changing due to interactions between matter and energy in the course of time, governed by laws of nature with no necessity of a coordinator or divine regulator. Jains also believe that there is life in other parts of the universe other than on earth; they have extensive knowledge and classifications of various living organisms, including microorganisms that reside in mud, air, and water. Jainism teaches respect for all forms of life and requires that we minimize the harm done to other living beings by practicing five major ethical principles.[25]

Jainism has been described as a spiritual pathway, with a love for life and dislike for the world. The living soul that permeates all reality is understood to be a life-giving spirit, which inhabits everything, but paradoxically can become trapped in *ajiva*, which means inert/nonliving matter. *Ahimsa* (nonviolence) is the hallmark of this spiritual discipline, and while refraining from belief in a Creator God, it strikes me that belief in the power of the Great Spirit is central to this ancient belief system. With this belief so central to Jainism, one wonders why Spirit power remains a largely undeveloped concept in some of the other great religions of Asia.

Hinduism

The oldest of the formal religions known to humanity is Hinduism. Today it flourishes mainly in India itself. It is a highly complex belief system, with an elaborate and amorphous understanding of the sacred, expressed in a range of iconic imagery used in temples for public worship, and in people's homes for devotion and personal sanctification.

Akasha is the Hindi/Sanskrit word meaning "ether," in both its elemental and mythological senses. In Hinduism it is one of the *Panchamahabhuta* (five great elements). Hindus believe that every person's spirit is part of the Great Spirit of the universe they call *Brahman*. This Great Spirit is everywhere. It is eternal, with no beginning and no end, and no form that can be pictured. The many gods and goddesses that Hindus worship represent one aspect of this Great Spirit. Three of the most important gods are *Brahma* the Creator, *Vishnu* the Protector, and *Shiva* the Destroyer. These three gods are known as the Trinity. The Trinity represents the three energies constituting the one God, and these energies are also found in each person. When these energies are balanced, an individual is closest to God.

Hindu's most holy spirit, Brahman, sometimes called "Bhagavan," is transcendent and immanent. He exists beyond the universe, pervading all nature and humanity. Brahman is considered all powerful, all knowing, all loving, and ever present in all things, as the activity of consciousness (see Bracken 1995, 131). He created the universe from himself and exists within each soul. Our creation and evolution are not separate from him, and he eventually absorbs the universe back into himself. Brahman is worshiped in both male and female form, which makes Hinduism the only major world religion where God is worshiped as a woman, although commonly regarded as male.

This brief description illustrates unambiguously the central role of the Great Spirit in the Hindu faith—yet in both scholarly research and popular belief, Brahman tends to be depicted as a supreme deity, assumed to be male rather than female, and frequently described as the all-powerful ruling God, on par with the supreme Divine Father of the monotheistic religions. Even in Hinduism, it feels like the patriarchal God has robbed the high ground from the Great Spirit.

What may be more relevant to the present work are the insights of Christian theologians exploring pneumatology from within the Indian cultural context. P. V. Joseph (2007) collates the research of three theologians—A. J. Appasamy (1891–1975), P. Chenchiah (1886–1959), and V. Chakkari Chettiar (1880–1958)—noting several comparisons between the Christian notion of the Holy Spirit and the Indian deity *Shakti*, usually described as the divine personification of creative cosmic energy and widely worshiped in India as the Great Divine Mother. Understanding the Holy Spirit in such feminine terms occurs in Syriac, Gnostic, and patristic sources (cf. Murray 2006); occasionally it occurs in Western feminist scholarship (e.g., Elizabeth Johnson; Elisabeth Schüssler Fiorenza), but it remains a rich insight from the East with a potential for a much deeper discernment.

Buddhism

Buddhism, on the other hand, sought to purify Hinduism of its excessive externalizations of image and worship in favor of the interior path of mindfulness aimed at breaking the cycle of *samsara* (the endless cycle of suffering). Buddhism spread across the whole of Asia, subdividing into several cultural adaptations, the better known being the *Mayahana* and the *Theravada* expressions, while also morphing into a range of other devotional outlets—the better known being Confucianism and Taoism.

Buddhist teaching seems somewhat ambivalent about the concept of Spirit. To describe what it might be, we need to use reason and human language, which invariably tie us up in the desire to know— and all desire eventually leads to suffering and alienates us from spiritual meaning. Enlightened ones do not need to resort to the human process of trying to understand: they have already achieved a fullness of wisdom. To move in this direction, the seeker needs to grow in awareness by cultivating mindfulness.

In early Buddhism there are two important *suttas* (scriptures attributed to the Buddha) dealing with mindfulness: the *Anapanasati Sutta* (mindfulness of breathing) and *Satipatthana Sutta* (attending with mindfulness). Both suttas emphasize four dimensions of mindfulness: the body, feelings (*vedana*), emotions or mental states, and wisdom. Although both strands include the physical body, the development of mindfulness is linked specifically to the breath. Having found a suitable place for meditation, the breath is the primary tool for discovery and transformation. The instructions focus on getting to know the breath, becoming intimate with it, and using it as the means to shift attention and energy to the process of enlightenment.

There are ancient and elaborate instructions on how to tame the mind and use it to cultivate liberation through nonattachment—that is, noticing when the mind is clinging to our experience and when it isn't. *Impermanence* is a key teaching in Buddhism, often portrayed negatively as the unreliable nature of everything in creation. The flip side of impermanence is the *real*, which defies all human attempts at recognition or definition. Is this not exactly what several indigenous traditions understand by the notion of the Great Spirit?

The Buddha was essentially silent on the relationship between body and spirit. He encouraged his followers to find out from direct experience, rather than talking about it. Meditation—especially mindfulness meditation—is the royal pathway to the wisdom that procures liberation, and in that process the breath is the foundational layer to which the devotee needs to return time and again.

Pause for a Moment

Can you recall when you first became acquainted with the Asia's great religions? It happened for me about thirty years ago, when I first learned Transcendental Meditation, having to engage shortly thereafter with a barrage of criticism for betraying my Christian faith and turning instead to the worship of Hindu gods. Fortunately, I was so convinced of the value of the meditation practice that I easily weathered that storm, paying the price, however, of keeping the matter a secret from my closest friends for almost ten years. Why do we have to be so secretive about what touches the sacred within?

Islam

Today Islam ranks among the great religions of Asia, dominating the religious scene in countries such as Indonesia and Malaysia. The Muslim faith is uncompromising in its devotion to the One God. Unlike most other major religions, it has no doctrine of the Trinity. Allah is the one ultimate God to which all creation is subject. With this emphasis, the unity of God is safeguarded, but perhaps more important, the power of God to rule and govern is unambiguously endorsed.

However, the Qur'an alludes to the notion of God as Holy Spirit in two quite specific ways:

1. Allah, the Almighty One, uses the Holy Spirit as the medium for spirit power—for example, the life principle in the developing fetus. That is why abortion is prohibited in Islam, because the fetus is endowed with the spirit of life. "But He fashioned him in due proportion, and breathed into him something of His Spirit" (Qur'an 32:9; also 38:72; 66:12).
2. The Holy Spirit is used to provide divine guidance for believers who already submit to and enjoy the good favor of Allah: "The Holy Spirit has brought the Revelation from thy Lord in truth,

in order to strengthen those who believe" (Qur'an 16:102);
"By His command doth He send the Spirit [of inspiration] to
any of his servants he pleases" (40:15).

Like the angels, the Holy Spirit in Islam is actually created by
Allah. Allah uses this supernatural "force" to awaken and sustain
spirit power, mainly if not exclusively in human creatures. The
divine status and cosmic nature of the Spirit, which we note in other
religious traditions, is totally absent in Islam. The Islamic sense
of Holy Spirit is the very antithesis of what I am exploring in the
present work.

Ancient Chinese Beliefs

I opened this chapter with reflections based mainly on the Indian
context of Oriental belief systems, and the evidence for the existence
of the Great Spirit that may be unearthed from that source. It seems
an obvious starting place when dealing with the great Eastern
religious traditions. However, such an approach carries a certain
degree of injustice, because it is China, not India, that provides the
oldest evidence in Asia for religious belief and sentiment.

China is considered one of the world's oldest civilizations. The
first Chinese civilization is believed to have originated in the Yellow
River Valley, in the Neolithic era, dating back at least ten thousand
years. Chinese spirituality is better evaluated through artistic
expression rather than through formal religious practice. A mystique
and sacredness in Chinese heritage that impresses even the rational
agnostic is manifested in several ways.

Ancient Chinese architecture is the most magnificent and splendid
aspect of Chinese culture. One architectural wonder is the Great Wall
of China, which was completed during the Ming dynasty. Chinese
traditional arts represent the country's rich heritage. Jade and
pottery were extensively used in Neolithic times, while bronze was
introduced only in the Shang dynasty. China has had a remarkable
track record for ornate garments; archaeological evidence shows
the presence of bone sewing machines, ornamental shells, and stone
beads as early as eighteen thousand years ago.

It was believed that Yellow Emperor had invented martial arts for the first time in about 2600 BCE (before the Shang dynasty). Around 550 BCE, Sun Tzu described the techniques of the martial arts in terms of supremacy in the battlefield. This warrior connotation is still associated with the practice, overshadowing a much earlier understanding exhibiting a more distinctive spiritual flavor: a disciplinary training for both spirit (*shen*) and mind (*xin*). Inner strength belongs to the realm of spirit while mind is used for external expression of a wisdom that originates essentially in the inner being.

When we come to consider the philosophy of Chinese medicine, this distinction between the inner and the outer in ancient Chinese thought becomes much clearer. The concept of *Qi* (Chi) is a central element of Chinese philosophy and healing arts—going back into the dim and distant past. Qi is life force—that which animates and energizes everything in creation, the energetic flow operating unceasingly at the molecular, atomic, and subatomic levels of existence. In Japan it is called *ki*, and in India, *prana* or *shakti*. The ancient Egyptians referred to it as *ka*, and the ancient Greeks as *pneuma*. In Africa it is known as *ashe*, and in Hawaii as *ha* or *mana*.

In China, the understanding of Qi is inherent to the written/spoken word itself. For instance, the literal translation of the Chinese character meaning "health" is "original Qi." The literal translation of the character for "vitality" is "high-quality Qi," while the character meaning "friendly" is "peaceful Qi."

Practitioners of Chinese medicine and of meditation forms such as *qigong* have identified many different kinds of Qi. Within the human body there is the Qi that we're born with, called *Yuan Qi*, or ancestral Qi. The Qi that we absorb during our lives from food, water, and air, and from qigong practice is called *Hou tain Qi*, or postnatal Qi. The Qi that flows at the surface of the body, as a protective sheath, is called *Wei Qi*. Each internal organ also has its own qi/life force—Spleen-Qi, Lung-Qi, and Kidney-Qi, for example. According to Taoist cosmology, the two most fundamental forms of Qi are *Yin-Qi* and *Yang-Qi*—the primordial feminine and masculine energies. Many qigong practices utilize Heaven Qi and Earth Qi, as well as the Qi that emanates specifically from trees, flowers, lakes, and mountains (see more in Orr 2005).

Several web pages allude to the fact that early Chinese beliefs centered on earth, nature, and localized spirits. A vivid and tangible sense of spirit power characterizes Chinese culture in every sphere. Not surprisingly, therefore, creation myths do not feature strongly. Those that do exist appear well after the foundation of Confucianism, *Taoism,* and folk religions. Long before the formal religions, belief in the energizing Spirit seems to have been the central feature of Chinese life and culture.

China is associated with three dominant religions, all with roots in Buddhism. First comes *Shinto*, a set of popular devotions widely practiced in Japan today, but originally belonging to China—hence the derivation "shin tao" (the way of Kami). Central to the practice is the notion of *kami* (see http://en.wikipedia.org/Kami), normally translated as spiritual essence, which can also denote God or Spirit. Shinto's spirits, considered to be millions, are collectively called *yaoyorozu no kami.*

Kami is considered as an innate supernatural force, the realm of the sacred that permeates all reality, including gods, spirit figures, and human ancestors. Although kami is present in all dimensions of the created order, certain places are considered to have an unusually sacred spirit about them and therefore become objects of worship: mountains, trees, unusual rocks, rivers, waterfalls, and other natural edifices. In most cases they are on or near the grounds of a special shrine.

In addition to the many public shrines in Japan, there is the *kamidana*, a house shrine (placed on a wall in the home) that is a "kami residence," acting as a substitute for a large shrine on a daily basis. In each case the object of worship is considered a sacred space inside which the kami spirit actually dwells, the focus within the home for respect and devotion.

More widely known is *Confucianism,* a Chinese ethical and philosophical system developed from the teachings of the Chinese philosopher Confucius (551–478 BCE).[26] It is a complex system of moral, social, political, and religious thought, with authentic humanness as its primary goal. This quality of human flourishing requires a clear, ethical sense of order with leading males playing a crucial role. Loyalty (*zhōng*) is deemed to be the supreme virtue, promoting the order and harmony through which the human community could thrive.

Confucius sought to retrieve the meaning of the past by breathing vitality into seemingly outmoded rituals. His love of antiquity was motivated by his strong desire to understand why certain rituals—such as the ancestral cult, reverence for heaven, and mourning ceremonies—had survived for centuries. He had faith in the cumulative power of culture, as exemplified particularly throughout the Chou dynasty. Confucius regarded heaven (*T'ien*) as a positive and personal force in the universe; he was not, as some have supposed, an agnostic or a skeptic.

Few followers of Confucius today have a clear belief in any divine existence, yet they believe in the world of spirits and souls, and some even practice ancestor worship. The religion of ancient *China* was a form of nature worship, with spirits associated with natural phenomena such as mountains and rivers, land and grain, the sun, the moon, and the stars. All were considered subordinate to the supreme Heaven-god, *T'ien*, also called *Ti* (Lord), or *Shang-ti* (Supreme Lord). T'ien was the upholder of the moral law, exercising a benign providence over all creatures, spirits included.

Confucianism veers toward monotheism, with the ruling God from on high, thus relegating spirit power to a subservient role. Not so *Taoism*, the other major religion in China. Its roots are believed to lie in shamanic traditions that predate even the Hsia dynasty (2205–1765 BCE).

Tao literally means "way," but it can also be interpreted as road, channel, path, doctrine, or line. Essentially, Tao denotes the flow of the universe, or the force behind the natural order. It is the influence that keeps the universe balanced and ordered. Tao is the inner dynamism of Qi, the cosmic life energy through which everything is sustained and flourishes. As an ethical system, Taoism emphasizes the Three Jewels of the Tao: compassion, moderation, and humility. Human well-being is intertwined with the well-being of the entire created order. Harmony with the universe, or the source thereof (Tao), is the intended result of many Taoist rules and practices. Reverence for ancestor spirits is common in popular Taoism.

There is an undefined sense of belief in deities, considered to be embodied primarily in kings and outstanding virtuous people. It is not the deities that are significant, however, but the transpersonal force, the Tao, that has many affinities with the notion of the Great Spirit in several indigenous traditions.

Indigenous Religions of Asia

One of the largest ethnic groups in Asia is known as the *Mien* people (also called the *Yao*), forming several tribal communities in Thailand, Laos, Vietnam, and China. Like their counterparts elsewhere, their spirituality is strongly focused on the Great Spirit, belief in ancestors, and reverence for the creation imbued with spirit energy. There are thousands of indigenous tribal groups spread throughout the Asian subcontinent, some influenced by the Vedic/Hindu culture of India (as in Indonesia), while others have clearly been influenced by the infiltration of Islam and Christianity in more recent times.

Asian tribal groups are characterized by many of the same values and customs we observe in other cultures: a cult of the ancestors, nature spirits, rites of passage, healing and exorcism, and cohesive community spirit. Several Asian groups believe in a supreme God, typically referred to as the Creator or Father of all, yet frequently described as the Great Spirit or the Great Earth Mother. The supreme God is simultaneously transcendent and immanent, the source of all things, the progenitor of the tribe and source of all fecundity. (For more, see http://www.sjweb. info/Documents/dialogo/pastoralapproach.doc).

Several studies have been done on Polynesian myth and ancient beliefs, and in more recent times through one of their best-known survivors, the Maori of New Zealand. A brief overview of Polynesian spirituality gives a good indicator of other indigenous expressions throughout Oceania and mainland Asia—especially where Christian missionary influence has impacted.

We note a strong distinction between the God who reigns in the heavens and the one dwelling on earth in human forms. The Maori *Rangi*—considered to be a thinking, living being, having its own peculiar form—dwells in the heavenly realm. On the other hand, the creator on earth is perceived to be of human form, known as *Tahiti Taa-roa*. There is also the spirit world, *Amed* as *Mana*. Every human being, every god and spirit, every animal and plant, every stone, star, hill, and valley, differed from every other in its class because each had a specific amount and a different kind of mana.

The power and dignity of a sacred chief depended on his mana, part of which he inherited from his godlike ancestors. The mana of the priest was shown by his knowledge of things to come and of how the people should act. He obtained his mana by study and by rites that brought him close to powerful spirits. The mana of the orator, the poet, the teacher, the fisherman, the canoe builder, the house builder, and the farmer was shown by each person's respective skill. The unjust ruler, the dishonest priest, and the unskillful workman were said to have lost their mana through some ignoble action or perhaps never to have had mana.

Although the Polynesians do not separate the natural from the supernatural, we detect a strong Christian influence leading to the prioritization of the ruling sky-God (and his earthly representative) over the all-pervasive Spirit, whose influence on creation tends to be described in piecemeal fashion rather than holistically. We encounter much emphasis on how the spirit pervades each (male) person and object, but little on the cosmic or planetary significance of the Great Spirit as evidenced in other traditions.

The employment of the notion of *tapu* (similar to taboo in Hawaiian traditions) suggests a dualistic split between the sacred and the secular—again with a likely Christian (Western) influence. The strong association with spirit force being linked with the fate of the dead in an afterlife is unlikely to be of indigenous origin.

Polynesians sometimes equate the earth-God with the Great Mother. This theme recurs in several Asian traditions, with the Mother occasionally identified as the Great Spirit. According to Crace Odal (http://www.urduja.com/spirit/mutya.htm), the Filipino notion of the Mutya has ancient spiritual roots (chiefly among those who speak Tagalog) in which a Mother Goddess figure also represents the pristine Spirit (*diwa*), the source of all life and vitality in the universe. According to Young Lee (1996, 105), "Asians tend to seek their divinity in a warm hearted mother rather than in a stern father." They experience the Holy One as close and intimate, yet awesome and even fierce in her destructive capacity. Imaged as a caring and protective mother, the divine pervades all reality in the power of creative energy, a distinctive feature of the Great Mother. In Asian spirituality, the Great Mother is the equivalent of the Great Spirit in several other indigenous traditions, an insight also entertained by the psychologist Carl Jung in his reflections on the Holy Spirit (Jung 1956, 459; more in Appendix 3), with parallels in early Christian thought (Murray 2006).

In India, Hindus address her as *Shakti, Maya, Kali,* and *Durga.* She is also known as Wisdom, *Aum,* Amen, and the Word of God. By whatever name we adopt, her nature is deemed to be one of the unfathomable mysteries of life. Almost everything that can be said of the Great Mother must be couched in metaphors. She is described in terms of waves, clouds, lights, fire, voices, and music. Her existence preceded language. Therefore it stands to reason that she operates without recourse to, or dependence on, words. No amount of intellectual understanding can substitute for a direct and personal experience of her.

Sri Ramakrishna is a widely recognized source for a deeper understanding of the role of the Great Mother in ancient Vedic wisdom (Isherwood 1980). According to Hindu mysticism, the Mother operates the world, creating, preserving, and destroying everything there is. (The Father is the source of creation, but remains ever no-thing, uncreated, un-manifest, im-material).

Having created the universe, the Divine Mother dwells within it; she penetrates and permeates everything that is, every material form. According to Sri Ramakrishna, after the creation the Primal Power, the Mother, dwells in the universe itself. She brings forth this phenomenal world and then pervades it. The essence of the Mother is a universal creative vibration, symbolized by the sacred syllable Aum, which calls matter into being, sustains it for a while, and then releases it back into the general dissolution of the Father.

According to Swami Nikhilananda, the essence of the Divine Mother is shakti or energy; "Shakti is the creative power of the cosmos and prime mover of creation. Without her, nothing can stir or be imbued with life" (Madhu Khanna in Ahmed 2002, 40). Several Christian theologians in India note the connection between the Christian notion of the Holy Spirit and the Hindu concept of Shakti (Kim 2006).

In prehistoric times, the tree was a primary symbol of the Great Earth Mother, which might suggest a carryover from the notion of spirits (like the *devas* and *yakshas*) inhabiting trees, which is found in Hinduism, Buddhism, and Jainism; this concept is also widely attested in the Philippines. In ancient times, Filipinos made offerings to particular trees in which certain benevolent deities, or even certain ancestral spirits, were thought to reside. Other trees were thought to house malevolent spirits, and care was taken to avoid sleeping under them. These animistic sensibilities also extended to several snakes, birds, and animals.

Shamanism and the Great Spirit

Finally I offer a brief overview of shamanism in the Asian context. The word *shamanâ* is from the Tungus tribe of Siberia. Siberia is regarded as the locus classicus of shamanism. Many different ethnic groups inhabit Siberia; its Uralic, Altaic, and Paleosiberian peoples observe shamanistic practices even in modern times. When the People's Republic of China was formed in 1949 and the border with Russian Siberia was formally sealed, many nomadic Tungus groups that practiced shamanism were confined to Manchuria and Inner Mongolia.

From its Siberian origins, Shamanism spread into Asia, mainly through Tibet where the tradition still flourishes. Laos also has had a long tradition in shamanism, where spirit belief and worship are widely practiced. Much of the popular literature for Laos and Thailand focuses on the shaman's role in appeasing or dispelling evil spirits, who are perceived to be the source of misfortune and sickness. Good spirits, on the other hand, inhabit the heavenly realm, and the shaman can implore them to benefit human life on earth.

In Malaysia, associated mainly with an ethnic group known as the *bomohs*, shamanism is linked primarily with healing, a role attributed to shamans in many parts of the world, ancient and modern. In Japan and South Korea, shamanism still flourishes where most shamans are females. Here the shamanness is often regarded as a liminal, borderline figure who is consulted for major business, financial, and personal decisions. The shaman(ness) may also be asked for prayers for an abundant harvest, or for success in secular affairs.

Korean shamanism, which dates back to at least forty thousand years, is distinguished by its wisdom to solve human problems through a meeting of humanity and the spirits. The gut is a shamanistic rite where the shaman offers a sacrifice to the spirits. Through singing and dancing, the shaman begs the spirits to intercede in the fortunes of the humans in question. The shaman wears a very colorful costume and normally speaks in trance.

For the shaman, the spirit world is ultra-real, not to be controlled (as often perceived by those analyzing the phenomenon), but to be embraced and negotiated through ritual and trance. The shaman does not fear the spirit world, but knows it can only be accessed through transcendent behavior that honors its numinous and powerful character. Although shamanistic literature does not refer explicitly to the notion of the Great Spirit, the awareness of, and engagement with, spirit influence confirms strong evidence for a similar understanding. Spirit influence is pervasive, and when invoked appropriately in ritual, contributes to the healthy function of person and planet alike.

Although shamanism flourishes in several parts of the contemporary world, I outline its significance within the Asian context where, among other things, it helps to highlight what I believe to be a subtle but enduring sense of Spirit power at the core of Asian spirituality.

~⤸~

Pause for a Moment

Why are we so addicted to monotheism that we consistently fail to appreciate the diverse richness of the Asian-based faith traditions? In the modern world, notes Jose Maria Vigil (2010, 183ff.), many believers have a plural religious experience. They have double belonging and sometimes even a multiple sense allegiances. There is nothing exceptional in the experience of double or multiple religious belonging. Is it fair or responsible to dismiss such diverse allegiance as relativistic? Is this not a judgment made on the basis of a former imperialism rapidly outgrowing its usefulness?

~⤸~

The Subverted Spirit

The Western worldview, and monotheistic religion generally, tends to view Eastern spiritualities in a negative light. Words like "pagan" and "polytheistic" are used rather liberally, frequently by commentators with little or no personal experience of the Asian context. The following statement by the U.S. process theologian Joseph Bracken can lead to several misunderstandings: "[There prevails in the East] a deep seated desire not for union with God as a supremely intelligent and compassionate being, but for unity with, even absorption into, the Infinite as a strictly impersonal principle of existence and activity" (Bracken 1995, 137).

If Bracken were to use the word "transpersonal" instead of "impersonal," then the ensuing analysis, reflection, and discernment would be of a totally different caliber. The major religions of Asia and the several spiritual strands briefly reviewed above cannot and should not be judged in the light of Western monotheism. To do so is to perpetuate the patriarchal, postcolonial mind-set of the West, seeking to impose upon the amorphous diversity of Asia an individualistic personalism that is alien to the Asian worldview and increasingly problematic for the West itself.

Like the ancient traditions of Africa, Asian spiritual wisdom is characterized by age, depth, and complexity. The recurring theme in diverse spiritual traditions is that of spirit influence. It is a transpersonal recognition, not an impersonal one. Although believed to be mediated primarily through people, several ritual practices use resources from the material creation, because intuitively at least they discern the spirit influence to be intimately connected with the created order of the universe itself.

In the case of Africa and Asia, a deeper authentication of the indigenous belief in the spirit world will not result from subversion of ancient beliefs to the truths of monotheistic religion. To the contrary, the deeper wisdom will be rediscovered and reclaimed by aligning the inherited spiritualities with the enduring wisdom that the notion of the Great Spirit embodies. To that end, the indigenous peoples of the modern world are holding a treasure with a significant potential for future spiritual maturation, particularly for those who seek a dynamic spirituality to help us make sense of the complex twenty-first century world.

Chapter 10

The Great Spirit in Christianity

God-talk in expressions of Pneumatology is able to widen the metaphorics beyond the human and so can create wideness and freedom in the open spaces of theological imagination.

— SIGURD BERGMANN

The Holy Spirit sanctifies and transforms the humanity of Jesus from the beginning that he might be the Wisdom of God in our midst.

— DENIS EDWARDS

FOR MUCH OF CHRISTIAN history the individual existence of the Holy Spirit was rarely emphasized. The Spirit belonged to the Divine triune configuration, known as the Holy Trinity. In conventional language it translates into Father, Son, and Holy Spirit. The Father is widely recognized as the one who brings everything into being, the God who gives birth to, and rules over, all creation from above the sky. He is the ultimate principle of power and control.

Next in the hierarchy comes the Son, the historical Jesus, beloved Son of the Father, divinely chosen and designated as the Christ (Messiah) whose primary task is to rescue and redeem sinful humanity by the power of his cross and resurrection. Only when Jesus has accomplished salvation for humanity and is glorified alongside his heavenly Father can the Spirit come in its fullness. This unique event marks our Pentecostal situation.

In this brief outline (as articulated in the Christian Creed), the Spirit falls into a kind of ambiguous role. The Spirit can only come in its fullness at the original Pentecost some two thousand years ago, yet Genesis 1:2 clearly states that the Spirit is the one who organizes

137

all that is emerging at the dawn of creation. How do we resolve this contradiction?

According to the doctrines of the early church, the Holy Spirit has another preexistence—being the power that emanates from the love of Father and Son, cocreated to the degree of becoming a full "person" in its own right, equal to Father and Son. And yet the Spirit's coming into our world is only possible after Father and Son have done their unique tasks. A rather strange theological quagmire!

The shift to a different understanding, in which the Spirit enjoys greater substance and significance in its own right, is described by Philip Clayton (2008, 137ff.) in these words:

> The key modern resource for the theology of Spirit is the switch from substantivalist thinking to a subject-based ontology. During this period the Spirit came to be linked in the first place with human subjects and with their experience. This is a tremendous transformation from the medieval period, where the Spirit represented an objective metaphysical principle. . . . The Spirit, which in the Middle Ages, had served as a principle of demarcation between the human and the superhuman, the natural and the supernatural, now became the principle of unity between the two, the basic principle of all being. We exist as Spirit and pervasively in Spirit. Spirit now becomes the basic ontological category, that which unites all living things.

Upgrading the Holy Spirit

In the latter half of the twentieth century, theologians began a process of what might be described as upgrading the Holy Spirit. While still retaining the traditional ordering of Father, Son, and Holy Spirit, a more creative role for the Spirit came to the fore. The German theologian Jürgen Moltmann is an oft-cited name in promoting and developing this new pneumatology:

> God the Holy Spirit . . . is *in* all created beings. . . . [If] we understand the Creator, his creation, and the goal of that creation in a trinitarian sense, then the Creator, through this Spirit, *dwells in* his creation as a whole, and in every individual

created being, but by virtue of his Spirit holding them together and keeping them in life. The inner secret of creation is this *indwelling* of God. (Moltmann 1985, xii)

For Moltmann, the Spirit uniquely represents God's indwelling of the whole creation, an approach described by Denis Edwards (2004, 140ff.) as a panentheistic pneumatology. The indwelling of God in creation is facilitated primarily by the Spirit, described by Moltmann as "the principle of evolution . . . the Spirit of the universe, its total cohesion, its structure, its information, its energy" (1985, 16, 100). God the Holy Spirit has the exclusive quality of saturating creation, and it is God as Spirit through whom creation experiences this special immanence and indwelling of God. While striving to rehabilitate the Holy Spirit as a dynamic force, impacting the whole of creation, Moltmann still retains the conventional view of the Trinity: the Father creates through the Son in the power of the Holy Spirit.

Through the energies and potentialities of the Spirit, the Creator is himself present in his creation (Moltmann 1985, 9). The Holy Spirit is nonetheless also the Spirit of Christ and requires the redemption wrought in Christ to act effectively in the world. Moltmann understands the Spirit as being God's *shekinah* (a Hebrew word denoting God's universal presence on earth, particularly in the temple) resting upon Jesus, just as it did in the tabernacle and temple in Israel's early history. Both chronologically and theologically the operation of the divine Spirit is the precondition or premise for the history of Jesus of Nazareth. This Spirit brings to Jesus the overflowing life and bounty of the divine, allowing him to be filled with power for ministry.

According to this reformulation, it looks like the Spirit lies between the Father and Jesus, the Son. The Father needs the Spirit to make real in the world the vitality and bountifulness of all creation, yet the divine perichoresis (community of being) is incomplete without the redemption wrought in and through Jesus, which is also activated by the Spirit and requires the power of the Spirit for its full realization.[27]

Several other scholars followed Moltmann's lead in revamping and expanding the notion of the Holy Spirit, while retaining the inherited paradigm of the Christian Trinity (e.g., Dunn 1998;

Karkkainen 2002; Kovel 1991). Many of those same scholars seek a retrieval of the Eastern Orthodox approach to pneumatology, which views the work of the Spirit as integral to the process of divinization (*theosis*). While in Orthodox thought, theosis seems to apply to humans in particular, the relational empowerment embodied in the Trinity is also perceived to impact upon the whole of creation.

Trinity as an Archetypal Statement

In our time, the work of rehabilitating of the Holy Spirit continues with renewed momentum. The current ecological crisis makes us more aware of, and responsive to, the Spirit at work in all creation (Edwards 2004; 2006; Johnson 2008; Wallace 2005). We are challenged to re-vision the Holy Spirit in more expansive terms, which in turn requires a fresh appraisal of the traditional ordering of Father, Son, and Holy Spirit.

For too long the Holy Spirit has been couched in a kind of suspended animation, kept at the periphery of Trinitarian theology, and almost an afterthought in terms of Christian salvation. To understand what contemporary theologians are attempting we first need to revisit the notion of the Trinity and the central role it has played in the evolution of Christian belief, especially in early Christian times.

Elizabeth Johnson (2008, 202–25) provides a fine overview of our current theological understanding of the doctrine of the Trinity. Tracing the history of its doctrinal development, she notes how the role of the Father predominates, not merely as creator, but as the primary metaphor for all divine action in the world. The Son then emerges as the primary agent of the Father, designated with the unique role of mediating salvation for humans. Inevitably the Holy Spirit is relegated to a third place, with an often ambiguous and unclear function.

Johnson continues to locate the Trinity within the economy of salvation rather than within the role of divinization emphasized by the Orthodox tradition. However, she considers love to be the central feature of the salvific process, and reconceives the Trinity as a template for this saving love. Archetypally, therefore, the Trinity encapsulates the foundational significance of relational love, a reconceptualizing of the Trinity first popularized by Catherine LaCugna (1991), and subsequently by several theologians throughout the closing decades of the twentieth century.

As an archetypal statement, the doctrine asserts that the divine life force is first and foremost a relational matrix—not an individually heroic reality on the one hand, nor a linear patriarchal construct on the other. As an archetypal claim, it attempts to describe not merely the essence of the Divine but a core dynamic at work in the whole of creation, symbolically in the triune configuration. The number *three* signifies a relational construct, with rich archetypal meaning (http://en.wikipedia.org/wiki/3_(number)). Three is a sacred number in several religious traditions, ancient and modern. In fact, all major religions, with the notable example of Islam, have developed something akin to a doctrine of the Trinity.

Divinity, therefore, is first and foremost a capacity for deep relating, embodying in itself a primordial commitment to relationality, and desiring it throughout the whole of creation, and not merely within human beings. There are several possible ways for naming this triune process, as Elizabeth Johnson notes (2008, 219–21). They include a brightness, a flashing forth, and a fire (Hildegarde of Bingen); the revealer, the revelation, and the revealedness (Karl Barth); primordial being, expressive being, unitive being (John Macquarrie); eclipse, word, and presence (Nicholas Lash), Mother, Lover, and Friend (Sallie McFague); Creator, Liberator, and Advocate (Letty Russell). Perhaps best known of all is the Pauline greeting, "The grace of our Lord Jesus Christ, the love of God, and the fellowship of the Holy Spirit . . ." (2 Cor. 13:13).

In all these renderings, Jesus serves as a bridge linking God the Father to the world (via the church), where the ongoing task of salvation (or divinization) is mediated through the Holy Spirit, often indicated by metaphors of advocacy or unity. The respective roles of Father and Son seem more specific and concrete; that of Holy Spirit is more open-ended and less defined—perhaps not capable of definition in precise terms.

Enter the Church

For mainline Christian theology, the Holy Spirit is at work in the world, primarily through the agency of the church. John Zizioulas (1985) speaks of the church as "instituted" by Christ and "constituted" by the Spirit. Until recent times, the Pentecostal tradition (see chapter 12) considered the church to be the exclusive abode of the Spirit, launched from the initial Pentecost moment as described in Acts 2:1–11. The precise role of the Spirit remained largely undefined, apart from St. Paul's frequent allusions to the fellowship of the Spirit. The Spirit was deemed to be a force for unity, holding together the people of God in faithful service to the one true Church.

This view of the Holy Spirit became a lifelong enterprise of the French theologian Yves Congar, whose three-part magisterial study (initially published in French in 1979) was considered, in its day, to be groundbreaking and revolutionary. For Congar, Christians come to know the Spirit as a universal life force through participation in the life of the church. Although Congar also acknowledges the Spirit at work in creation, the presence of the Spirit in the life of the church is deemed more real and complete (Congar 1983). The church therefore needs to function in a way that facilitates this fellowship through greater mutuality and participation of all its members. Congar has been rated as a major influence in the reform of Catholic ecclesiology in and after the Second Vatican Council (1962–1964). Denis Edwards (2004, 87–103) provides a fine overview of Congar's pneumatology.

In Paul's development of early church life, the Spirit was seen as the primary agent for gathering the people, calling them to conversion, guiding them wisely, awakening in them gifts (charismata) for the good of the whole group, and facilitating the development of faith through worship and sacrament. John's Gospel highlights the additional factors of convicting the world of sin, and being the people's advocate before God as the *Paraclete*. According to the Catechism of the Catholic Church, the mission of Christ and the Holy Spirit is brought to completion in the Church, which is the Body of Christ and the Temple of the Holy Spirit (cf. *The Catechism* 1994, 733–740). Through the Church's sacraments, Christ communicates his Holy and sanctifying Spirit to the members of his Body.

From the ecclesiastical point of view, the Spirit is primarily about people—helping them to be faithful to God (and to Jesus) by treating each other in a dignified and morally responsible way. The anthropocentric emphasis is quite distinctive. Involvement of the Holy Spirit in other life forms, in other religions, or in the wider creation is rarely considered. On the other hand, the Orthodox tradition envisages a wider remit for the work of the Spirit and seems to have played a significant role in the Christian revamping of the Holy Spirit in the latter half of the twentieth century.

The Orthodox Wisdom

Instead of viewing the three persons of the Trinity, each having a unique and distinctive role, the shift to a relational understanding marks a new departure particularly in reference to the Holy Spirit (Fox 2001; Burgess 1989). The Spirit is more integrated into the relational matrix and gradually comes to be understood as playing a pivotal role in empowering such relationality. The empowerment is activated within the Trinity itself, but also in all God's dealings with the created order of universal life.

Reviewing the Eastern approach, Stanley Burgess (1989, 1–9) identifies five distinctive features of the theology of the Holy Spirit in the Orthodox tradition:

1. The Eastern view emphasizes the unity as opposed to the individuality within the Godhead, while recognizing the reciprocal nature of Trinitarian persons, adopting the notion of perichoresis, which literally means "to dance around."[28]
2. Eastern anthropology is far less sin-focused than its Western counterpart, and looks forward to the renewing of the image of God: the divinization, rather than the salvation, of the human.
3. Since the divine Spirit is the giver of life, its main soteriological operation is the divinization of human beings (theosis).
4. Although there is some divergence of opinion among the Eastern Fathers regarding the role of the Holy Spirit, they have always emphasized the experiential nature of the divine Spirit.
5. The symbolic significance of the Spirit is more highly developed (e.g., in liturgy) in the Eastern Orthodox tradition.

Like other Christian counterparts, however, the Orthodox view of the Spirit also exhibits a strong anthropocentric flavor. People and their spiritual well-being are at the forefront. However, we need to supplement these insights with another outstanding feature of Orthodox spirituality: the sacred nature of energy and the key role of the Holy Spirit in energizing the energy. Several seminal texts spring to mind:

> It is God who has given to nature the *energy* which produces its forms. Created beings are made by God to participate in His *divine energy*. (St. Maximos the Confessor)

> The *divine energy* is purifying and sanctifying. (St. Gregory of Sinai)

> Wisdom and spiritual knowledge are both gifts of the one Holy Spirit, as are all the divine gifts of grace; but each has its own distinctive *energy*. (St. Diadochos of Photiki)

> The *energy of grace* is the power of spiritual fire that fills the heart with joy and gladness. (St. Gregory of Sinai)

According to St. Gregory Palamas, *divine energies* are the "processions, manifestations, and natural operations of the one Spirit." He calls these "divine communications." He taught that they are "essence-bestowing, life-bestowing, and wisdom-bestowing energy and power." St. Gregory Palamas further explains, "The energy that creates individual essence, life and wisdom, and sustains created beings, is identical with the divine volitions . . . and the gifts of supernal Goodness, the cause of all."[29] Parallels with developments in quantum physics—also focusing on the incomprehensibility of energy—were noted in the opening chapters.

Spirit Christology

Thus far, I have highlighted an emerging trend in Christian theology toward a more expansive understanding of the Holy Spirit. How to integrate this enlarged vision with Christology has become particularly significant, and in the closing decades of the twentieth century, *Spirit Christology* became quite a controversial theological topic.

For much of the Christian era, the function of the Spirit are essentially subservient and instrumental to the work of the incarnate Christ. According to both the Lukan and Johannine accounts, the Spirit comes *after* Christ in the divine economy: "For as yet there was no spirit, because Jesus was not yet glorified" (John 7:39). Historically the subordination of the Spirit is asserted unambiguously through the famous *filioque* clause, adopted at the third Synod of Toledo in 589 CE, specifying that the Holy Spirit proceeds "from the Father *and from the Son*"—a modification not accepted by the Eastern Church, and an inherited doctrine upon which contemporary theologians certainly do not hold a shared consensus (see Hodgson 1994, 288ff.).

The notion of a triune God—Father, Son, and Holy Spirit—was developed for the greater part at the Council of Nicaea in early Christian times. The Father comes first. He begets the Son, and the love relationship between Father and Son is personified in the Holy Spirit. There is a clear line of descent, elaborately articulated through the sophisticated language and concepts of Greek metaphysics, which in later centuries translated into Scholasticism.

Although the Father holds the honored, superior place, in the ensuing Christian faith Jesus quickly acquired an exalted status known as *Logos Christology*. Philo of Alexandria (20 BCE–50 CE), a Hellenized Jew, used the term *Logos* to denote the creative principle. The Platonic concept of imperfect matter made the material world inaccessible to God, so Philo taught that the Logos was necessary as an intermediary between God and his creation. Logos Christology, carried through to a full victory by Clement and Origen, was a method of making the universality and uniqueness of the Jesus event understandable to the ancient Greek mind.

Logos symbolizes rationality, logic, and reason, favored concepts of patriarchal ordering and structure. Logos Christology, on the one hand, seeks to protect the divine and human natures of Jesus while prioritizing Jesus as the unique son of the Father through whom alone humanity can be saved. These ideas are captivated in a statement of Cardinal Josef Ratzinger (before becoming pope):

Only creative reason, which in the crucified God is manifested as love, can really show us the way. In the necessary dialogue between secularists and Catholics, we Christians must be very careful to remain faithful to this fundamental line: to live a faith that comes from the "Logos," from creative reason, and that, because of this, is also open to all that is truly rational. (http://www.Catholiceducation.org/particles/politics/pg0143.html)

In the latter half of the twentieth century, Spirit Christology was introduced to offset what was perceived to be the one-sided emphasis of Logos Christology. Many of those attempting a new integration of Spirit and Jesus (e.g., Moltmann 1981; 1992; Lampe 1977; Dunn 1998; Haight 1999; Welker 1994; 1999) found themselves pushing boundaries that were unacceptable to those guarding the clarity and power of the Logos position. Generally speaking, the teaching authority of the Catholic Church and the majority of Pentecostal theologians tend to prioritize and defend the Logos position.

Some of the above-named scholars claim that before the Council of Chalcedon (451), there was a Spirit Christology. It focused primarily on the experience of Jesus as anointed by the Spirit. But this Christology was short-lived and ill fated after the rather metaphysical and contentious debates that led to the Christological doctrines.

An example of Spirit Christology is the work of G. W. H. Lampe (1977), who claims that the Spirit properly describes not one of the three divine persons but the whole activity of God in his relation to humanity. As a consequence, Lampe's conception of the Spirit is that of a general presence of God within creation, a position also adopted by theologian Paul Tillich.[30] Along similar lines, Maurice Wiles (1982) suggests that the Holy Spirit denotes the personal and relational nature of God perceived to be present in all of creation. Although scholars such as Lampe and Wiles connect the Spirit with the wider creation, the impact on human beings seems to be their primary interest. For a more recent and detailed development of these ideas, see the double-volume work of James G. D. Dunn on Christ and the Spirit (1998; 2002).

In Christological studies, the Jesuit scholar Roger Haight is a frequently cited advocate of Spirit Christology. Seeking to transcend the excessively rational thought forms of Scholasticism, Haight embraces a symbolic process to highlight God's universal presence in the world, primarily through the power of the Spirit—a presence that cannot be restricted to three entities, whether persons or other mediations, and a presence humans may come to know and internalize through a range of religious experiences, ancient and modern.

In his classic work, *Jesus, the Symbol of God*, Haight (1999) contends that in a postmodern culture with its pluralistic consciousness, one can no longer claim the superiority of Christianity over other religions, or demand that Christ be the sole mediator for all religious systems. As a result, the dogmatic statements of faith, particularly in the area of Christology, need to be rethought and reinterpreted in a cultural and linguistic context different from the one in which they were first formulated. Haight defines a Spirit Christology as one that is open to other mediations of God. In cultural terms, the Spirit is spread abroad, and it is not necessary to think that God as Spirit can be incarnated only once in history. In the power of the Spirit, the revealed truth of God enters our contemporary world through several avenues, and our Christian theology needs to embrace the pluralistic consciousness of our time (more in Haight 2008). Kirsteen Kim (2006) outlines the potential of a Spirit Christology for a fresh sense of mission in India today. The Indian Jesuit scholar Jacques Dupuis (1997), keenly aware of the religious diversity in modern Asia, advocates a similar commitment to the development of a Spirit Christology.

Wisdom from the East

The link with the East—with the other great world religions—launches us into an even deeper level of discernment. The emerging insights are scarcely known to Western scholars; insofar as they are, they tend to be cautiously noted or surreptitiously dismissed. I refer to an alternative construction of the Trinity boldly asserted by a number of Asian Christian theologians. They begin not with God the Father, but with the Holy Spirit. Here are three contemporary formulations of this controversial claim:

1. "The Father, although he is formally known as the Godhead, becomes the background of the divine activity. It is the Spirit

that evokes our spirit and empowers us to act in response to God's will. Thus, in reality the Spirit is more active and more important in our Christian life than the Father is" (Young Lee 1996, 214).

2. "We may be able to put the Gospel message across more meaningfully if we begin from the Spirit, rather than the historical Jesus. And after all, it is the role of the prevenient Spirit to prepare the world to receive Christ" (Kim 2007, vi).

3. "With regard to the structure of the treatise of the Trinity, I suggest that we reverse the traditional order. Rather than beginning with the Father, then moving to the Son, and ending with the Holy Spirit, given the principle that we should root our Trinitarian theology in our experiences of salvation, we should begin with our present-day experiences of the Holy Spirit, and then show how the Spirit is the Spirit of Jesus, and end with Jesus' revelation of the mystery of God the Father" (Phan 2004, 38).

Pause for a Moment

What is your first reaction to the suggestion of reordering the Trinity, beginning with the Holy Spirit and not with God the Father? If the reordering resonates with your inner truth, how might we reconstruct our understanding of Pentecost (as the first imparting of the Holy Spirit on the Church) or the Sacrament of Baptism as the first imparting of the Spirit on the Christian person? In an attempt to engage these questions in a more discerning way, I suggest that an understanding of the indigenous notion of the Great Spirit proves to be crucially important.

In this newly proposed configuration, the Spirit comes to the fore—an alternative approach also endorsed by U.S. scholars Elizabeth Johnson (1992, 120–21) and Marc Wallace (2005, 45); by Sallie McFague of Canada (1993, 20); and more circumspectively by an Australian, Denis Edwards (2004, 27). This is the living reality of Holy Mystery that has energized creation for time immemorial.

In conjunction with contemporary science and its growing interest in the concept of infinity, we can suggest that the Spirit is without beginning or end. It is an infinite presence, not impersonal as the philosopher, Ken Wilber, intimates, but rather *transpersonal* (more in chapter 13). We encounter the Spirit first and foremost in the creative energy of universal life, in what today we regard as an essentially open-ended multiverse. That which energizes the living energy is what conventionally we name as the Holy Spirit of God.

This starting point protects us against the suffocating anthropocentrism that has not merely undermined the grandeur and beauty of the Holy Mystery, but which has often inflated human arrogance to the point of utter self-destruction. In the name of the ruling divinity we have set ourselves up as next to the angels, endowed with the divine right to rule and govern as we believe the patriarchal God has commissioned us to do. We often end up playing God— whether in religious, scientific, or economic terms. Time and again, we have invoked religion to validate our imperial domination.

With the Holy Spirit at the forefront, we re-vision afresh the creative power of the Holy One. Rather than investing divine power in a male progenitor, with exclusive rights over the "seed" from which all is begotten, we are invited to transcend the anthropocentric dominance in favor of cosmic and planetary creativity. For instance, Ilia Delio (2011, 41) proposes that God the Father "is what we might call a *singularity*, an indeterminate beginning of God that is itself without beginning." The creative Divine Originator—whether conceived as Father or Mother—itself is sprung from a more primordial energizing source.

Re-visioning the Creator

Empowered by the Spirit of living energy, the Holy Mystery cocreates with, and within, the emerging patterns of the energy flow. The more suitable metaphor for this process is that of *birthing* rather than *procreating* through phallic prowess. The Creator Father gives way to the image of the Great Mother, with the earth itself as a primary expression of her embodied presence (cf. the seminal work of Reid-Bowen 2007). Throughout much of the Paleolithic era, this seems to have been the understanding of God that our ancient ancestors embraced.

In metaphysical terms, the Father/Mother metaphor seems to serve as the principle of creativity. Why do we need to isolate and highlight this principle? Presumably because creativity is so foundational to the meaning of all existence (cf. Kaufman 2004). Without creativity there would be absolute nihilism. We may also add the theological conviction that the very nature of God is to create. God cannot but create. Indeed we can extend the insight even further, acknowledging that nothing in creation has meaning apart from the capacity for cocreating.

Thus far I have been using the words "creating" and "cocreating" interchangeably. In conventional Christian theology, the Father creates without intermediary or assistance. God is the absolute One with no need of any other. In relational terms he always relates downward (and it is always *he*). How much of this imagery belongs to our patriarchal projections, with ensuing descriptions of God as endowed with absolute power, ruling like a king on a heavenly throne? The concept of a Sky God ruling and controlling from afar is very much an invention of our patriarchal era. Sociologist and scholar of ancient history Steve Taylor (2005) claims that no evidence for such divine imagery exists before six thousand years ago. Before that, the focus seems to have been on the Great Earth Mother Goddess, whose primary modus operandi was that of cocreation rather than direct creation.

The distinction seems to be eminently important for the pneumatology arising from the reflections of this book. In the creation initiated by the Father God, everything belongs to the Father. He creates *ex nihilo* (from nothing), and all his actions have a direct impact without any intermediary. Even Jesus can only be the type of intermediary the Father desires. In the case of the Mother imagery, for which *birthing* is probably a more generic metaphor, the creativity is exercised in conjunction with the emergent nature of that which is already there. What was already there? Plato's *khora*, which we encountered in chapter 2: pure energy, for which Catherine Keller coined the term *ex profundis* (out of the depths) rather than *ex nihilo* (out of nothing). The energy is profoundly erotic, precisely because it is infused with the living Spirit of the divine, the primordial source of all being and becoming.

One wonders if the author of the book of Proverbs was working with fertile ideas such as these when he attributes to Lady Wisdom the distinctive role of being there at the side of the Master Craftsman when he first brought the world into being (cf. Prov. 8:22–31)? Is this the Spirit of infinite existence? Is the Master Craftsman cocreating with an energy already pregnant with possibility? Indulging in erotic playfulness (see Prov. 8:31) with coevolutionary possibilities already unfolding and emerging?

Several contemporary theologians link the notion of the Holy Spirit with Sophia Wisdom in the Hebrew Scriptures: Elisabeth Schüssler Fiorenza, Elizabeth Johnson, and Denis Edwards, among others. There are various allusions to the motherly nature and identity of the Holy Spirit in early Christian lore (cf. Gelpi 1984). For instance, St. Jerome, a contemporary of Augustine's, and two church fathers of an earlier period, Clement of Alexandria and Origen, quoted from the pseudepigraphal *Gospel of the Hebrews*, which depicted the Holy Spirit as a mother figure, a notion briefly considered by Jürgen Moltmann in his book on the Trinity (Moltmann 1981, 164–65; see also Beck 2007, 190–92).[31] Contemporary scholars, however, favor the Wisdom literature of the Hebrew Scriptures as the basis for a more fertile line of inquiry. It helps to transcend the androcentric/patriarchal bias of Logos rationality, opening us to the nurturing and empowering mutuality embodied in the Wisdom (Sophia) tradition.

We must still be wary lest we replace one powerful figurehead with another. As noted several times throughout this book, the Holy Spirit denotes empowerment, not linear power of any type. Consequently, the relationship with this empowering Spirit must be re-visioned anew. One way to do this is to invoke a fertile insight from the Canadian theologian Sallie McFague, who proposes that the metaphor most appropriate for our relationship with the Holy Spirit is that of *friendship* (see McFague 1987, 165).

Adopting this metaphor, God the lover of the world gives us the vision that God finds the world valuable and desires its wounds healed and its creatures free. God, as friend, asks us, as adults, to become associates in that work. The right name for those involved in this ongoing sustaining, trustworthy, committed work for the world is neither parents nor lovers, but "friends" (cf. John 15:15).

And What about Jesus?

As these brief notes indicate, the newly proposed expansive view of the Holy Spirit focuses our attention considerably more on the Spirit than on the Father or Jesus. Even scholars who adopt a Spirit Christology fail to develop an understanding of Jesus congruent with their own expanded vision, and less so with the larger landscape being explored in the present work. *Incarnation is still postulated primarily on the historical Jesus of two thousand years ago.* I proposed in an earlier work (O'Murchu 2008) that Incarnation—denoting God's unambiguous affirmation of the divine in the human—needs to be redefined and reconceptualized in terms of our human evolutionary story of 7 million years, and not merely within the context of the past two thousand years. This approach links Jesus more explicitly with the human dimension of creation, understanding the human, however, as deeply embedded in the Spirit-filled dynamics of all creation.

Apart from the famed Teilhard de Chardin, I am aware of only one Christian theologian adopting a broadly similar view: Karl Rahner, for whom anthropology and Christology dovetail closely. Rahner is well known for his transcendental anthropology, in which he views humans as open and receptive to divine influence made real and tangible in and through the historical person of Jesus. In that context he writes,

> Jesus then must be truly human, truly a part of the earth, truly a moment in this world's biological process of becoming, a moment in humanity's natural history. It is perfectly legitimate to employ the notion of an event through which God's self-communication and acceptance reaches a point in history which is irrevocable and irreversible. (Rahner 1978, 218)

For Rahner, anthropology (the human qua human) remains seriously deficient until it matures into its fuller realization in Jesus as the primordial Christ; also, Christology without its grounding in anthropology lacks credibility and meaning (see Rahner 1975, 195–200). The mystery that underpins our humanity and which comes to fullness in the historical Jesus is fundamentally the same mystery. In theological and Christological terms Jesus is not so much about the planet and the cosmos as about humanity, albeit as creatures whose fuller potential cannot be realized without a planetary and cosmic grounding.

Restricting Jesus to the human dimension of cosmic and planetary life inevitably is viewed as reductionistic and contrary to the divine status of Jesus. I acknowledge it is at variance with the tradition of mainline Christian theology, which strikes me as being quite imperialistic, patriarchal, and dualistic, to a degree that seriously undermines the primacy of the Spirit and a range of more creative ways for re-visioning Jesus's significance. The human way of being in the world is the most highly developed form of self-reflexive consciousness we know to date. It seems eminently important that we explore the grounding of this "humanum" in the divine life of our inherited Christianity. The obvious link seems to be through Jesus as an archetype of all that is fully human (explored at length by Walter Wink 2002). In the fullness of that humanity, divinity becomes more transparent and visible.

The distinction between the divine and human in Jesus is a theological question beyond my competence as a social scientist. What seems eminently important in my faith experience is the humanity of Jesus and the enormous challenge it poses to live human life in a radical new way. If Christians had been doing that more faithfully over the past two thousand years, they might well have made a much more significant impact in shaping the world as a more God-like place. Our failure to make such an impact may well have to do with our preoccupation with the divinity of Jesus, the basis for several patriarchal power games, and frequently a gross distraction from the Christian task of building on earth God's new reign (in Jesus) of justice, love, empowerment, and liberation.

The Trinity Seen Anew

I am proposing that we re-vision God at work in creation primarily in the power of Holy Spirit and, second, that we re-vision our Christian task as a discipleship in solidarity with, and within, the radical empowerment of Jesus's humanity. In that way we are likely to make far more visible and credible the divine empowerment of the Holy Mystery in our midst. Much of the theological rhetoric, characteristic of Scholasticism past and present, needs to give way to an experiential appropriation of a living and vibrant faith, inspired primarily by the pervasive Spirit of the Holy One in our midst.

In a fertile insight from Catherine Keller (2008, 149), "The Spirit begins to push free of Trinitarian shibboleths while intensifying the radical relationality that is the whole meaning of the Trinity." It is not so much a case of the Spirit breaking loose from its ecclesial moorings as rather from what Philip Clayton (2008, 250) describes as "the metaphysical superstructure." Set free from the congestion of patriarchal rationalism, the Spirit breathes afresh, and as biblically promised it will blow where it wills. In that archetypal dispersion we encounter once more the deep wisdom of the indigenous Great Spirit. Fortunately for us today, it is not merely a new attempt at glancing backward; more important, it is a contemplative gaze into the future, abetted with the insightful vision of modern science and cosmology.

My suggested revamping of the Trinity begins with the dimension of living Spirit, the foundational energy that inspires even God's own creativity, encapsulated in the notion of a Father/Mother creator. That creativity expressed in our self-reflexive humanity—from a Christian point of view—was lived out in an exemplary way by the historical Jesus. All three Trinitarian dimensions form an archetypal unity, with relationality at its very foundation, and that explosive relationality is what we witness every day in the grandeur of the creation that surrounds us.

Conventional Christianity has lost the real power of the Spirit, and correspondingly the incarnational wisdom of the body—as cosmos, planet, and person. That underlying creativity—without beginning or end—is the eroticism of Holy Mystery that has been brutally subdued by excessive rationalism, anthropocentrism, and patriarchal domination. We can no longer keep the erotic in prison, and the Spirit that blows where it wills is revisiting the spiritual landscape with a disturbing but timely wisdom. Let's strive to discern more deeply.

Chapter 11

The Erotic Spirit in Creation

The world is an adventure in God's Eros that cannot merely be resolved into inner-divine peace.... As Eros, God's primordial nature is the beginning of every creature, is its future, and is the reflection of its best possible existence.

— ROLAND FABER

The movements of the Spirit are erotic and rhythmic. Spirit pushes against ossifying and binary logic. The oscillations of the Spirit in the deep reveal that God is entangled, related, and implicated in the becoming of the world.

— CATHERINE KELLER

A COLLEAGUE DREW MY attention to the following statement from the papal document *Redemptoris Missio*, published in July 1990:

The Spirit manifests himself in a special way in the Church and in her members. Nevertheless, his presence and activity are universal, limited neither by space nor time. . . . The Spirit, therefore, is at the very source of man's existential and religious questioning, a questioning which is occasioned not only by contingent situations but by the very structure of his being. The Spirit's presence and activity affect not only the individuals but also society and history, peoples, cultures and religions. (John Paul II, *Redemptoris Missio*, No. 28)

Already in 1990, the Catholic Church had adopted an expanded view of the role and influence of the Holy Spirit. Beyond the horizon

155

of the Church itself, the activity of the Holy Spirit is "universal, limited neither by space nor time." Although the statement has a distinctive anthropocentric flavor, it clearly envisages the Spirit at work in the wider creation, even in the unlimited realms of space-time. To suggest that such an alignment with the Spirit involves "religious questioning" sounds like a bold statement by contemporary standards, never mind the more conservative stance of twenty years previously.

That same year, the German theologian Jürgen Moltmann was completing a book on the Holy Spirit, in which he defines the experience of the Spirit in these words: "An awareness of God in, with, and beneath the experience of life, which gives us assurance of God's fellowship, friendship, and love" (Moltmann 1992, 17). Already in a theological treatise on creation, Moltmann identifies four characteristics of the Spirit at work in the created universe (1985, 99–100):

1. The Spirit is the principle of creativity on all levels of matter and life. From within the evolutionary process the Spirit liberates new possibilities.
2. At every evolutionary stage, the Spirit facilitates interactions, inspiring a dynamic of cooperation and community. The Spirit of God is the "common Spirit of creation."
3. The Spirit is "the principle of individuation," in which each organism retains unique identity—unique, yet united through a creative wholeness, the polyphonic orchestra of creation.
4. All creations in the power of the Spirit are intentionally open, so that all things can grow and flourish and reach their full potential as God intends. The principle of intentionality is inherent in all open systems of matter and life.

In chapter 3 I alluded to Pannenberg's intuition that field forces in creation evoked a sense of spirit power animating and directing the creative energy of the universe. To the best of my knowledge, Pannenberg was the first contemporary theologian to suggest a direct link between our understanding of the Holy Spirit and modern science. Several other scholars have taken up this suggestive line of inquiry—some scientists, others cosmologists, and still others theologians.

Together they forge a fresh synthesis to launch the theology of Holy Spirit into new, fertile territory, while unintentionally rehabilitating for our time the ancient notion of the Great Spirit.

The Erotic Spirit

In Genesis 1:1–2, the Spirit is described as the One that draws forth order from the emerging chaos of creation. This is probably a patriarchal view that misses a deeper truth. Ronald Faber (2008, 229ff.) invites us to re-vision the Spirit as an erotic force, not merely a principle of order. The Spirit awakens, stimulates, arouses, and engages the many processes of creativity with passion and intimacy. The erotic foreplay for the birthing of possibilities is a prerogative of the Spirit. Several indigenous cultures view the Spirit this way, and this is the primal perception of the Asian wisdom in its notion of the Spirit as a Great Mother (cf. Ahmed 2002).

In mainline Christian spirituality, the erotic denotes primitive instinctual drivenness—a wild, uncontrolled release of passion, with demon-like sexual desire as one of its primary expressions. Eros denotes everything that is disordered and disorderly—the subliminal id in Freudian psychology, the source of sin and temptation, the relentless drive that begets compulsions and addictions, driving humans to insanity and beyond. The erotic is central to the fundamental flaw, the basis of original sin, that which has infected humans ever since the original fall. Its sexual expression is the mechanism through which the flaw is transmitted to successive generations, not merely to other humans but to the entire material creation. Humans are flawed—and so is everything in the material universe.

Long before the antisexual rhetoric of Christianity, eros enjoyed another existence. It was deemed to be the archetypal virtue through which the gods themselves bonded voluptuously, birthing forth the galactic universe in its elegance and beauty, a beauty often infused with violence and paradox. In this context the erotic alludes to a foundational creativity of ageless existence—eternal like the divine life itself—and it has definite connotations of exuberance, elegance, passion, wildness, and prodigious fertility.

Indeed, creation is alive with the glory of God, a creative urge, a ceaseless becoming, long predating every myth of origin humans ever conceived. Central to that creative erotic birthing drive is that divine life force we aptly name the Great Spirit. S(he) marks the "beginning" of everything—even that of the Godhead itself.

Using female metaphors is likely to direct us along more authentic paths in our desire to discern the meaning of the erotic Spirit. For instance, Roland Faber, belonging to the tradition of process theology, uses the image of the Holy Mystery as Sophia (Wisdom), in his attempt to develop a pneumatology for our time. Here he is in league with several contemporary scholars revisiting the notion of Sophia Wisdom in the Hebrew Scriptures.

Many years ago, scripture scholar Ronald Murphy highlighted the neglected nature of the Wisdom literature as a topic deserving serious study and discernment. Scholars such as Elisabeth Schüssler Fiorenza and Elizabeth Johnson mined the likely links with the narrative (story) strategy that Jesus adopted, with his elaborate use of parables, proverbs, and witty sayings, suggesting that Jesus was embracing and emulating the creative wisdom of the Sophia tradition. They suggest, moreover, that Sophia is the more ancient and foundational version of the Greek Logos, and that the deeper meaning of the Logos in John's Gospel can best be accessed by grounding it in the Hebrew concept of Sophia Wisdom.

In more recent times scholars such as Denis Edwards invoke the Sophia tradition as a basis for ecotheology, the interface between religious wisdom and the pressing ecological and environmental issues of our time. Sophia Wisdom is not merely a personification in human terms. She embraces the whole creation, wherein she is its fecund source and its enduring animation.

Although Edwards never refers to the Goddess tradition, his insights closely resemble recent scholarship on the Great Earth Mother Goddess. This subject is controversial, often dismissed as new age romanticism, a kind of speculative nostalgia for a utopian past based on flimsy evidence from studies of Paleolithic times. This ancient wisdom poses quite a threat to the conventional patriarchal worldview, especially as articulated in religion, and not surprisingly tends to be ridiculed and dismissed out of hand in several major religious traditions. A number of studies, however, view the tradition of the Great Earth Mother in more metaphorical and archetypal terms, generating insights that complement and deepen our reappropriation of Sophia Wisdom. At the forefront is the seminal work of the British scholar Paul Reid-Bowen (2007).

Reid-Bowen interprets the current fascination with the Great Earth Mother as an archetypal awakening arising from the pain and suffering of the tortured earth body itself. Humans who internalize this same experience—women for the greater part, and mothers in particular—are often drawn to a kind of mystical awakening whereby a fresh sense of the divine evokes images and connections with a motherly experience of the Holy One rather than the prevailing masculine imagery that dominates formal patriarchal religion. Instead of an urge to worship some God in a distant heaven, these people find themselves lured into an intimately convivial relationship with the embedded divine in the heart of creation itself. That new spiritual intimacy is a feature of the eroticism explored in the present chapter.

Spirit of the Wild

By its very nature, the erotic veers toward relationality and thrives in the relational mode. Intense bonding is its primary drive, of which bondage may be considered its dark side. It flourishes on trust and seems to transcend any and every notion of human control. It is endowed with a quality of wildness that feels scary to rational humans, who need to remember the timely words of Thomas Berry, "The wild is a great beauty that seethes with intelligence. . . . For without this wild energy, life's journey would have ended long ago" (Swimme and Berry 1992, 127).

In this ancient understanding, the erotic belongs first and foremost to the divinity. It could be described as the default mode in which the Holy Mystery functions, defying all attempts at human comprehension. To the rationally minded, this concept is too crazy to be taken seriously; to those aligned to inherited notions of contemplation and meditation, it feels too hyperactive to be of God; to religionists, it is too speculative and unruly to be real; to nonreligionists, it is further evidence that makes religion even more irrational and incredulous. How do we discern the significance of this issue? Where do we even begin?

Religion is unlikely to provide a helpful starting point, except perhaps in some of those wild prophetic and contemplative endeavors of which we get sneak previews in the scholarly literature—as in Jeffrey John Kripal's description of the mystical calling:

> Mystical communities and literatures have offered some of the most successful, if still ethically ambiguous, venues in which alternative sexualities and genders have expressed themselves. I thus read mystical texts, first and foremost, as cultural sites of sexual and gender liminality, as semiotic openings to a more polymorphous erotic existence that would be impossible within the more orthodox parameters of the social register in question. . . . What is particularly striking about such appearances, at least with respect to male mystics, is the remarkable manner in which they line up along a rather clear homoerotic structure. (Kripal 2001, 17, 70)

Addressing the broader human sphere of emotion and sensuality, John V. Taylor (1972, 51) remarks, "The Spirit is not adverse to the elemental world of our dreams, the raw emotion of our fears and angers, the illogical certainties of our intuitions, the uncharted gropings of our agnosticism, the compulsive tides of our history. These are his *milieu*." This is the proverbial chaos of the original creation with which the Spirit works so creatively. Our wild passions are not pathologies to be incarcerated, nor satanic drives to be moralistically denounced, but graced endowments through which we rework our evolutionary becoming toward greater integration, not to eliminate our wildness but rather to place it at the service of a greater, Spirit-inspired creativity.

~

Pause for a Moment

What sense can you make of the last sentence—that we should not "eliminate our wildness but rather place it at the service of a greater, Spirit-inspired creativity"? Is this possible in cultures scared of any type of social deviancy where "wild" behavior is tamed by medication, and those who rebel against

the norms of the dominant culture tend to be incarcerated?
What might a new sexual ethic look like, inviting humans to
integrate our wildness rather than suppressing (or repressing)
it as suggested in conventional Christian morality?

The more we understand the workings of the universe, the more
we are exposed to the enormity and sheer elegance of mystery going
wild. We see the evidence in the explosive eruptions of the galactic
and planetary domains where unceasingly the erotic birthing weaves
paradoxical patterns of birth-death-rebirth. Thanks to sophisticated
technology like that of the LHR collider at CERN, Switzerland, we
are beginning to piece together a universe that grows and flourishes
through musical metaphors of branes and strings that re-echo the
creative melody of the divine life force itself.

Sophia's Erotic Creation

Instead of personalizing the Great Goddess, as those tracing
Paleolithic sources tend to do, Reid-Bowen (2007) opts for a less
personalized portrayal, with a more ingenious and persuasive
outcome. As already indicated, he attributes the modern Goddess
fascination with a primal hunger for a quality of mothering for
which millions of people are yearning. Why such a primal hunger
at this time? Because, avers Reid-Bowen, the earth body itself is
exploited, damaged, weak, and vulnerable, leaving all its dependent
creatures—including humans—feeling vulnerable and threatened
themselves. The cult of the Earth Mother, therefore, is based on a
cultural projection (as much religion tends to be) seeking divine
protection and empowerment in the face of our disempowerment as
earth-planetary creatures. In such a case, the Goddess serves as an
archetypal symbol of the earth body itself, calling all the creatures
who inhabit it to more caring, responsible, and sustainable ways of
behaving.

While theology (spelled with an "o") emphasizes the patriarchal
metaphysical characteristics of God as distinctive, other, remote,
and superior, *thealogy* (spelled with an "a") privileges immediacy,
presence, embodiment, and indwelling. The Goddess is perceived as

a living body enlivening an embodied cosmos, the generative force for creativity and transformation. In this analysis the Goddess is not a person as conventionally understood, but the entangled, energized life force in whose erotic fecundity every creature is invited to participate.

Denis Edwards describes Sophia as wisdom at work in creation, while Paul Reid-Bowen offers quite an original exposition of the Goddess as Nature (thealogy). Both strands are uniquely illustrated in Marc Wallace's re-visioning of the Holy Spirit as that which lives and breathes in the creativity of nature itself (Wallace 2002; 2005). Revisiting the metaphors used in the Scriptures to describe the Spirit—vivifying breath, healing wind, living water, purgative fire, and ministering dove—Wallace (2002, 220) concludes,

> At the behest of the Spirit it is time for a reversal of this convenient hierarchy: rather than placing nature at *our disposal*, it is now the natural world itself, in all its power and poverty, its grandeur and fragility, that *disposes us* to interact with it as equal co-partners. The Spirit is calling us to become friends of the earth rather than stewards of its resources. . . . I have proposed a shift in emphasis toward a *biocentric* redefinition of the Spirit as God's agent of interdependence and unity within all creation.

The biocentric Spirit is the living energy sustaining all creation in its formative and emergent nature. In this unfolding process, humans and the natural world are one: the world's forests are the lungs we breathe with, the ozone layer is the skin that protects, and the earth's lakes and rivers are the veins and arteries that supply us with vital fluids. Endowed deeply with Spirit energy, the earth body is the primary embodiment from which all other embodied creatures—including humans—receive life, vitality, and everything needed to grow and flourish. That integral endowment of the Holy Spirit in creation is the primary landscape that shapes and molds everything that comes into being:

> The Spirit is the "soul" of the earth—the wild, life-giving breath of creation—empowering all life-forms to enter into

a dynamic relationship with the greater whole. In turn the earth is the "flesh" of the Spirit—the living landscape of divine presence—making God palpable and viscous in nature's ever widening circles of seasonal changes. To experience the full range of nature's birthing cycles, periods of growth, and seasons of death and decay—to know the joy and sadness of living in harmony with nature's cyclical processes and flow patterns—is to be empowered by the Spirit and nurtured by nature's bounty. The Spirit is the hidden, inner life of the world, and the earth is the outward manifestation of the Spirit's sustaining energies. (Wallace 2005, 127)

The Spirit of Nonduality

As already indicated, the erotic in its archetypal meaning denotes deep bonding. I wish to suggest a close parallel with the pervasive and enduring *oneness* described in several texts of classical mysticism. In Vedic wisdom it is often described as *Advaita*, the Sanskrit word for "nonduality." For the rational mind, this concept is difficult to grasp, and those of us formed and educated in the West do not easily transcend the dualistic splitting so endemic to our culture and history. We tend to view everything in isolation, standing apart from, and over against, every other. We often identify objects (and people) in terms of their opposite. We are so preoccupied with highlighting differences, we often forget and even undermine the commonalities, which potentially are far more enriching and empowering, not to mention more reconciling and productive of peace and progress.

The philosophy of nonduality or nondualism, as it is sometimes called, claims that there is just one formless and limitless Spirit, and that everything in the universe—every person, animal, plant, and tree, everything animate and inanimate—is within it, sprung from its pregnant source, and sustained by it. This one Spirit manifests in and through myriads of forms, all interconnected at a deeper level, being originally of the same source. This philosophy, Eastern in origin and called *advaita-vedanta* in India, is known by several names in other great spiritual traditions: *tian ren heyi* in ancient Chinese philosophy, *ein sof* in ancient Judiasm, *monism* in ancient Greece (see Thales,

Heraclitus), and *tawhid* in Sufism. It is a central feature of all the world's great mystical traditions (see Krumpos 2011).

A great deal of esoteric speculation is devoted to the notion of illusion as a central feature of nonduality. This approach can seriously distract from the deeper significance borne out in the spirituality of the Great Spirit. It strikes me that we are dealing not so much with illusion as with what Paul Ricoeur often referred to as the *surplus of meaning*. Because our minds and spirits have not been trained (attuned) to discern spirit power at the heart of creation, then tragically we often relate with life in an illusory way. We misread the evidence, regarding separateness and objectivity as real, when in fact these features are merely illusions. The realism is embodied in erotic birthing, process in flow, and relational wholeness. In the language of modern physics, the whole is greater than the sum of the parts, and it is primarily in the whole that the eroticism of the Great Spirit births the nonduality that holds all life in creative unison.

In this state we inhabit a different consciousness. We see with different eyes. We look out for commonalities rather than differences—for the bigger picture rather than the disparate parts— and we begin to seek connections beyond the dualisms that fragment and violently divide. This stance is not utopian, whereby we can dodge the struggles of life and abide only in serenity and calm. To the contrary the mystic knows all too well the pain and ecstasy of creation. Mystical faith is not about transcending life's struggles but rather abiding more deeply within them, as elegantly and sensitively explored by the U.S. theologian Shelly Rambo (2010).

Here the spirituality of nonduality is really put to the test. How do we hold together the beauty and the pain that characterize our world in every evolutionary moment, particularly in the face of so many innocent millions numbed by oppression and cruel suffering? Elsewhere in this book I refer to this phenomenon as the great paradox of creation-and-destruction, which can also be named as the recurring cycle of birth–death–rebirth. Many commentators suggest that the Spirit's task is to draw order and meaning from disorder and absurdity. The Spirit is in the good and the wholesome, but not in that which we humans categorize as negative and immoral. Is this not another neat distinction made in the name of humanly invented dualisms? We split off that which we don't like, that which we cannot control, and we go on to insinuate that God also engages in such splitting. I suspect this is not how the erotic Spirit of nonduality operates.

The great paradox of creation-and-destruction (Swimme and Berry 1992) is a complex and largely neglected theological topic that I have described in other works (O'Murchu 2002; 2010). While many disciplines, religious and secular, deem the paradox to be an aberration of a sinful and deranged world—or, more accurately, out of balance because of human fickleness—I believe we need to see it afresh and reclaim it anew as an integral aspect of creation in its emerging growth and development. God's creativity is in the destruction and death as well as in the birthing of novel and emergent forms.

Paradoxically the same Spirit that can be fierce and bewildering explodes in the cacophonous disintegration occurring extensively in the galactic realm, in the elegant and painful death of stars and the sometimes violent dispersal of stellar debris. "The evolutions and catastrophes of the universe," writes Moltmann (1985, 16), "are also the movements and experiences of the Spirit of creation." That same Spirit breathes alike in the Category 2 hurricane, but also in the gentle breeze that stirs rippling waters. More difficult to comprehend is the Spirit's instigation of redemptive pain and suffering on the human level, as distinct from the cruel and meaningless sufferings that humans invent against themselves. In this latter case more than any other, humans need the Spirit's greatest gift of all, the grace of discernment.[32]

This process can also be described as the unceasing cycle of birth–death–rebirth. This is not a deviation but an inherent aspect of the wisdom within which all life unfolds, develops, and endures. In religious language the cyclic pattern is a divinely bestowed aspect of universal life (not be confused with intelligent design), and therefore not an evil to expunge. Rather it is a paradox to be embraced and befriended and in that way transformed into a powerful evolutionary force without which everything would cease to be.

Marc Wallace (2002, 171ff.) faces this dilemma with remarkable honesty and transparency: "God is engaged as both lover and betrayer, defender and judge, friend and enemy. On the one hand, to live the life of faith in the face of radical evil is to attune oneself to the life-giving power of the Spirit in all living things—while, on the other hand, always remaining aware of the possibility that this power can engender ruination as well as renewal, destruction as well as healing." Shelly Rambo (2010) also engages the paradox and its manifestation in human trauma and suffering, suggesting that "the Middle Spirit" negotiates the chaos and formlessness, empowering people to "remain" grounded in the paradox, awaiting the hope born from within the struggle itself. Both Wallace and Rambo echo the mystical spirituality of the dark night, and both see the Spirit as central to the ensuing hope and transformation that may transpire.

The Befriending Spirit

As noted in the last chapter, Canadian theologian Sallie McFague advocates befriending as a primary feature of the Holy Spirit. The Spirit is the great friend, not merely to humans but to everything in the universe. How do we learn to befriend a Spirit force that begets in erotic birthing, radical freedom, and paradoxical creativity? We certainly cannot do it on the basis of the rational mind alone, nor on the basis of the anthropocentric, patriarchal philosophies that have dominated our world for the past five thousand years.

Befriending is a deeply perceptive, nonviolent stance, leading to interventions that are gentle, reflective, and noninvasive. It asks deep questions and is not bewildered when nature offers an answer that is unexpected and unusual. Befriending honors soulfulness (cf. Moore 1992; 1994), the need for complexity, messiness, and untidiness as dimensions inherent to life's evolution. And it knows how to befriend decline, death, and termination. The mystics are among the few who have managed to attain such wisdom.

A befriending stance empowers people to deal differently with the great paradoxes of creation and the suffering that ensues. It is a mysticism that enters deeply into pain and anguish, not with martyrlike resignation, but with an inner resilience for truth, justice, and the desire for deliverance from the systemic forces addicted to manipulation and control in our world. Mahatma Gandhi's *satyāgraha* comes to mind: that sense of fierce spirit that supports and empowers us in the face of human oppression (cf. Rynne 2008). Befriending is based on a wisdom of the Spirit largely unknown in the world of our time. For the greater part, formal religion is unacquainted with this mystical vision; religion instead tends to seek violent saviors to redeem humankind from its self-imposed myopia. As Rene Girard (and other contemporary thinkers) intimate, redemptive violence exacerbates rather than reduces the meaningless suffering in our world.

The mythologies of the Great Earth Mother Goddess often allude to her voluptuous erotic impulses, a strange blend of instinctual wildness and fierce tenderness, culminating in a life force of prodigious fertility. This imagery for the divine predates our patriarchal religions by thousands of years, providing further evidence for the notion of a creative eroticism within the divine life itself. I want to discern the possibility that ultimately we are referring to a central feature of the primordial Spirit—the birthing eroticism, named positively as love in all the great religions—which needs to be supplemented with the Spirit's fertile darkness, exemplified in the destructive impact of the universal paradox outline briefly above.

In the Christian Gospels, light and darkness tend to be juxtaposed as binary opposites. In the spirituality of the Great Spirit they need to be held as one—two sides of the same coin. Nature needs both, universal life needs both, and a credible spirituality for our time needs to honor both. Dualistic divisions, and the splitting of reality that ensues, is a human device of our culture of divide-and-conquer, with destructive consequences posing enormous problems for humanity today. In our confused attempts to bring about light (good) by eliminating the dark, we actually exacerbate the dark forces that have made our world such a violent place. In integrating light and darkness, creation itself flourishes; that also is the prescription for humanity to grow and flourish in a more enlightened and Spirit-filled way.

Invoking the Paraclete

Before Jesus's Passion, he promised that the Father and he would send his disciples "another Counselor" (John 14:16, 26; 15:26; 16:7). The Counselor—or Paraclete, from the Greek word *parakletos* (meaning one who gives support)—is a helper, adviser, strengthener, encourager, ally, and advocate. Jesus himself may be considered to be the first Paraclete, and he is promising a replacement who, after he is gone, will carry on the teaching and testimony that he started (John 16:6–7).

Every commentary on John's Gospel elaborates at length on the significance of the Spirit as Paraclete. Apart from John's Gospel, the word is rarely used in the New Testament, and there are not many precedents for it in older Jewish writings. It seems to have come into Christian usage from Greek culture, wherein it denoted advocacy or interceding for people in need. The Spirit as comforter or counselor is a popular interpretation of the Johannine context, coming to the rescue of those in need and leading them toward salvation (which in Christianity can only happen in and through Christ). The Spirit is very much the active force, and humans are the passive recipients of a power that God alone can give.

This emphasis is quite different from the tradition of the Great Spirit, where the focus is more along the lines of the befriending described above. The Spirit is the friend who stands in solidarity with all creation, inspiring and challenging people to be in solidarity with each other and with creation—in order to realize a more hope-filled future, a nuance that Shelly Rambo also adopts (2010, 103–5). There is no semblance of passivity here. Mutual empowerment is the goal, in a process whereby people in the empowerment of the Great Spirit are called to mutually empower each other and all other creatures as responsible cocreators.

The work of cocreation is to be undertaken with passion and intense commitment, which is the erotic undercurrent of living by the Spirit—very different from *apatheia*, admired as a virtue in early Christian times. Matthew Fox (1999, 551) captivates this more vibrant eroticism in his outline for how we are called to live in accordance with the Spirit. The following, he suggests, are some of the primary features:

- Live with the wonders of cosmology (a relation to the whole) and live grounded to the earth and ecology.
- Live with passion (better lustful than listless), which derives from our yearning for union on the personal level.
- Live with moral outrage and stand up to injustice.
- Live with compassion and resist fear.

- Live with telling your truth and resist being gagged by consumerism and its sellers.
- Live with giving birth and develop all your creative powers of intellect and imagination.
- Live for the building of community among all light beings. Resist competitive and envious relations with others.

⤝⤞

Pause for a Moment

How do you feel about making the above list a daily prayer, a kind of "examination of conscience" for striving to remain more faithful to the urgings and lure of the Great Spirit?

⤝⤞

Christian theology and popular devotion have both colluded in keeping the erotic Spirit tamed, and keeping its enthusiasm sheltered in an ecclesiastic enclave, seeking to protect its divinity to justify power, and its holiness to justify escape from our sinful world. The Spirit, however, belongs primarily to our world and not to any church or religion. In the indigenous tradition of the Great Spirit, the Spirit imbues creation in each and every vibration of its evolutionary unfolding. The Spirit has fared better in creation than in the Church.

Today, the Church itself may be under attack from the Great Spirit. Reminiscent of the book of Jeremiah (1:10), the Spirit seems to be pulling down archaic edifices in order to build anew. In doing so, we face another mammoth task: to be faithful to the Spirit that blows where it wills. One area of seismic shift is within the Pentecostal movement, initiated in the 1960s and flourishing with incredible pace across the Christian world. We explore that topic in our next chapter.

Chapter 12

A New Pentecost?

*Whereas for most other Christians, the presence of the Spirit
is just that, presence; for Pentecostals the presence of the Spirit
in their midst implies empowerment.*

— VELI-MATTI KARKKAINEN

*The Spirit is defined by its movement and not by its essence.
The Spirit is the vibration, the flow, the flight, and the unfolding
of God that is unending and unconfining.*

— SHELLY RAMBO

ANY OVERVIEW OF THE role of the Holy Spirit in contemporary
theology or spirituality must include the significant impact of
the Pentecostal movement in modern Christianity. Many consider
it to be the fastest-growing aspect of modern Christian faith. While
several official churches struggle to survive due to depleting numbers,
Pentecostal gatherings often attract huge numbers and lure spiritual
seekers away from mainline religions. In the space of thirty years
(1970–2000), Pentecostals' institutional membership grew from 74
million to 500 million.

Public media focus on the exuberant nature of prayer and worship
at such gatherings and judge superficially the nature of fervor
and unusual practices like speaking in tongues. Critics frequently
insinuate that popular Pentecostal movements attract people of
insecure disposition, seeking clear-cut, simple answers in matters of
faith and seeking emotional release through music, dance, and so
on. However, the question must also be raised: Is it possible that
the Holy Spirit is using this outlet to revivify other faith systems

that have become congealed through overinstitutionalization, that Pentecostals bring freshness and vitality into overlegalized religions, and that the Spirit is actually breaking new ground in and through such movements? The Pentecostal revival certainly deserves an informed and thorough discernment, and in that testing of the spirits we need to come with an open mind and a receptive disposition.

Historical Background

We are dealing with a phenomenon that initially came into being in the early twentieth century. Many trace it to an event in the United States known as the Azusa Street Revival, which took place in Los Angeles, California, and was led by William J. Seymour, an African American preacher. It began with a meeting on April 14, 1906, and continued until about 1915. The revival was characterized by ecstatic spiritual experiences, accompanied by speaking in tongues, dramatic worship services, and interracial mingling. The participants were often criticized by both secular media and Christian theologians for behaviors considered to be outrageous and unorthodox, especially at the time. Today, the revival is considered by historians to be the primary catalyst for the spread of Pentecostalism in the twentieth century.

Seymour and the other revivalists at the Apostolic Faith Mission on Azusa Street held to five core beliefs:

1. Salvation by faith
2. Sanctification (or Holiness) of the believer
3. Tongues as evidence of Baptism with the Holy Spirit
4. Faith healing as part of God's redemption
5. The "very soon" return of Christ

The early Pentecostal revival was understood by its participants as restoring to the church these mighty acts of the Spirit. The manifestation of tongues, healings, miracles, and other spiritual gifts distinguished the early Pentecostals from other Christian churches and traditions. Invoking the Spirit in the exuberance and vigor of the gathered group (church) gave the early Pentecostals a sense of being more truly in touch with the fervor and truth of the

Christian faith as exemplified in the opening chapters of the Acts of the Apostles.

Among firsthand accounts were reports of the blind having their sight restored, diseases cured instantly, and immigrants speaking in foreign tongues: German, Yiddish, and Spanish. There were many accounts of uneducated black members interpreting the tongues with a quality of insight and wisdom that proved transformative and empowering for other participants.

The *Los Angeles Times* (April 18, 1906) was not so kind in its description:

> Meetings are held in a tumble-down shack on Azusa Street, and the devotees of the weird doctrine practice the most fanatical rites, preach the wildest theories and work themselves into a state of mad excitement in their peculiar zeal. Colored people and a sprinkling of whites compose the congregation, and night is made hideous in the neighborhood by the howlings of the worshippers, who spend hours swaying forth and back in a nerve racking attitude of prayer and supplication. They claim to have the "gift of tongues" and be able to understand the babble.

By 1913 the revival at Azusa Street had lost momentum, and by 1915 most of the media attention and crowds had left. Seymour remained there with his wife, Jennie, for the rest of their lives as pastors of the small African American congregation, though he often made short trips to help establish other smaller revivals later in life. After Seymour died of a heart attack on September 28, 1922, Jennie led the church until 1931, when the congregation lost the building. To all, it seemed as if the nine-year wonder had run its course.

At the same time, thousands of people were leaving Azusa Street with the intentions of evangelizing abroad. So many missionaries went out from Azusa Street (some thirty-eight left in October 1906) that within two years the movement had spread to over fifty nations, including Britain, Scandinavia, Germany, Holland, Egypt, Syria, Palestine, South Africa, Hong Kong, China, Ceylon, and India. Christian leaders visited from all over the world.

Doctrinal differences abounded, and many separate organizations and denominations sprang from the initial revivals (see the comprehensive overview of Hollenweger 1997). The Church of God in Christ was formed in 1907, the Assemblies of God and United Pentecostal Church emerged in 1914, and the Pentecostal Church of God was formed in 1919 at the Sharon Bible School. Today, there are more than 500 million Pentecostal and charismatic believers across the globe, close to a quarter of the world's 2 billion Christians. Some researchers suggest that the movement is growing at a rate of 13 million a year, or thirty-five thousand a day. The Pentecostal denomination is currently second only to the Roman Catholic Church.[33]

In 1947, Pentecostals worldwide held a conference in Zurich, Switzerland (not attended by the Oneness groups who claim that God is *One* person, namely Spirit, and not *Three* as conventional Christianity claims). Many leaders hoped to establish an organization for Pentecostals similar to the WCC that was then in formation. They were unable to do so because of the strongly congregational-centered Pentecostals of Scandinavia and Brazil. Since that time, Pentecostal leaders have gathered in a worldwide Pentecostal World Conference (PWC), where a small presidium has discussed items of mutual interest and concern. In 2004 the PWC formally took the name Pentecostal World Fellowship.

True to Christian Origins

Pentecostals tend to see their movement as reflecting the same kind of spiritual power, worship styles, and teachings that were found in the early church. For this reason, some Pentecostals also use the term "apostolic" or "full gospel" to describe their movement. Pentecostalism is theologically and historically close to the charismatic movement, and sometimes the terms "Pentecostal" and "charismatic" are used interchangeably.

Within Pentecostalism, speaking in tongues generally serves two functions. One relates to the initial evidence of the baptism in the Holy Spirit, when a believer speaks in tongues for the first time. Many Pentecostal denominations (especially in the United States) consider this to be the initial sign that the believer is filled with the

Holy Spirit. The other function has to do with the gift of tongues itself, when a person gives to a congregation a "message in tongues," a prophetic utterance given under the influence of the Holy Spirit. Pentecostals base their understanding of the gift of tongues and its operation in the church on the teachings of St. Paul as outlined in 1 Corinthians 12:4–12; 27–31; also I Corinthians 14:1–27.

Besides the gift of tongues, Pentecostals may also use glossolalia as a form of praise and worship in corporate settings. Some participants pray aloud in tongues while others pray simultaneously in the common language of the gathered Christians. This use of glossolalia is seen as an acceptable form of prayer and therefore requires no interpretation. Congregations may also corporately sing in tongues, a phenomenon known as "singing in the Spirit."

The majority of Pentecostal churches have chosen not to participate in any ecumenical organization, partly because of their restorationist perspective on the history of the church, whereby existing churches are perceived to have fallen away from God's intentions through compromise and sin. Another reason is the antagonism of several existing churches uneasy with, or suspicious of, the testimonies recording what God had done in individual lives. As a result, sectarian thinking has dominated much of the movement; ecumenical contact tends to be shunned, and several Pentecostal churches operate in relative isolation.

Key Beliefs Today

Pentecostals emphasize the teaching of the *full gospel* or *foursquare gospel*. The term "foursquare" refers to the four fundamental beliefs of Pentecostalism:

1. Jesus saves, according to John 3:16.
2. Jesus baptizes with the Holy Spirit, according to Acts 2:4.
3. Jesus heals bodily, according to James 5:15.
4. Jesus is coming again to receive those who are saved, according to 1 Thessalonians 4:16–17.

Pentecostals, like other evangelicals, generally adhere to the Bible's divine inspiration and inerrancy. A literal interpretation of scripture is quite widespread. Of particular significance is the text of Acts 1:4–5, 8: "On one occasion, while he was eating with them, Jesus gave them this command: 'Do not leave Jerusalem, but wait for the gift promised by the Father, which you have heard me speak about. For John baptized with water, but in a few days you will be baptized with the Holy Spirit. . . . But you will receive power when the Holy Spirit comes upon you; and you will be my witnesses in Jerusalem, and in all Judea and Samaria, and to the ends of the earth."

A central feature is the direct personal experience of God through baptism in the Holy Spirit. For Pentecostals, this "infilling" is a definite experience that happens after salvation. It gives access to the spiritual gifts described in the Bible—tongues, healings, exorcisms—and provides those who have been filled with power to serve and to witness.

For Pentecostals, Jesus is the only Savior and Mediator. All other religions are false, and sometimes denounced as satanic. The church is the only vehicle capable of communicating the truth of God's word. "Most often," writes Veli-Matti Karkkainen (2009, 170), "Pentecostals have succumbed to the standard conservative/fundamentalist view of limiting the Spirit's saving work to the Church."

Prophetic utterance is a regular feature of Pentecostal gatherings. It is generally considered to be an act of the Holy Spirit using a human vehicle to speak a divine word. Prophetic revelations may come through visions, dreams, impressions, or verbal proclamations—the intention being to edify, encourage, and comfort; to provide correction and warning; and to serve as direction and an agenda for prayer. The text of Joel 2:28–32 is often invoked as the basis for this practice: "In the last days, God says, I will pour out my Spirit on all people. Your sons and daughters will prophesy, your old men will dream dreams. Even on my servants, both men and women, I will pour out my Spirit in those days, and they will prophesy."

Pentecostals generally follow a very strict moral code. They look with contempt on the culture of modernity and its technological achievements and consumerist orientation—despite the fact that they liberally and extensively use modern mass media. The use of tobacco and alcohol is generally forbidden. Pentecostals practice adult baptism by immersion, and the Lord's Supper, which they call "ordinances" rather than "Sacraments."

Pentecostals seem excessively preoccupied with Satan, demons, and spiritual warfare. Their fascination with signs and wonders often relates to acts of exorcism and deliverance. Some of this extreme fervor seems related to a rather literalist approach to the *second coming of Christ*. Most believe that Christ will invisibly return and rapture his saints to heaven, leaving all other humans in a state of tribulation for a seven-year period. Subsequently, Christ will visibly return with his saints, who will reign on earth with him for one thousand years. During this reign the nation of Israel will be saved, and a time of universal peace will ensue. Judgment Day will follow later, with the good being rewarded and evil ones condemned eternally. After this time, Satan and his demons are destroyed forever.

Impact on Conventional Churches

For the millions attracted to the Pentecostal movement, the particular beliefs are not the appeal as much as the worshipers' sense of engagement and empowerment. Frequently, the experience of Pentecostal worship can be excessively emotional, overdramatized, and devoid of any sense of decorum, restraint, or control. Psychological projections often dominate, and the theological tenor may seem superficial and even dangerous. Some people become utterly delirious, and the leaders (and preachers) often come across as imposing, controlling, and manipulative.

This perspective is often the conclusion of the neutral observer. The experience of the engaged participant is quite different. A huge emotional release often occurs for people locked into pain, suffering, oppression, or fear. A distinctive sense of fellowship and solidarity is present, the intimate and empowering kind of community that many churches promise but few deliver. The church provides an outlet for spontaneous praise and celebration often suppressed in mainline churches, where worship formulas can be excessively verbose. This empowerment of rank-and-file members is documented by Anderson (1992), while the Nigerian researcher Ogbu U. Kalu (2008) describes the empowering impact on African people, precisely by affirming their primal worldview and the spontaneity they naturally employ in times of worship.

On the shadow side is the sense of escape from the drag and drudgery of life—especially for people in poorer situations. Instead of devoting itself to liberation through justice, the Pentecostal gathering can reassure by loudly condemning the satanic forces to which all problems are attributed. Sectors of the movement also promote what has come to be known as the *prosperity gospel*, the promise and false allure of health and wealth that will result from fidelity to the movement.

The final discerning question, however, has to do with the central phenomenon that Pentecostals claim to be proclaiming: the Holy Spirit! Is the Holy Spirit at work in this movement in a way that calls all Christians (and maybe all faith believers) to a new sense of awareness and engagement? One of the movement's finest scholars, Amos Yong, answers affirmatively (Yong 2005). Despite the exaggerated elements and the excessive attention to literalism, might the Holy Spirit be using this instrument to awaken new zest, hope, and vitality?

Brazil is the country with the most Catholics in the world, as well as the nation with the most Pentecostals: some 24 million faithful, in comparison to only 5.8 million in the United States. In 1980, 89 percent of the Brazilian population called itself Catholic; in the 2000 census, the figure fell to 74 percent, and by 2007, when the pope visited the country, to 64 percent. In 1980 John Paul II had crowds of 2 million people, but by 2007 Benedict XVI could draw only eight hundred thousand.

However, Pentecostals are a social and political force, not just a religious movement. In a historical irony, the largest political party on the South American continent, the Workers Party (PT), created by the Catholic Church and other entities, came into power with a Pentecostal vice president, José Alencar. The Universal Church of the Kingdom of God to which he belongs controls seventy television and fifty-plus radio stations, a bank, and several newspapers, and has thirty-five hundred temples. Its Record TV Network vies for the largest audience against the legendary Globo Network and earns $1 billion a year.

Of the 550 total legislative representatives in Brazil, 61 are Pentecostals, and 91 call themselves militant Catholics. The vice president's Brazilian Republican Party (PRB), created in 2005 and linked to the Universal Church, is the fastest-growing political force in the country. The PRB grew in less than a year "from a thousand members to a hundred thousand," something no other party has been able to achieve.

This has remained Amos Yong's pressing question: Is it possible that the Holy Spirit is active not only among Christians of all denominations but also among believers of the non-Christian world religions? I'd like to widen that question, keeping Brazil as a timely example: *Is modern Pentecostalism a symbolic cultural statement for a new wave of Spirit energy?* That aspect of divine-universal life, so long subverted and subdued, may be revisiting our world with a timely vengeance. Beyond the external religious veneer, which tends to be the focus of scholarly research, is this new spirit breakthrough/ awakening not merely a fresh sense of religious devotion but also presenting new horizons for politics, economics, media, social policy, and education? As a cultural phenomenon, modern Pentecostalism may yet prove to be one of the most prophetic movements of the twenty-first century.

───

Pause for a Moment

What is your inherited understanding of the Pentecostal move-ment? Do we unfairly judge it by impressionistic externalized behaviors? How might we engage Pentecostals in a dialogue that would facilitate growth and empowerment both for them and for those of us who belong to other Christian persuasions?

───

Revivalist in What Sense?

Glimpsing this wider international impact, Miriam Adeney (2009, 124) writes,

In the burgeoning populations of Asia, Africa and Latin America, many people are brought to Jesus by the Pentecostals. These churches emphasize the Spirit. When Pentecostals worship they open up their emotions and throw their whole bodies into the activity. They sing passionately, they sway, they shout, they dance, they cry, they may even collapse into the arms of others who will pick them up and support them. When the service is over and they walk out the church door and down the streets to their own neighborhoods and businesses, they expect the Spirit to walk with them, and they call on him to heal, to exorcise evil powers, to protect from dangers, to right wrongs, to guide, to reconcile and to strengthen. The Spirit also propels them to reach out to the needy.

Is Pentecostalism an antidote to what Harvey Cox once described as the "ecstasy deficit"? When religion loses its mystical fervor and becomes ensnared in bureaucracy and legalism, instead of lifting up the spirit within, it can become a burden of unworthiness and guilt, trapping the devotee in lethargy and disillusionment. Miller and Tetsunao (2007, 25), suggest that the rise of Pentecostalism is a new thing the Spirit is doing in our time rather than a reaction or response to a spiritual deficiency. One scholar describes the revival in these terms:

> Pentecostalism—by its democratization of religious life, promise of physical and social healing, compassion for the socially alienated, and practice of Spirit empowerment—has the ingredients for a powerful moral imagination that can address the concerns of the disinherited, frustrated and assertive persons who in large part make up the movement. (Douglas Peterson in Karkkainen 2009, 57)

Modern Pentecostalism seems to be going through many of the developmental processes one notes in most forms of religion. An initial fervor, which to the outsider may seem strange and even bizarre, gives way to gradual formalization and more structured institutionalization. That can also promote a kind of maturity whereby the religious system transcends its denominational enclave in order to move toward partnership with other sources of wisdom and inspiration. One sees this in the expanding desire to link ecumenically and in the direction of multifaith dialogue (Karkkainen 2009; Yong 2005). Of particular interest to this author is the desire to dialogue with the newly emerging insights of science and cosmology (more in Smith and Yong 2010; Vondey 2010).

I have already alluded to the pioneering work of Amos Yong, a Pentecostal minister and scholar of Chinese-Malaysian origin who has lived in the United States since his early teenage years. Having finished his doctorate in theology at Boston University, he went on to teach theology at Regent University, in Virginia Beach, Virginia, a school committed to Pentecostal-Charismatic scholarship. Yong is among the leading Pentecostal scholars seeking to discern the universality of the Spirit at work in the world, especially in the different religions and in the dialogue between science and religion.

Where most Pentecostals see the devil's work, Yong sees the possibility of the Spirit's breakthrough. Concretely, that means Christians should be open to learning from, and be enriched by, the Spirit's work in world religions. Dialogue must take place alongside evangelism, he argues, so that all the religions—including Christianity—can embrace a more mutually responsible mode of discernment.

Within Pentecostalism, Amos Yong is viewed very much as all visionaries are perceived in religious circles: with a mixture of admiration and trepidation. He is not alone, however. At least at the scholarly level, one detects expanding horizons leaning very much to the broader understanding of the Spirit I am exploring in this book. As yet, it is unclear where Pentecostalism will move in our postmodern world, but it may well prove to be one of the more generic and creatively disturbing movements pushing the Spirit not to one side but right to the top of the Trinitarian pyramid. Even Pentecostals would not be too happy with that image, because they are also seeking the dissolution of the pyramid, collapsing it into the circle, the relational matrix in which the empowering Spirit plays a crucial role to the benefit not merely of humanity but of the entire spectrum of God's creation.

Chapter 13

Personal Obstruction

Many of the problems of the world are due to spirit gone amok.
— THOMAS MOORE

The self is a will to belong.
— DANIEL DAY WILLIAMS

SPIRIT HAS GONE AMOK in our world mainly because of human beings. The very creatures who claim to be uniquely spiritual and capable of responding to the Spirit's urgings in a manner superior to, and transcending, all other creatures are the very ones who may be getting it drastically wrong. Our inflated anthropocentrism undermines our true nature, grounding us in a highly dysfunctional relationship with the surrounding web of life, but also leading to gross confusion on what constitutes our inner core of meaning and our relationship with divine transcendence.

In public discourse, and particularly in the economic and political domains, humans are defined by their capacity to be productive agents in the battle for the survival of the fittest. In that functional role, we are defined by our genetic makeup, with its fierce determinism toward survival at any cost (the selfish gene). Belligerent competition is the order of the day for the solitary selves who can endure the heat. Even when we have to work in cooperation with others—according to the leading theories—we are doing it ultimately for our individual good. The solitary self is the only true emblem of authentic humanity (see the informed critique of Midgley 2010).

Despite impressive evidence to the contrary, the violent embattled individualism still holds pride of place. Even scholarly research substantiates an alternative approach, as in Joan Roughgarden's notion of the genial gene (2009), Jeremy Rifkin's elaborate defense of the human capacity for empathy and cooperation (2009), or Paul Gilbert's claim that compassion rather than competition defines more accurately the deeper orientation of the human spirit (2009). These resources surface another view of what it means to be human, one that is also grounded in rigorous scientific research. It invites and challenges us to redefine our human personhood in the direction of altruism, sociality, and relationality.

We need to evaluate afresh the fundamental issue of personal identity. When we describe a relationship or connection as *personal*, we are working with several assumptions, deemed to be so basic and widely adopted that most people never dream of questioning the assumptions. Several layers of cultural accumulations need to be exposed, dismantled, and reframed. The whole enterprise of what it means to be a person needs to be imagined new.

Defined by the Web of Life

Like every other organism in creation, humans are begotten out of the creative vacuum. We don't come into the world; we come out of it. With these assertions, one runs the risk of losing most readers of these pages. It all sounds so far-fetched, fanciful, esoteric, unreal, and impractical. The actual problem is not one of superficiality but of profundity, a quality of wisdom, insight, and understanding that transcends so many ideas taken for granted in our excessively rational, anthropocentric culture.

Humanity's future is in great peril, unless and until we become transparent to the enlarged context to which we and all other creatures belong—the web of life that defines even our personal identities in minute detail. Like everything born out of the vacuum, we are energized to relate; relationships define our identity at every level, and the spirit-filled aspect of those relationships is an integral dimension. All that is born of the Spirit cannot but be spiritual.

Humans have a long historical story that illuminates the central ideas of this chapter. The story percolates through a range of sciences, notably paleontology, anthropology, evolutionary studies, ethnography, and so on. Our dependence on all other life forms in the universe is already well documented. The carbon from dying stars provides the organic basis of our human lives (and of all other organic forms). The energy of sunlight is the basis of all we eat for nourishment and good health. Bacterial organisms that first evolved as single-celled creatures about 3.5 billion years ago, and multicellular creatures that initially evolved about 2 billion years ago, still form the foundations of all we are and do. We are intrinsically connected with everything else in the great web of life.

The immediate ancestors to our human evolution comprise a range of animals and primates in a complex set of life lines still subject to intense scholarly scrutiny. Of enormous importance is the observation that there is no direct line of descent, a widespread misconception. Humans are not descended either from monkeys or chimpanzees. Evolution seems to work through what we might metaphorically call quantum leaps rather than lines of direct descent.

In the case of humans we share an estimated 98.3 percent of the same DNA with chimps, bonobos, gorillas, and orangutans. These other primates may be considered as our first cousins. Scholars think that there is a common ancestor somewhere in the background, but a range of attempts at locating it have drawn a blank. Evolution yields little evidence for anything resembling direct lines of descent, no more than quantum physics can accommodate our need for a cause-and-effect rationale.

Innately Relational

All this information offers a timely reminder of a complex and intricate background, grounding us as the amazing complex creatures we are. *We are defined by our capacity to relate* (cf. Budja 2010; McFadyen 1999). Our individuality is grounded in an intricate web of relationships. This foundational relational matrix precedes our biological coming into being. Long before egg and sperm meet, fields of influence are urging the formative influence that cocreates the new organism.

Where does the cocreation begin? All the formal religions attribute human origins to the power of divine creating, thus postulating a distant engineer-like divinity that manufactures everything in creation. This mechanistic metaphor is alien to the Spirit that blows where it wills and that energizes with the creative energy of the universe, evolving from the creative vacuum long before material form was known.

That same Spirit is the lure of all the laws of attraction, including those forces of human attraction whereby male and female embrace the creative process through which human life is conceived. Biologically, we understand well how this process takes place, and those who explore the process of human procreation from wider angles (beyond the biology) have long suspected that the process is immensely more complex than mere biological reproduction.

The Spirit is also the lure of sexual endeavor, including its human expression. In humans, sexuality serves many purposes above and beyond biological reproduction, a claim that is difficult to unravel holistically, so conditioned are we with biological determinism. At the heart of all sexual power (drive, instinct, etc.) is the lure of the erotic, explored in chapter 11.

In ancient times, eros was considered to be a divine power, the very dynamism that drew all life into an intricate, intimate web. The power for bonding is the soul of the erotic endeavor, theologically expressed in the notion of the Trinity—with its various equivalents in several of the great world religions. As indicated in chapter 11, the erotic life force belongs uniquely to what we call the Great Spirit, or Holy Spirit of God.

I want to suggest that the process of human reproduction begins with this ancient divine erotic lure. It translates into sexuality in every life form, and in humans it veers toward mystical union, always imbued with deep erotic intent (cf. Kripal 2001), without necessarily leading to physical sexual union. When it does lead to such union, informed by the primordial urge to cocreate—which often is subsumed in the deep subconscious—then this is where an individual human life begins. Long before the biological process is activated, a Spirit-infused erotic lure awakens the will-to-life, and the conception of new life subsequently ensues.

Spirit and Person

Amos Yong (2009) observes that the *ruach elohim* in Genesis 1:2 is neither a reference to the person of God, nor to a personal agent of God, but rather something akin to "the storm of God" or "God's wind." He claims that reputable Old Testament scholars such as Gerhard von Rad and Claus Westermann share the same view. Clearly, the writer of Genesis, and commentators over several centuries, understands the work of *ruach elohim* to be a profound form of creativity, incorporating all that is personal, while also transcending it, as Catherine Keller vividly illustrates (2003, xvii ff.).

"The Spirit is not less than humanly personal," writes Denis Edwards (2004, 178), "but infinitely more. A personal other, someone who draws us into love . . . the Spirit is not simply an impersonal power but a *personal presence* interior to each creature, creating communion with all in ways that are appropriate for each of them" (Edwards, 2004, 119). In a similar vein, Philip Clayton (2008, 149) writes, "Infinite Spirit may include personal predicates and qualities within it, but as such it is also more than personal—trans-personal. This is one reason why traditional theology was right to maintain that God consists of three divine persons rather than that God is a personal being."[34]

In daily life we tend to judge personalism by external behavior and performance, which frequently leads to an exaggerated anthropocentricism. Humans are deemed to be superior to all other life forms, forgetting, as noted frequently in this book, that human meaning is totally dependent on meaningful relationships with the larger realities of planet and cosmos and the diverse life forms embodied therein.

In the above quote from Denis Edwards, I want to draw attention to the aspect of interiority, which more than anything else defines authentic personalism. In their outline of the universe story, Swimme and Berry (1992) highlight three processes (as noted earlier in this volume) that characterize life at every level: *differentiation*, *interiority* (*autopoiesis*), and *communion*. Differentiation denotes individual uniqueness, neatly captivated in the biblical statement: every hair on your head is numbered.

Interiority highlights the within-ness from which all life forms receive their will-to-exist, and the accompanying behaviors that favor their growth and flourishing. In humans, this dimension has the added ingredient of self-reflexive consciousness, free will, and the option of personal conscious choice. When this option becomes excessively individualized we run the risk of jeopardizing the deeper meaning of our life's work. Here the third element highlighted by Swimme and Berry becomes crucial: *communion*. All our efforts are to be directed not for individual gain, but for interpersonal and transpersonal mutuality. Communion is the goal of emergent flourishing.

I draw the readers' attention also to the distinction between the *individual* and the *person*—to a point where confusion often reigns supreme. The fulfillment of all my individual rights does not guarantee my personal integrity. To the contrary, it can catapult me into an alienating, arrogant loneliness, generating a kind of internal battle of assertion and willpower, yet never winning in a truly satisfactory way. My personal flourishing, on the other hand, requires frequent and consistent mutuality—with other persons, but also with other creatures, and with the entire web of creation in its planetary and cosmic dimensions. This is a new definition of human personhood, one largely unknown to humanity at this time, and it seems to embody a personalism in which the Holy Spirit stands the best chance of influencing and leading us in a truly empowering way.

Enter the Transpersonal

The notion of the transpersonal tends to be associated with the human potential movement of the 1960s—more specifically with the psychological theories of Abraham Maslow, Carl Rogers, Roberto Assagioli, and more recently the integral theorist Ken Wilber. In fact, the word "transpersonal" was first used by William James in 1905, and it owes its current popularity mainly to the pioneering work of the psychologist Carl Jung (more on Jung in Appendix 3).

The transpersonal denotes that we are dealing with states or areas of consciousness beyond the limits of individualized, personal identity, and beyond all material expression, as Van Lommel (2010) illustrates so vividly. Ego functioning in daily life focuses on the individual and that person's needs. We assume that if every person is happy and fulfilled in themselves, then society at large will function effectively. In this anthropology, humans are at the forefront; the created universe exists to serve human need and well-being.

We consider the ego-functioning ideology as a philosophy that has been tried and tested across many millennia. However, this ideology is actually a very recent development, well named by Herbert Marcuse (1964) as "one-dimensional man." Humans are perceived as functionaries who can perform effectively and productively in an industrial technological culture, people who can operate machines and manage structural institutions, beginning with the family, and culminating in processes of government, national and international.

The mechanistic undercurrents of this model progressively led to the anxiety and dissatisfaction with life popularized by existential philosophy, and evoked the desire to embrace a larger view of human beings and their role in the created universe. Making the transition was to prove more problematic than we might have imagined. One-dimensional man was an external construct whose inherent limitations could easily be recognized; however, a more subtle influence with a much more stubborn resistance was built into its survival ability. I refer to the understanding of the human person developed in classical Greek philosophy.

Aristotle wanted humans to separate themselves from their enmeshment in the natural world, to stand apart from it and behave in a manner superior to it—primarily through the use of reason. Aristotle viewed humans, created by God, as rational creatures who could rise above the sentiment and emotion that belonged to earthly enmeshment—and embodied primarily in women. Thus there began to emerge a new sense of the human, represented foremost in the rational, productive male—productive in sowing the seed of new biological life, for which females served primarily as biological organisms for the purposes of reproduction and home-based domestication, and productive in managing society at large (the *polis*) in a rational, orderly way.

In a very real sense, Marcuse's one-dimensional man becomes the crowning achievement of Aristotle's rational patriarch. But Aristotle's legacy is much more secure than Marcuse's because in all governmental systems in the modern world, secular and religious, Aristotle's anthropology still reigns supreme. Consequently, educational systems throughout the modern world support and promote the Aristotelian view of the human, leading to the culture of fierce competition that causes so much anguish and pain in our time.

The notion of the transpersonal, therefore, is first and foremost a declaration against a way of being human no longer deemed to be meaningful, empowering, or authentic. Millions are disenfranchised by this fiercely competitive anthropology; people are not relating authentically with each other or with the living earth. Ethically, the strong win and everybody else loses out, in a brutal strategy that leads to violence, poverty, and widespread disillusionment. The more we try to rectify the mess we have created by exerting more effective human control mechanisms, the more we seem to be driving the whole thing out of control.

The picture is quite pessimistic. Even some critical thinkers believe that humanity has already gone past the point of no return and is catapulting headlong into the next major extinction (cf. Leakey and Lewin 1996). Crisis management has become our default mode. To keep despair at bay, drastic options need to be considered. Invoking the transpersonal is one such strategy.

The transpersonal is not just about transcending the limitations inherent in our highly individualistic and competitive culture. Rather it seeks to redefine what it means to be human. It views human meaning and integrity not merely in an autonomous, self-reliant, rational way of being, whereby maturity is perceived as the ability to stand on one's own individual resources. Instead, it proposes that we can only become authentically—and fully—human in an integral relationship with all the dimensions of the universe to which we belong. Thus Peter C. Hodgson (1994, 284) redefines the challenge facing us:

> Spirit is nothing but relations; it is precisely relationality, the moving air that permeates and enlivens things, the open space across which the wind of Spirit blows. The open space is the condition of possibility of relations; without it, everything would collapse into sameness. By entering into relations, Spirit loses its vagueness, takes on specificity and shape: it is this to which the language of "person" is pointing.

Pause for a Moment

To what extent have you been aware of the inherited cultural impact of dualistic splitting? If something does not feel personal, why do we hurriedly conclude that it must be impersonal?

Can you internalize the meaning and significance of the transpersonal? Can you apply this new idea to your life experience, embracing a more awesome and at times more frightening vision of reality?

∽

Belonging is the defining element in this new understanding. We become who we are—and what our potential makes possible—through our ability to belong. Isolation and individual autonomy undermine the potential for belonging. Belonging in this context is not merely a form of human camaraderie, but is defined fundamentally as a cosmic inheritance, a planetary disposition, and a spiritually bestowed endowment. In a word, we are programmed to belong. In the closing decades of the twentieth century, this same consciousness began to impact on our theology of the Trinity, as exemplified in the works of scholars such as Catherine LaCugna, Patricia Fox, John D. Zizioulas, and David Cunningham (a useful review appears in Johnson 2008, 202–25).

The capacity for belonging underpins our propensity for relationship. Relationships define every moment of our existence (cf. Budja 2010). Our being and becoming are defined by several field influences that connect us to the web of life and sustain our every endeavor. We are at all times the sum of our relationships, and relationality is the medium through which we grow and flourish. The transpersonal elevates the meaning of personhood to a new cosmic and global context. In this new domain, the dualistic split between the personal and the impersonal holds no meaning.

Reclaiming the transpersonal is essential for humanity to move forward meaningfully, but its credibility is not based merely on its practical usefulness for our collective future; it has even a stronger base in our ancient past, which Aristotle, in his shortsightedness, sought to ridicule and undermine. For most of our time as earthlings we lived and behaved in a convivial relationship with the enveloping creation. As I indicate in a previous work (O'Murchu 2008), our immersion in creation did not degrade our humanity; instead it enhanced and supported its evolutionary unfolding in several creative and dynamic ways. Today, we are blessed with a more thorough understanding of the creation to which we belong, but tragically that enhanced wisdom has not empowered us into the convivial way of living in which our ancient ancestors flourished over several millennia.

The Transpersonal Spirit

Our ancient moorings are becoming ever more accessible, thanks to the pioneering work of anthropologists and paleontologists in our time. The evidence increasingly points not to a primitive barbaric species but to creatures who cocreated authentically and elegantly because of their affinity to the natural processes of the universe. Moreover, those ancient bonds were profoundly spiritual in nature. Their convivial relationship with the living earth endowed them with an understanding and appreciation of the divine presence in their very midst. Thomas Berry (2006, 118) captivates the sense of that primordial sacredness when he writes,

> Humans, in this earlier period of human development, experienced themselves as owning nothing, as receiving existence itself and life and consciousness as an unmerited gift from the universe, as having exuberant delight and unending gratitude as their first obligation. It was a personal universe, a world of intimacy and beauty. A universe where every mode of being lived by a shared existence with all other modes of being. No being had meaning or reality or fulfilment apart from the great community of life. This primordial earth community itself existed through the presence of the indwelling spirit whence came its sacred character.

Long before the indigenous peoples of our day, our ancestors knew intuitively the empowering presence of the Great Spirit. They certainly did not perceive the Great Spirit as an impersonal force, nor are they likely to have inquired into the precise sense in which the Spirit could be defined as personal. Those metaphysical distinctions were of no interest to our ancestors, not do they preoccupy indigenous peoples of our day. In the absence of the dualistic mind-set, the transpersonal becomes the more fertile soil in which people can grow, flourish, and cocreate with the spiritual life force that outwits all our categories and distinctions, philosophical and theological alike.

Paradoxically, our attempt to preserve a more person-centered approach to religion and the divine life in our midst is the very thing that militates against our spiritual depth and empowerment. Reclaiming a more central role for the Great Spirit—the goal of this book—hopefully can help us now to embrace a larger sense of personhood. It will bring alive in a more profound way the Holy Mystery within which we live and move and have our being. More significant, perhaps, it will engage us with a new anthropology—one that has much more to offer as we desire to cocreate a more peaceful and empowering future for our earth and all who share life upon it.

Chapter 14

The Spirit That Blows

I once said, perhaps rightly: the earlier culture will become a heap of rubble and finally a heap of ashes, but spirits will hover over the ashes.

— LUDWIG WITTGENSTEIN

The Spirit is the indwelling of God at the heart of the process of ongoing creation, empowering and luring all things into an unforeseeable future.

— DENIS EDWARDS

IN CONCLUDING THIS book I want to highlight the fact that the exploration undertaken does not lend itself to a conventional sense of closure. The entire book has been a pilgrimage into horizons that stretch the inner spirit—of human and earth—toward the Great Spirit of unlimited possibilities. This is the One who in the oft-quoted words of scripture, "blows where [it] wills" (John 3:8). And we follow the lure, because nothing else is likely to satisfy the hunger and thirst that sustain our inner being.

As we saw frequently in this volume, the personal and transpersonal dimensions of the Spirit are complementary sides of the one reality. Energizing, luring, and blowing are among the pregnant metaphors adopted by those who detect the emergence of a new synthesis between the personal and the transpersonal, between cosmology and pneumatology, within our growing sense of an organic, open-ended universe imbued with an universal spirit force that pervades and empowers on a universal scale.

Theology itself has not arrived there yet. In fact, most theologians seem quite some distance away, still concerned about reserving pneumatology to the Christian faith, and locating it within the landscape of the Trinitarian-God configuration. Within that theological locus, it is difficult to transcend the patriarchal, hierarchical structure with the Creator at the top, and inevitably the Spirit occupying the lowest place on the triadic ladder.

Inspired by the pneumatology of Gregory of Nazianzus (329–389), the Swedish theologian Sigurd Bergmann aims at a fresh synthesis around "the ecology of the Holy Spirit as transparency of place" (2006, 302–21). He proposes that we dispense with the notion of the Spirit's immanence in nature and re-vision the Holy Spirit as the divine life force that makes all space more transparent to ultimate meaning. In turn, we transcend the metaphysical scrutiny about the Spirit's place within Trinitarian life, on the one hand, and within the church, on the other. The Spirit's place is not so much about location, understood metaphysically or geographically, but about transformation toward greater transparency. The transformative impact of the Holy Spirit cannot be restricted in any sense—it is born out of unlimited freedom and creativity, described by Moltmann as the principle "of creativity, of evolution, of individuation and of intentionality" (1985, 100).

Horizons of Greater Transparency

In conclusion I want to offer a synthesis built around the various new horizons explored in this book. To conventional Christian readers, the emerging insights may seem novel and speculative, and for some they may feel unorthodox to the point of being outrageous or even heretical. In truth, nothing in this book is totally new. I am attempting a synthesis of ideas that were afloat for much of the twentieth century. Some can be traced back to early Christian times, as Sigurd Bergmann does in the case of Gregory of Nazianzus, and others to the prehistoric depths of human mythology.

In this final attempt at collating the material, I humbly acknowledge that indeed there is nothing new under the sun. Precisely because I believe in the all-pervasive fertility of the Holy Spirit, then everything is new and we should never cease from exploring and discovering afresh that empowering novelty. As I glance backward I feel the tug and pull to open up to the many horizons that beckon in our time. At every stage, however, I am seeking out that greater transparency, which hopefully will empower us all to befriend more authentically the Holy Mystery, arising *ex profundis*, and befriending us in every realm of the creation that surrounds us.

First Horizon: The Indigenous Notion of the Great Spirit

Human learning today has become highly sophisticated. The rigor and detail of science permeates every sphere of knowledge. Yet we live in a culture of mass information, where the wisdom shared in the human community is vastly more complex and enriching than scientific learning can ever hope to captivate. Other forms of wisdom also impinge upon our daily lives, inform our daily behaviors, and enhance the breadth and depth of our wisdom.

Human society has long looked down upon those who don't measure up and don't aspire to the standards and values of our so-called civilized world. We put much of our valued experience beyond the pale. We relegate, disown, and often denounce ways of being in the world that have the potential to enhance our well-being, possibly in significant ways. Indigenous cultures fall into this category.

Although only a minority in terms of current world population, first-nations people feature much more strongly in our awareness today. Many of their land-based values and their more grounded sense of the sacred embody values we know are crucial for this time and for the future of our civilization. In this book I have incorporated just one aspect of those complex diverse cultures, namely belief in a divine life force, universally known as the Great Spirit.

The notion of the Great Spirit conveys a sense of freedom, playfulness, engagement, and grounding often missing in formal religious systems. It weds transcendence (the beyond) and immanence in an unique way. It articulates sacred power (even frightening and awesome at times), always mediated in the experience of empowerment. The notion of the Great Spirit transcends the legalism in which religion is often bogged down, yet is unambiguously clear on its key values. Perhaps most significant for the present work, it honors the long-held belief in the Holy Mystery, while seeking new articulations grounded in the world of daily life.

Second Horizon: The Spirit in Creation

The Great Spirit is perceived to inhabit creation without being confined to it. It is panentheism rather than pantheism. Contrary to the dualistic split so characteristic of monotheistic religion, there is no heavenly abode for the gods that needs to dwell above the sky outside this sinful creation. The Great Spirit is at home in creation, as long as we remember that it is not a static place but an evolving, emergent universe.

Here science and cosmology adumbrate the indigenous wisdom. Everything in creation originates as energy, taking physical and material shape under its empowering impetus. As field theories indicate, the energy is not random, although often chaotic. It is infused with pattern and a preferred sense of direction. When we ask what energizes the energy itself, it is difficult to avoid the answer: *the Holy Spirit of God*. We are now into a multidisciplinary mode of discernment that still feels strange—and threatening—to many people of our time.

The strange and exciting nature of this insight can be gleaned from the work of Mark Hathaway and Leonardo Boff (2009, 323), who suggest that *energy* should become the first descriptive feature of the Holy Spirit; second, *passion*; and third, *spirit*. They go on to describe the role of the Holy Spirit in these words:

> In cosmological terms, spirit can be understood as the capacity of the primeval energies and of matter itself to interact with each other in such a way that they self-create, self-organize, and constitute themselves into open systems (i.e., autopoiesis) that communicate with each other and which form an increasingly complex fabric of interrelationships which ultimately sustain the entire cosmos. . . . The cosmos, in this sense, is overflow with spirit because it is interactive, pan-relational, and creative. (Hathaway and Boff 2009, 316).

The vibrant Spirit—from a human point of view—first manifests in the cosmic creative vacuum. Within the vacuum, the energizing

Spirit weaves the relationships and patterns that beget every structure and life form we observe in the world around us. Moreover, that same Spirit interconnects all the creative beings—from subatomic particles to the vast galaxies—in the grand adventure of the evolving creation.

New insights in cosmology tease us into engaging more deeply with the great scientific insights of our time. Learning to relate with a vast creation, which feels impersonal but also dauntingly intimate, requires a spirituality not easily discerned in formal religion. The mystics in all the religious systems were acquainted with this archetypal wisdom, but for the greater part, mystics are not cherished in the formal religious systems we know today.

Third Horizon: The Spirit in Personhood

We are still heavily inundated in functional personhood. We judge ourselves and each other by how well we perform. Moreover, the performance is valued in terms of how much brute force we can exert or how much wealth we can accumulate. Herbert Marcuse's one-dimensional man is still alive and well. And as Mary Midgley (2010) convincingly illustrates, we all suffer the pain of alienation endemic to that anthropology.

Psychology and the social sciences alert us to other ways of seeing who and what we are, and what we might choose to become. A relational understanding of the person has so much more to offer us than the lone-ranger image so endemic to the anthropology of classical Greek times. Once we embrace this new way of being human, we glimpse other horizons where relationality dictates the prevailing values. Creation itself begins to look different, and so does our understanding of God (the Holy Mystery).

Relational personhood is an event rather than an entity, an evolving process rather than a biologically defined organism. It never ceases to grow, change, and develop, and in that process it moves toward a desired future, the lure of that living force we call the Holy Spirit. The Spirit impels from both within and without. That which dwells in the human heart, according to conventional spirituality, is one and the same Spirit that indwells the whole of creation. In fact, the Spirit's presence in creation predates humans by billions of years.

Fourth Horizon: The Spirit in Religion

When spirit power flourished in prehistoric religion, we dismissed it as animism. Unfortunately, we still tend to do the same with modern forms of ancestor worship. Our intellectual literalism, on the one hand, and our imperial theological arrogance, on the other, ill dispose us for the deeper discernment needed to uncover deeper truth.

The sense of Spirit in several prehistoric religions is visceral, earthy, and tangible. People feel a sense of sacredness and intuitively they know that their senses are not deceiving them. When we became excessively rational in dealing with our senses we lost our capacity for *synesthesia* (Abram 1996; see http://en.wikipedia. org/wiki/synesthesia) and the innate wisdom of Spirit power was reconceptualized in metaphysical categories deeply alien to divine spirit and human intuition.

We projected God above the sky and began to invent a metaphysical ladder to access the all-powerful hero. The Spirit could never measure up to such grandeur and opulence, and eventually was relegated to third place, largely forgotten for most of the Christian era. Now the Spirit is back with a vengeance, or so it seems, and I hope this book is at least a small contribution to the spiritual and theological adjustments will need to be made.

Fifth Horizon: From Third to First in the Trinity

This rearranging of the Trinity seems to have originated with Asian Christian scholars. A more pervasive sense of God as Spirit characterizes several of the great Eastern religions, and is also discernible in a vast range of Asian indigenous spiritualities. While the notion of a personal God is of paramount importance for Westerners (i.e., Christians), Eastern wisdom finds the Western notion of personhood too narrow, biologically reductionistic, and tainted with patriarchal, imperial intent. The God concept of the Far East is perceived as a cosmic life force, inclusive of all life forms including human persons. It is transpersonal rather than impersonal.

The Asian view of the Holy Spirit connects readily with all the dynamic forces at work in creation, because it is already perceived to be a cosmic life force. The creative dimension is significantly honored in the cultures of Asia, but not attributed to a divine originator (the Father) as explicitly as in the West. And instead of the third person, envisaged to serve the Christian task of salvation and redemption, the Eastern divinity tends to embody a god (or goddess) who embraces and transforms the great paradox of creation and destruction: Shiva and Kali of Hinduism, Nu-Kua in ancient Chinese mythology, Tiamat in Babylonian mythology.

Sixth Horizon: Even Jesus Is Empowered by the Spirit

In conventional Christianity, Jesus is effectively the primary divine reality. He makes real and tangible the Father who abides in a distant heaven, and Jesus mediates the power of the Spirit for all believers. It is in and through Jesus—not through the Father or the Spirit—that salvation is wrought and new life is made possible. In daily prayer and devotion, Jesus is the focus, and the Christian Gospels provide the primary guideline for responsible behavior as Christians seek to imitate the virtues and good deeds of Jesus as outlined in the Gospels.

St. Paul, the first Christian commentator (theologian), presents a somewhat different picture. He states explicitly that Jesus came on earth in the power of the Spirit, bore witness, and was raised from the dead. (More on St. Paul in Appendix 2.) So, too, with John, the author of the fourth Gospel: although Jesus is portrayed as a divine hero, his mission begins after baptism in the power of the Spirit, and Jesus is often portrayed as the one who paves the way for the fuller life bestowed through the power of the Paraclete. Raimundo Panikkar (2004, 122) captivates the central role of the Spirit in the life of Jesus in these inspiring words:

> The Master is about to leave without having finished hardly anything whole, almost abandoning his disciples. The people have abandoned him because it has become too risky to follow him; the synagogue declares him a heretic, indeed blasphemous; the political representatives despise him; and his "own" do not understand him. He has not left them anything durable, no institution; he has neither baptized nor ordained, much less has he founded anything. He has left both the Spirit

and himself as a silent presence in the Eucharistic act. . . . He promises his disciples only one thing: the Spirit.

The life and ministry of Jesus was the work of the Spirit and in the end gave way to a fuller realization of the Spirit's empowerment—even in the face of apparent failure. This portrayal of Jesus as a Spirit-filled person gradually gave way to the individualized hero of patriarchy, reaching its ideological climax in Constantine's elevation of Jesus, crowned as *pantocrator* of the universe, a royal status that remained largely unquestioned until the mid-twentieth century.

Seventh Horizon: Sacramental Empowerment

Paradoxically, the church has covertly attributed to the Holy Spirit a role of primary significance. This is nowhere as obvious as in the celebration of the Eucharist and its foundational theology. From earliest times, the church understood the Holy Spirit to be the primary agent of change and transformation in the Eucharistic liturgy. That central role of the Holy Spirit is known as the *epiclesis*, literally meaning the *invocation*.

Through the ritual invocation of the Holy Spirit the bread and wine become the body and blood of Jesus—whether we name the process as transubstantiation or transfiguration. It is widely believed that Eucharistic transformation is activated by the priest solemnly pronouncing special words of consecration, exercising a specially bestowed divine power by virtue of ordination. That, too, is the formal teaching of the church, leaving Christians in an intriguing theological double-bind. According to the tradition, change is activated through the *epiclesis*, yet the formal teaching also claims it is activated by the *priest*.

In fact, the dilemma is even more complex. The Catholic Church (and some other denominations) requires not one but two invocations of the Holy Spirit (the double epiclesis). The first invokes the Holy Spirit upon the gifts, and the second upon the people as a worshiping community, that all may be more united and focused on what they are about as participants in the Eucharistic celebration. Historically, the invocation of the Holy Spirit was first upon the people and laterally upon the gifts.

However we seek to unravel the intricacies of this tradition, one thing seems unambiguously clear: the community cannot worship, and Eucharistic transformation cannot take place, without the empowerment of the Holy Spirit. The Holy Spirit is the primary agent in all sacraments. In the power of the Spirit we are empowered to exercise our ritualistic and liturgical responsibilities as a Christian people.

Eighth Horizon: The Spirit That Lures

According to Christian faith, the fullness of the Holy Spirit was given at Pentecost for the first time two thousand years ago. Since then, the gifts of the Spirit are dispensed first and foremost through the church. In this view, the Holy Spirit belongs primarily (if not exclusively) to the holy realm of religion, which for some Christians means the exclusive domain of Christian revelation. How the Spirit works in creation is of little consequence to many Christian churches; indeed, some see no reason for holding that view in the first place.

The Spirit, therefore, is in the past, and all authentic faith is built on the solid foundations of the past. Strangely, this is precisely what Darwinian evolution—in its conventional formulation—also claims. We build on those life forms that have stood the test of time and that, time and again, have proved to be the fittest to survive. In fact, it is within the context of the Darwinian paradigm that Georgetown professor of theology John F. Haught has promoted the notion of the lure of the future (Haught 2003; 2010; Faber 2008).

For Haught, evolution is not just driven from the past (what we might call the classical position) but also empowered by the lure of the future. Here we evidence the Spirit at its most inventive and innovative. I suspect in fact that the lure of the future is far more significant than the drive from the past. The Spirit that blows where it wills is the surprising catalyst, forever breaking open novelty and extravagance—and not merely in the foreseeable future, but far beyond our conventional notion of space-time, as cosmologists press forward into new visionary horizons of an open universe without beginning or end.

We are driven from the past, but also lured from the future—the future that lures and invites us to move forward, informing every aspect of our being and becoming. We strive for something more because deep in our hearts the Spirit lures us to do so. The restlessness within us is a divine one, the fruit of the enlivening, energizing, and empowering Spirit, the same Spirit that blows where it wills and never ceases to amaze and surprise us. At all time, the Spirit is always several steps ahead of us.

~

Pause for a Moment

As you reflect on the experience of having read this book, what resonates with you, and what are you resisting? What can you carry forward into your faith experience, and what may not fit for you? More important, perhaps, what have been the life learnings of earlier times that made the insights of this book more accessible to you? What are the challenges to continue as a seeking, searching, Spirit-imbued person?

~

Holy Restlessness

The new horizons outlined in this chapter can be detected in the words of St. Gregory of Nazianzus (Orations 41:9), as quoted by Sigurd Bergmann (1995, 120):

> The Holy Spirit, then, always existed, and exists, and always will exist: invisible, eternal, incomprehensible, unchangeable, without quality, without quantity, without form, impalpable, self-moving, eternally moving, with free will, self powerful, all-powerful.

Far from being the hidden force behind the divine power of the Creator and the redeeming power of Jesus, the Spirit seems to me the most overt aspect of Holy Wisdom in our world and in our human experience. In every movement of creation the Spirit is manifest in the pregnant energy of life. In every attempt at spiritual connection—whether secular or religious (in some sense)—the Spirit is operative.

Today, the Pentecostal movement seems to be playing a significant role in the revival of the Spirit in religion and culture alike. Despite a range of reservations from within and outside Christian denominations, the Pentecostal movement is a sign of our time, requiring a considerable and concerted quality of discernment. To urge us in that task it is worth heeding the words of two contemporary theologians:

> [Pentecostalism] has succeeded because it has spoken to the spiritual emptiness of our time by reaching beyond the levels of creed and ceremony into the core of human religiousness into what might be called "primal spirituality," that largely unprocessed nucleus of the psyche in which the unending struggle for a sense of purpose and significance goes on. . . . My own conviction is that Pentecostals have touched so many people because they have indeed restored something. (Cox 2001, 95, 81)

For many decades the Pentecostal movement was merely known for its aggressive evangelistic and missionary work; enthusiastic charismatic spirituality; and lay-led, nonacademic way of proclaiming the Gospel. Academia and Azusa Street seemed to be at odds with each other—or at least in different worlds. During the past two decades or so, Pentecostal theology has emerged and is about to establish its place among other traditions. A younger generation of Pentecostal theologians, many of them educated in some of the best theological schools and thus knowledgeable of wider Christian traditions, have done some exciting work in reflecting theologically on the Pentecostal "experientialism" (Karkkainen 2009, xxiii).

Pentecostalism invades religious orthodoxy, shaking tired and weary foundations, and deeply disturbing established faith patterns. It invites a new baptismal enthusiasm, which the masses embrace with exuberance and ecstasy. Like all human developments—religiously inspired or otherwise—Pentecostalism has its pitfalls, its deviations, and its ecclesiastical power games. But it embodies a fervor, a freedom, and an awakening that connect spiritual experience with a more enduring truth. The movement symbolizes an awakening of the Spirit that none of the major religions seem capable of matching.

If the Pentecostal movement can embrace some of the wider horizons depicted in this book, an interdisciplinary engagement with the social and physical sciences—as scholars such as Amos Yong, Veli-Matti Karkkainen, and Wolfgang Vondey are beginning to do—then the movement may be poised for a unique prophetic breakthrough with a significant cultural impact throughout the twenty-first century. It will not have been the first time that the Spirit broke new ground—another reminder that Pentecost is not so much a one-time event, but a reawakening that occurs time and again in the Spirit-inspired dynamics that characterize the whole of God's creation.

The Final Word

Humanity is being taken to the place where it will have to chose between suicide and adoration!

— TEILHARD DE CHARDIN

When it comes to the Great Spirit, there is no final word. Every ending is effectively a new beginning. The Spirit scrambles all our categories, distinctions, theories, and dogmas. Destruction and the need for reconstruction belong innately to the great paradox of birth–death–rebirth. Learning to live with the fluidity and flexibility of the Spirit's creativity is a lifelong task; having to do that in a world so fixated on, and addicted to, order, structure, and rigidity requires continuous discernment, if we stand any chance of being faithful to our Spirit-filled context.

So I end reminding us once again what the landscape context looks like. Spirit power is the wellspring of all possibility, the restless pulsation of every movement in creation and of every desire in the human heart. It is the power of becoming that awakens every stir of imagination, wisdom, and creativity. It is the indwelling of God, but a great deal more, because without this Spirit power even the Mother/Father God cannot cocreate the creation to which we, humans, intimately belong. The Spirit is the originating power even of the triune Godhead itself.

Appendix 1

Spiritualism and the Great Spirit

THROUGHOUT THIS BOOK, several ideas relate to the key beliefs of a movement known as *spiritualism*. Sometimes described as a religion, spiritualism claims that the spirits of the dead reside in the spirit world and have both the ability and the inclination to communicate with the living. Anyone may receive spirit messages, but formal communication sessions, popularly known as séances and facilitated by mediums, provide what is deemed to be more authentic insight—particularly in relation to the afterlife.

Most spiritualists adopt seven guiding principles:

1. The Fatherhood of God, primary source of divine power
2. The family of humankind, all equal before God
3. Communion of spirits and the ministry of angels
4. Continuous existence of the human soul through the spirit body
5. Personal responsibility, which does not stop at death
6. Compensation and retribution hereafter for all good and evil deeds done on Earth
7. Eternal progress open to every human soul

Spiritualism flourished in the latter half of the nineteenth century, mainly in the United States and Europe, reaching an estimated strength of 8 million followers mostly drawn from the middle and upper classes. Many prominent Spiritualists were women, supporting causes such as the abolition of slavery and women's suffrage. Spiritualism is currently practiced primarily through various denominational Spiritualist churches in the United States and the United Kingdom, and is often affiliated with the burgeoning Pentecostal movement described in chapter 12.

Spiritualism is a distinctively Christian phenomenon, and although it adopts neither formal institutions nor scriptures, it embraces the sense of personal allegiance to divine guidance more typical of conventional Christianity. Its focus is very much on human personhood and the reassurance of ultimate salvation for each individual.

Positively, it can be viewed as another compensatory development for a culture lacking more generic belief in the Great Spirit. When the dynamism of the Spirit is not consciously acknowledged and responsibly accommodated, spirit-inspired movements are likely to arise to fulfill the unmet need. Discerning their authenticity continues to be a major challenge for all cultures that take Spirit power seriously.

Appendix 2

Does St. Paul Have Anything to Offer on the Great Spirit?

"IN PAUL'S THEOLOGY OF the Spirit," writes Kirsteen Kim (2007, 19), "being 'in the spirit' is decisively different from being 'under the law' or 'in the flesh' (Rom. 7–8; 1 Cor. 2–3; 2 Cor. 3; Gal. 3–5), not in the sense of being an alternative way of life, but rather an altogether higher quality of living." In Paul's theology, the Holy Spirit belongs integrally to the triune God of Father, Son, and Holy Spirit. Although Jesus is the primary agent through which salvation is made possible, everything Jesus does and accomplishes is in accordance with the guidance and empowerment of the Spirit. In the power of the Spirit, Jesus reveals the love of the Father and makes conversion and salvation possible, and in the power of that same Spirit, Jesus is raised from the dead.

All of this seems to suggest that, for Paul, the Spirit is primarily some type of divine life force that exercises a power of influence above and beyond that of Jesus. No Pauline commentator would agree. First, they claim that for Paul, the Holy Spirit is definitely a person, not some type of life force, and although Jesus acts in the power of the Spirit, effectively the Spirit can only bring about change in those who submit to, and follow, the teaching and example of Jesus.

Yet for Paul, the Spirit is not merely central to his vision, but commands a spiritual significance that is deeply personal and globally expansive. The Spirit inhabits the whole of creation and seems to influence every movement that forges harmony and unity— admittedly realized for Paul primarily in the community of the church. Paul seems to be connected into an understanding of the

Spirit exceeding the denominational concerns of Christianity itself, or indeed the specific preoccupations of any formal religion.

For Paul, being "in Christ" and "in the Spirit" seems to convey one and the same experience (1 Cor. 3:16), often described by commentators as a kind of Pauline mysticism. Gordon Fee (1994) concludes his monumental study noting that, for Paul, the Spirit is the key to all Christian spirituality, enabling the believer's own spirit to be truly one with God in worship and communion, individually and as a community.

Despite the unanimity of Christian scholarship claiming that Paul's pneumatology is distinctly and uniquely Christian, I detect in Paul's spiritual vision a stretching toward larger horizons—personal and transpersonal—that carry strong resonances with the primal faith in the Great Spirit. When it comes to Pauline scholarship, the jury is still out on several critical issues; perhaps his understanding of Spirit empowerment should be added to the list.

Appendix 3

Carl Jung and the Holy Spirit

CARL JUNG WAS A profoundly religious man, with an understanding of religion that exceeded the tenets of religious orthodoxy in his day. More accurately, Jung was enthralled by the notion of the spiritual, as a transformative power that impacted not merely on humans but on every movement of the human spirit in its convivial relationship with nature and with the power of universal consciousness.

A substantial proportion of volume 11 of *Jung's Collected Works* (Jung 1956) is a reflection on the concept of the Trinity from a psychospiritual point of view. For Jung, this doctrine is replete with psychological meaning. The Father symbolizes the psyche in its original undifferentiated wholeness. The Son represents the human psyche, and the Holy Spirit, the state of self-critical submission to a higher reality. Jung also noted parallels to the Christian notion of the Trinity in the Babylonian, Egyptian, and Greek mystical traditions.

Jung depicts the Holy Spirit as that mysterious force that unites opposites and allows the transcendent to enter space and time, in a process he describes as "continuing Incarnation" (Jung 1956, 412–15). The Spirit is also the empowering source of that personal growth process known as *individuation*, the relational maturation of the human within the entire context of planetary and cosmic life. Here we encounter a quality of unity very close to what the Eastern mystics call nonduality.

Larry Gates (1994) has examined in some detail Jung's concept of the Holy Spirit, but restricts his reflections to Jung's analysis of the Trinity outlined briefly above. In this regard Jung remains quite close to the conventional Christian paradigm while stretching the meaning and significance of three figures of Father, Son, and Holy

Spirit. When it comes to the Great Spirit, as explored in the present work, Jung has nothing to contribute in a direct way, but I suggest his indirect contribution is potentially substantial.

Central to Jung's expansive vision is the notion of the *collective unconscious*, which more aptly should be called "cosmic consciousness." It may be described as that envelope of intense awareness informing the creative energy through which everything in creation comes into being and flourishes thereafter. The reader will recall that this is exactly the depiction of the Great Spirit we encountered in the opening chapters of this book. Jung himself does not speculate on the inner dynamics of the collective unconscious, but he does acknowledge its divine source.

The inherent wealth of meaning in the collective unconscious becomes clearer as Jung develops his concept of the archetypes. Essentially these are energy movements, patterns of meaning, that recur time and again in human consciousness, symbolism, dreams, and rituals. People cannot escape their impact because we belong integrally to the great envelope of the collective unconscious. Bringing into awareness our rootedness in this archetypal foundation is the primary goal of Jungian psychotherapy. It strikes me that the archetypes have a great deal in common with the field influences identified by modern physics, a connection Jung himself acknowledged when he wrote,

> Sooner or later, nuclear physics and the psychology of the uncon-
> scious will draw closer together as both of them, independently
> of one another and from opposite directions, push forward into
> transcendental territory. (Jung 1956, 412)

In this brief Appendix I simply want to highlight another fertile avenue within which we can explore a study of the Great Spirit. It is beyond the scope and remit of the present work, but I highlight it in the hope that someday, some Jungian scholar might consider embracing what should prove to be an exciting and inspiring piece of research.

Notes

[1] I acknowledge the dynamics of Darwinian evolution: natural selection, niche formation, and survival of the fittest, but instead of seeing them as primary, I suggest that they be viewed as some of the strategies nature adopts to facilitate the tripartite process of growth-change-development. Whether on the macro or micro scales of cosmic evolution, growth takes place through change leading to an increase in complexity. It cannot be reduced to the dynamics usually identified as Darwinian, it's more accurately neo-Darwinian (since the original insights of Charles Darwin are still subject to a range of different interpretations). The more we study the evolutionary process, the more we encounter surprise and novelty in its complex emergence.

[2] I deliberately include the notion of paradox in my marvel and appreciation of the natural world. In this regard I draw extensively on the seminal work of Brian Swimme and Thomas Berry (1992), who describe the paradox as the recurring cycle of creation-and-destruction, a process I name elsewhere as that of birth–death–rebirth (O'Murchu 2002; 2010). Unremittingly, we experience creation in turmoil, chaos, and suffering. Paradoxically, all this destructive activity seems essential to the elegance, beauty, and flourishing of creation. A simple but profound example is that of earthquakes. A viable earth is impossible without earthquake activity; if we get rid of earthquakes, earth life as we know it will also disappear. I name this contradictory phenomenon as a *paradox,* and not as a *flaw.* It strikes me that there are no flaws in God's creation, but there is an abundance of paradox, and apparently always will be. Distinguishing between *paradox* and *flaw* seems critically important, an observation I return to several times in this book.

[3] Inflation became established as the standard model of the very early universe in the 1980s. The inflation theory, developed by Alan Guth, Andrei Linde, Paul Steinhardt, and Andy Albrecht, offers solutions to these problems and several other open questions in cosmology. (More in Gribbin 2009, 121ff.; for a brief and informed critique, see Steinhardt 2011.)

[4] *Discernment* is a Christian term describing the process of better understanding what the Spirit of God is asking of us, and how we might best respond. It is widely understood to be an individual process, aided by

a spiritual guide or guru. In conventional usage it enables us to live closer to God in this life, guaranteeing a better chance of obtaining salvation in the afterlife. In the Christian context it is often associated with the spiritual guidelines developed by St. Ignatius of Loyola (in the fourteenth century) translated in our time into the practice of Spiritual Direction.

As used in the present work, I understand discernment within the three fold process developed initially by the Young Christian Workers: see–judge–act (see http://en.wikipedia.org/wiki/Young_Christian Workers). The primary emphasis and the most laborious undertaking involve the first part: the *seeing*. The discerning person, or group, strives to see the meaning of what is being discerned, adopting as deep and large a context as possible. In our time, this requires a multidisciplinary analysis, and may need to be pursued over time spans of months and years rather than days or weeks. At the personal level, it also requires the skills for deep listening, critical reflection, engaging dialogue, and the willingness to explore truth not merely from one but from within several spiritual traditions.

Only when the seeing has been done in depth (and, of course, it is an ongoing process) can we responsibly move to the next stage, *judging*, which is primarily about identifying and appropriating key values to carry forth the wisdom of our seeing. After that, the *action* (for empowerment) flows more easily.

The single biggest obstacle to discernment—in the Western world particularly, and in several of the major religions—is that humans have an addictive tendency to jump straight into *judging*, frequently giving little or no attention to the *seeing*. Consequently, we often end up with disempowering forms of *action* that today are crippling human growth and development in almost every sphere of life, and resulting in inestimable damage and destruction to the living earth itself.

⁵ In many mythologies the gods form a divine family, or *pantheon* (from the Greek *pan*, meaning "all," and *theos*, "god"). The story of a power struggle within a pantheon is common to a large number of world mythologies—for example, the Babylonian *Enuma Elish* centers on Marduk's struggle for supremacy and his eventual victory over Tiamat. Greek mythology features a similar story of struggle between generations. In Greek mythology, the earliest gods were Gaea (Earth) and Uranus (Heaven), and their children were called the Titans. The eldest of the Titans, Cronus, overthrew his father and was eventually overthrown by his own son, Zeus, who became the new master of the universe. Similarly, the Aesir—the pantheon of the Norse gods—had to overcome an older group called the Vanir before gaining power.

⁶ In mystical literature, authors often draw a distinction between the cataphatic, describing God in human language, and the apophatic,

sometimes described as negative theology. Briefly, negative theology is an attempt to achieve unity with the divine source through discernment and contemplation, encountering divine mystery in terms of what God is *not* (*apophasis*), rather than adopting the more cerebral processes of rationality and verbal description. More at http://en.wikipedia.org/wiki/Apophasis.

[7] The Higgs Boson created a media frenzy on December 13, 2011, when scientists at the scientific collider at CERN, Geneva, announced that they had detected in the collider debris traces of what looked like the Higgs Boson particle. The Higgs field gives mass to particles through a process known as the Higgs mechanism. This mass is the missing elusive aspect of what scientists call the *standard model of particle physics*. Reporting this breakthrough, it is noteworthy that heavy emphasis rests on the materiality or physical dimensions (e.g., mass) of particles (atoms)—a crucial part of the machinery of the subatomic world, according to Dr. Stephen Barr of Oxford University. Yet we know that over 99 percent of the atom is empty space, which may in fact be far more crucial to our understanding of the subatomic world than materiality or physicality, as suggested by Pim Van Lommel (2010, 283ff.). Identifying the Higgs Boson may be significant for mainline scientific progress, but there is a deeper and more pervasive truth to the subatomic world, which the media excitement overlooks and the reporting fails to acknowledge.

[8] Note that in the buildup to this conclusion—that the original creative force should be conceived as Spirit rather than the conventional God the Father—I am drawing on key insights from process theology, in which the divine creativity is envisaged as a dipolar phenomenon with primordial and consequent expressions. The *primordial* represents the true essence in and of itself; the *consequent* is the physical expression in an evolving world.

When it comes to pneumatology, the Holy Spirit—as Logos-Sophia—is postulated as the primordial dimension, and Pneuma as the consequent pole. In the consequent role, the work of the Spirit is seen primarily as one of saving-through-reconciliation (see Faber 2008, 239–41, 246ff.) with the historical Jesus as the primary agent of such transformation. Here Process thought seems to be retaining the Christian image of a flawed world that needs Christian redemption, and seems to be contradicting its own foundational desire to transcend and outgrow dualistic splits, while also undermining its own unique insights on the primordial role of the Holy Spirit.

[9] *Intelligent design* refers to a scientific research program as well as a community of scientists, philosophers, and other scholars who seek evidence of design in nature. The theory of intelligent design (ID) holds that certain features of the universe and of living things are best explained by an intelligent cause, not an undirected process such as natural selection. ID theory claims that the intelligent causes are necessary to explain the

complex, information-rich structures of biology and that these causes are empirically detectable. Certain biological features defy the standard Darwinian random-chance explanation, because those promoting an ID stance claim that they have been designed by a Divine, intelligent power. More at www.intelligentdesign.org.

The vast majority of intelligent design theorists are theists. They see the appearance of design that pervades the biological world as evidence for the existence of God. However, the intelligent design theory is not biblical creationism. There is an important distinction between the two positions. Biblical creationists begin with a conclusion that the biblical account of creation is reliable and correct, and that life on earth was designed by an intelligent agent—God. They then look for evidence from the natural realm to support this conclusion. For a valuable overview and critique, see John F. Haught (2003, 85ff.).

10   Scott A. Ellington (in Yong 2009, 7) offers some further intriguing insights on the notion of *ruach elohim* in Genesis 1. In conclusion he states, "The phrase *ruach elohim* is primarily associated not with God's creation, but with his empowerment—the imparting of a prophetic spirit." Veli-Matti Karkkainen (2009, 163) similarly remarks, "Whereas for most other Christians the presence of the Spirit is just that, *presence*, for Pentecostals the presence of the Spirit in their midst implies *empowerment*" (emphasis in original). When indigenous peoples invoke the Great Spirit, it is very much with the understanding of an empowering presence available to them in the whole of creation.

11   The Korean-American scholar, Grace Ji-Sun Kim (2009) describes Chi as "the Spirit which is part of the universe and permeates all living things as it gives life and energy" (122); that same Spirit is bridging the life-force between Creator and creature (Kim 2011, 45). Moreover, "The Spirit is the glorifying and unifying God. In this respect the Spirit is not an energy proceeding from the Father, or from the Son; it is a subject from whose activity the Son and the Father receive their glory and their union, as well as their glorification through the whole creation. . . . The Spirit opens the space in which God can dwell." (Kim 2011, 54).

12   Sigurd Bergmann (2006, 121) notes that Gregory of Nazianzus is uneasy about comparing the Spirit with energy (*Oration* 31.6). It is precisely the capacity for self-movement that distinguishes God's Spirit from energy as such, insofar as energy is understood as following upon an efficient cause. Unlike energy, God's Spirit brings about its own movement. I wonder if Gregory might not think differently if he had the benefit of the scientific insights that we have today.

13   This expansive cosmic view can lead to divergent, opposite insights. Specialists such as Swimme and Berry (1992), along with Primack and Abrams (2006), consider the cosmic influences as central

to the progressive nature of evolution. Broadly accepting the generic worth of such insights, Fred Hoyle (1950) postulates his theory of super-intelligence governing the evolutionary process, while Heinz Pagels (1981) reinterprets Plato's notion of the demiurge as a kind of cosmic code; no human mind, he claims, could have arranged for any message so flawlessly coherent, so strangely imaginative, and sometimes downrightly bizarre. This is the note taken up by John D. Barrow (2011), for whom the big galactic picture leads to very pessimistic conclusions, convinced as he is that everything will one day be consumed by a cosmic cataclysmic fireball. Although this will not happen for millions—in fact, billions—of years, it leaves scholars such as Barrow with a distinctive sense of fatalism and anomie, reminiscent of Steven Weinberg's oft-quoted remark: "The more the universe seems comprehensible, the more it seems pointless." David Deamer (2011), drawing on evidence very similar to Barrow's overview of life and its evolutionary trajectory, reaches a rather different conclusion, leading to a much more optimistic forecast.

[14] Paul Davies (2006, 253–54) cites the example of throwing a dead bird into the air. According to the laws of gravity it will fall in a predictable fashion. Throw a live bird into the air, and it is impossible to predict its behavior. Genetic and neurological factors partially explain what is happening, and they become less significant if the bird links with the patterned flow created by groups of birds in long-haul flights.

[15] *Satyāgraha* can be loosely translated as "soul force," "truth force," or "holding on to truth." It is a philosophy and practice of nonviolent resistance developed and conceived by Mahatma Gandhi, deployed during the Indian independence movement and also during his earlier struggles in South Africa. Satyāgraha theory influenced Nelson Mandela's struggle in South Africa under apartheid, Martin Luther King Jr.'s campaigns during the civil rights movement in the United States, and many other social justice and resistance movements around the world. For valuable insights on this and other aspects of Gandhi's life, see Rynne (2008).

[16] Hence, Davidson's understanding of DNA: DNA is not the primary energy complex for the patterning of life's forms, but only a part of the outworking of the more inward vibrations and patterns within the subtle energy fields, and is present as a kind of holographic, cellular intelligence within every cell of our body. *Prana* (breath) is the life-giving, organizational energy that patterns first the subtle elements and through them the biochemistry, physiology, and anatomical form and function of the living creature (Davidson 1989, 75). Worthy of note, too, is Pim Van Lommel's suggestion that we consider DNA as a primary site for a deeper investigation of how consciousness impacts cellular life and human behavior generally (2010, 284–302).

[17]   The total number of Iroquois today is difficult to establish. About 45,000 Iroquois lived in Canada in 1995. In the 2000 census, 80,822 people in the United States claimed Iroquois ethnicity, with 45,217 of them claiming an Iroquois background. Tribal registrations among the Six Nations in the United States in 1995 numbered about 30,000 in total. The Mohawk is one of the better-known branches, as is the Oneida tribe.

[18]   The Inuit are a group of culturally similar indigenous peoples inhabiting the Arctic regions of Canada (Northwest Territories, Nunatsiavut, Nunavik, Nunavut), Denmark, Greenland, Russia (Siberia), and Alaska. Inuit means "the people" in the Inuktitut language. The Inuit language is grouped under Eskimo-Aleut languages.

[19]   The Navajo are the largest Indian tribe in the United States. They live on the largest reservation in the United States, covering over three states on 17 million acres in the Four Corners area of the Southwest. The states include Arizona, New Mexico, Utah, and a small part of Colorado. The current population is estimated at 250,000.

[20]   The Osage Nation is a Native American Siouan-language tribe in the United States that originated in the Ohio River Valley in present-day Kentucky. Ancestors lived in the area for thousands of years. After years of war with invading Iroquois, the Osage migrated west of the Mississippi River to their historic lands in present-day Arkansas, Missouri, Kansas, and Oklahoma by the mid-seventeenth century. At the height of their power in the early eighteenth century, the Osages controlled the area between the Missouri and Red Rivers. They are a federally recognized tribe based mainly in Osage County, Oklahoma.

[21]   How the Christian notion of the Holy Spirit impacts upon indigenous African religion, specifically on the Yoruba belief system, is the subject of an informative study by African scholar Caleb Oluremi Oladipo (1996). Clearly, Christian influence has penetrated quite deeply, inhibiting Oladipo from reviewing what Spirit might have meant before Christianity arrived in the Yoruba culture. Currently, one can see how Christian influence has been integrated as the Yoruba people view God the Father as the Great Ancestor, Jesus as the Proto-Ancestor, and the Holy Spirit as the Grand Ancestor (Oladipo 1996, 102). According to Oladipo, the Holy Spirit is viewed as the ancestor par excellence, the one that truly continues the work of Christ, and guarantees the final spiritual destiny to which the Yoruba people look forward. How other African religions relate to the Holy Spirit—specifically under the recent influence of Pentecostalism—is reviewed by Allan Anderson (1991).

[22]   In offering the above list of African ethnic groups, I am striving to make information readily accessible to a general readership at the risk of doing so in a manner not congruent with African sensibilities. I am grateful to Dr. Robert Kaggwa of the School of Religious Studies, University of

Roehampton (London), for alerting me to this matter, in the light of which I want to draw the reader's attention to the following related factors: (a) Anthropologists tend to group African groups according to language and customs, e.g., Bantu, Nilotics, Hamites, Nilo-Hamites. These groups can be found in several different countries, alongside other groups with whom they may differ significantly, a complexity that is undermined in creating a linear list. (b) African scholars themselves are reluctant to speak of Africa as a homogenized whole, which to some smacks of a colonial fabrication. When it comes to indigenous belief systems, we are dealing with African traditional religions (plural, not singular), indicative of a diversity and pluralism very different from the imposed uniformity characteristic of religious monotheism. (c) Appropriate language is a challenge in all intercultural research. Although I occasionally use the word "tribe" in this book, I acknowledge that "ethnic group" would be more appropriate. "Syncretism" often carries connotations of religious self-righteous imperialism; I agree with Robert Kaggwa's suggestion about using the word "eclecticism" instead.

23   One example is the Maryknoll Institute of African Studies (MIAS), a research project based in Tangaza College in Nairobi, Kenya (http://www. Mias.edu), under the directorship of Maryknoll missionary priest Michael Kirwen (see Kirwen 1994).

24   The notion of cannibalism dates back to Columbus's accounts of a supposedly ferocious group of cannibals that lived in the Caribbean islands, particularly the Carib tribe in the Lesser Antilles—sometimes called the Caniba, from which we derive the word "cannibal." Cannibalism features in many mythologies, and is most often attributed to evil characters or as extreme retribution for some wrongdoing. A number of stories in Greek and Hindu mythologies involve cannibalism.

In modern Africa, cannibalism is often associated with tribal ritual practices; reliable evidence is difficult to establish. We may be on firmer ground when we adopt the insights from the scholarly research of William Arens (1979), who questions the credibility of reports of cannibalism and argues that the description by one group of people of another people as cannibals is a consistent and demonstrable ideological and rhetorical device to establish perceived cultural superiority.

Many of the allegations of cannibalism related to Africa pertain to warfare or intertribal conflict, where the practice of cannibalism is best seen as one of several barbaric practices arising from the context of prolonged political and social unrest.

25   These principles include:

Ahimsa: Behave in a nonviolent way toward everything in creation.

Satya: Speak the truth; avoid falsehood.

Asteya: Do not steal from others.

Brahma-charya (soul conduct): Remain sexually monogamous with one's spouse.

Aparigraha: Live a detached life. Make do with basics.

26   Cultures and countries strongly influenced by Confucianism include mainland China, Taiwan, Korea, Japan, and Vietnam, as well as various territories settled predominantly by Chinese people, such as Singapore. An estimated 1.5 billion people follow Confucian ideals.

27   Moltmann, it seems, wants to retain the priority and patriarchal ordering of the Trinity while rehabilitating the Holy Spirit in a more dynamic and creative role. Despite many inspiring and stretching insights about the role and work of the Holy Spirit, Moltmann ends up keeping the Spirit subdued to both Father and Son. The ensuing confusion—or perhaps lack of clarity—compels Bergmann (2006, 255) to remark, "One wonders whether Moltmann has written both too much and too little about the Spirit."

28   Derived from the Greek "peri-choresis," which translates as "peri," meaning "around," and "choresis," meaning "to dance" (the same root as choreography), early Christians used the word to describe the relationship between the persons of the Trinity as an eternal Holy dance of each person in the Trinity around and within the others. An image often used to express this idea is that of a "community of being," in which each person, while maintaining a distinctive identity, penetrates the others and is penetrated by them.

29   I am grateful to Samuel Canilang, CMF, director of ICLA in Manila, for sharing the above notes with me. Source information for these and several other quotes can be obtained from Canilang (2008).

30   In volume 3 of his *Systematic Theology*, Tillich attributes the diminished role of the Holy Spirit in Christian faith to the negative relegation of "spirit" in our understanding of human life. Consequently, he seeks to develop a theology of the Holy Spirit as spiritual presence, uniting the power of being with the meaning of being, such that Lampe can speak of "an incarnation of God as Spirit within every man as human spirit" (1977, 45).

31   A fourteenth-century fresco in a small Catholic church southeast of Munich, Germany, depicts a female Spirit as part of the Holy Trinity, according to Leonard Swidler of Temple University (www.pistissophia. org/The_Holy_Spirit/the_holy_spirit.html). The woman and two bearded figures flanking her appear to be wrapped in a single cloak and joined in their lower halves, showing a union of old and new bodies of birth and rebirth.

32   In these complex reflections we need to differentiate as clearly as possible between the suffering in the world that ensues from wrong human intervention and the suffering that is consequent upon the process of

earthly and cosmic evolution. For instance, a lot of human suffering can ensue from an earthquake, yet some human communities—U.S., Canadian, Malaysian—have adopted earthquake-resistant buildings that minimize human suffering and physical damage. Acknowledging that earthquakes are essential to the flourishing of Planet Earth, sections of humanity have learned to cope with the destructive impact of earthquakes. Others have not managed to do so because human resources have not been shared fairly and justly, and these poorer peoples are likely to suffer the cruelest impact from an earthquake. All of this forces us to ask, Where is the real problem? Not with God, I suggest, nor with the earthquake, but *with the human species itself.* When we humans fail to share our resources in a fair and just way, or when we make wrong, irresponsible interventions to support our own greed and selfishness, then we exacerbate the meaninglessness of suffering in the world. We have caused the problem. Resolving it is up to us.

33 Pentecostalism was estimated to number around 115 million followers worldwide in 2000; lower estimates place the figure near 22 million (e.g., Cambridge Encyclopedia), while the highest estimates place the figure between 400 and 600 million. The great majority of Pentecostals are in developing countries, although much of their international leadership is still North American. According to April 2006 edition of the online journal, Christianity Today (www.Christianitytoday.com/ct/2006/7.30. html), classical Pentecostals number 78 million; Charismatics, 192 million; and neo-Charismatics, 318 million. 147 million Africans are either Pentecostals or Charismatics. There are just under one million Pentecostals in the United Kingdom, and over 20 million in the United States. The largest Christian church in the world is the Yoido Full Gospel church in South Korea, founded and led by David Yonggi Cho since 1958, and today numbering over 800,000 members (www.ambassador4Christ.org/yoido_church.html). Two Pentecostal churches in Buenos Aires together attract 150,000 people each week (see www.svchapel.org).

The 2006 survey cited above revealed that 75 percent of Protestants in Latin America are Pentecostals, and nearly 30 percent of this region's population consider themselves Pentecostal or charismatic. One Pentecostal-style church in Brazil, the Universal Church of the Kingdom of God (UCKG), is now in more than ninety countries and claims to have 10 million followers. Its founder owns one of Brazil's largest television stations, a number of newspapers, and a sports team.

34 Physicist-cum-theologian Arthur Peacock (2001, 114–15) makes a similar plea for preserving the personal as foundational to, and inherent in, every conceptualization of the divine: "Does not the very intimacy of our relation to the fundamental features of the physical world, its so-called 'anthropic' features, together with the distinctiveness of personhood, point us in the direction of looking for a best explanation of all-that-is in terms

of some kind of entity that could include the personal? Since the personal is the highest level of unification of the physical, mental and spiritual of which we are aware, it is legitimate to recognize that this Ultimate Reality must be at least personal, or super-personal—that is, it will be less misleading to attach personal predicates to the Ultimate Reality than not to do so at all." Peacock seems to be viewing personhood in rather dualistic terms, suggesting that a failure to adopt personal features inevitably leads to the impersonal. As I suggest later in this chapter, there is a third option—the *transpersonal,* which enables us to transcend the dualism while inviting us into more empowering insights on the meaning of divinity and humanity.

Bibliography

Abram, David. 1996. *The Spell of the Sensuous*. New York: Random House.

Aczel, Amir. 2003. *Entanglement*. New York: Penguin/Plume.

Adeney, Miriam. 2009. *Kingdom without Borders: The Untold Story of Global Christianity*. Downers Grove, IL: IVP Books.

Ahmed, Durre S., ed. 2002. *Gendering the Spirit*. London: Zed Books.

Anderson, Allan. 1991. *Moya: The Holy Spirit in an African Context*. Pretoria: University of South Africa.

Anderson, Robert. 1992. *Vision of the Disinherited: The Making of American Pentecostalism*. Peabody, MA: Hendrickson.

Arens, William. 1979. *The Man-Eating Myth*. New York: Oxford University Press.

Barrow, John D. 2011. *The Reason Why: The Miracle of Life on Earth*. New York: Allen Lane/Penguin.

———, and Frank Tippler. 1988. *The Anthropic Cosmological Principle*. New York: Oxford University Press.

Beck, T. David. 2007. *The Holy Spirit and the Renewal of All Things*. Eugene, OR: Wipf & Stock.

Bergmann, Sigurd. 2006. *Creation Set Free: The Spirit as Liberator of Nature*. Grand Rapids: Eerdmans.

Berry, Thomas. 2006. *Evening Thoughts: Reflecting on Earth as Sacred Community*. San Francisco: Sierra Club Books.

———. 2009. *The Christian Future and the Fate of the Earth*. Maryknoll, NY: Orbis Books.

Betcher, Sharon V. 2007. "Grounding the Spirit: An Ecofeminist Pneumatology." In *Ecospirit: Religions and Philosophies for the Earth*, ed. Laurel Kearns and Catherine Keller, 217–32. New York: Fordham University Press.

Bracken, Joseph. 1991. *Society and Spirit: A Trinitarian Cosmology*. London: Associated University Press.

———. 1995. *The Divine Matrix*. Maryknoll, NY: Orbis Books.

Braden, Gregg. 2009. *The Spontaneous Healing of Belief*. Carlsbad, CA: Hay House.

Budja, Mihael. 2010. "The Archaeology of Death from 'Social Personae' to 'Relational Personhood'." *Documenta Praehistorica* 37, 43–54.

Burgess, Stanley M. 1989. *The Holy Spirit*. Peabody, Mass: Hendrickson Publishers.

Burns, Charlene. 2006. "Altruism in Nature as Manifestation of Divine Energia." *Zygon* 41(1): 125–37.

Canilang, Samuel H. 2008. *Gregory Palamas: Theo-Anthropology and Mysticism According to the Philokalia*. Manila: Claretian Publications.

Catechism of the Catholic Church. 1994. London: Geoffrey Chapman.

Chopra, Deepak. 1989. *Quantum Healing*. New York: Bantam Books.

Chown, Marcus. 2006. *Quantum Theory Cannot Hurt You*. London: Faber & Faber.

Clayton, Philip. 2008. *Adventures in the Spirit*. Minneapolis: Fortress Press.

Clarke, Chris. 2010. *Weaving the Cosmos: Science, Religion and Ecology*. Winchester, UK: O Books.

Clegg, Brian. 2009. *The God Effect: Quantum Entanglement*. New York: St. Martin's Press.

Comblin, Jose. 1989. *The Holy Spirit and Liberation*. Maryknoll, NY: Orbis Books.

Congar, Yves. 1983. *I Believe in the Holy Spirit*. 3 vols. London: Geoffrey Chapman.

Conway Morris, Simon. 2003. *Life's Solution: Inevitable Humans in a Lonely Universe*. Cambridge: Cambridge University Press.

Cox, Harvey. 2001. *Fire from Heaven: The Rise of Pentecostal Spirituality and the Reshaping of Religion in the 21st Century*. New York: DeCapo Press.

Davidson, John. 1989. *The Secret of the Creative Vacuum*. Essex: C. W. Daniel.

Davies, Paul. 1979. *God and the New Physics*. New York: Simon & Schuster.

———. 2006. *The Goldilocks Enigma: Why Is the Universe Just Right for Life?* London: Penguin.

Deamer, David. 2011. *First Life: Discovering the Connections between Stars, Cells and How Life Began*. Berkeley: University of California Press.

De Duve, Christian. 1996. *Vital Dust: Life as a Cosmic Imperative*. New York: Basic Books.

———. 2002. *Life Evolving: Molecules, Life, and Meaning*. New York: Oxford University Press.

Delio, Ilia. 2011. *The Emergent Christ*. Maryknoll, NY: Orbis Books.

Demaille, Raymond J. 1987. *Sioux Indian Religion: Tradition and Innovation*, Norman: University of Oklahoma Press.

Deutsch, David. 2011. *The Beginning of Infinity: Explanations That Transform The World.* New York: Allen Lane.

Dobbs, Betty Jo. 1991. *The Janus Face of Genius: The Role of Alchemy in Newton's Thought.* New York: Cambridge University Press.

De Waal, Frans. 2005. *Our Inner Ape: The Best and the Worst in Human Nature.* New York: Penguin.

———, ed. 2001. *Tree of Origin: What Primate Behavior Can Tell Us about Human Social Evolution.* Cambridge, MA: Harvard University Press.

Dowd, Michael. 2009. *Thank God for Evolution.* San Francisco: Council Oak Books.

Dunn, James G. D. 1998. *Christ and the Spirit—Collected Essays.* Edinburgh: T. & T. Clark.

———. 2002. Vol. 2: *Pneumatology.* Edinburgh: T. & T. Clark.

Dupuis, Jacques. 1997. *Towards a Christian Theology of Religious Pluralism.* Maryknoll, NY: Orbis Books.

Edwards, Denis. 2004. *Breath of Life: A Theology of the Creator Spirit.* Maryknoll, NY: Orbis Books.

———. 2006. *Ecology at the Heart of Faith.* Maryknoll, NY: Orbis Books.

Eliade, Mircea. 1963. *Patterns in Comparative Religion.* New York: Meridian Books.

Etler, Dennis A. 1996. "The Fossil Evidence for Human Evolution in Asia." *Annual Review of Anthropology,* 25 (October), 275–301.

Faber, Roland. 2008. *God as Poet of the World.* Louisville, KY: Westminster/ John Knox Press.

Fee, Gordon. 1994. *God's Empowering Presence: The Holy Spirit in the Letters of Paul.* Peabody, MA: Hendrickson.

Fox, Everett. 1983. *The Five Books of Moses.* New York: Schocken.

Fox, Matthew. 1999. *Sins of the Spirit, Blessings of the Flesh.* New York: Random House.

Fox, Patricia. 2001. *God as Communion.* Collegeville, MN: Liturgical Press.

Gates, Larry. 1994. "Jung's Concept of the Holy Ghost." *Journal of Religion and Health* 33(4): 313–19.

Gehman, Richard. 2005. *African Traditional Religion in Biblical Perspective.* Nairobi: East African Educational Publishers.

Gelpi, Donald. 1984. *The Divine Mother: A Trinitarian Theology of the Holy Spirit.* New York: University Press of America.

Gibbons, Ann. 2007. *The First Human.* New York: Anchor Books.

Gilbert, Paul. 2009. *The Compassionate Mind.* Berkeley, CA: New Harbinger Press.

Gould, Stephen J. 1989. *Wonderful Life.* New York: W. W. Norton.

———. 1996. *Full House: The Spread of Excellence from Plato to Darwin.* New York: Harmony Books.

Gregersen, Niels Henrick. 2006. "The Complexification of Nature." *Theology and Science* 4(1): 5–31.

Green, Brian. 2000. *The Elegant Universe*. New York: Vintage.

———. 2011. *The Hidden Reality*. New York: Knopf.

Gribbin, John. 2009. *In Search of the Multiverse*. New York: Allen Lane.

Haight, Roger. 1999. *Jesus, the Symbol of God*. Maryknoll, NY: Orbis Books.

———. 2008. "Holy Spirit and the Religions," in David H. Jensen ed. *The Lord and Giver of Life*. Louisville, KY: Westminster John Knox Press, 55–69.

Harvey, Graham. 2005. *Animism*. London: Hurst & Co.

Hathaway, Mark, and Leonardo Boff. 2009. *The Tao of Liberation*. Maryknoll, NY: Orbis Books.

Haught, John F. 2003. *Deeper Than Darwin*. Boulder, CO: Westview Press.

———. 2010. *Making Sense of Evolution*. Westminster John Knox Press.

Hawken, Paul. 2007. *Blessed Unrest*. New York: Viking.

Hawking, Stephen. 1988. *A Brief History of Time*. New York: Bantam Books.

Heffner, Philip.1993. *The Human Factor: Evolution, Culture, and Religion*. Minneapolis: Fortress Press.

Hodgson, Peter C. 1994. *Winds of the Spirit*. London: SCM Press.

———. 2004. "The Spirit and Religious Pluralism" in Paul F. Knitter ed. *The Myth of Religious Superiority*, Maryknoll, NY: Orbis, 135–150.

Hollenweger, Walter J. 1997. *The Pentecostals: Origins and Developments Worldwide*. Peabody, MA: Hendrickson.

Hoyle, Fred. 1950. *The Nature of the Universe*, Oxford (UK): Blackwell.

Hrdy, Sarah Blaffer. 2009. *Mothers and Others: The Evolutionary Origins of Mutual Understanding*. Cambridge, MA: Cambridge University Press.

Irwin, Lee, ed. 2000. *Native American Spirituality: A Critical Reader*. Lincoln: University of Nebraska Press.

Isherwood, Christopher. 1980. *Ramakrishna and His Disciples*. Hollywood, CA: Vedanta Press.

Johnson, Elizabeth. 2008. *Quest for the Living God*. New York: Continuum.

Joseph, P. V. 2007. *Indian Interpretation of the Holy Spirit*. Delhi: ISPCK.

Jung, Carl G. 1956. *The Collected Works*, Vols. 9–11 (edited by H. Read). Princeton, NJ: Princeton University Press.

Kalu, Ogbu U. 2008. *African Pentecostalism*. Oxford: Oxford University Press.

Karkkainen, Veli-Matti. 2002. *Pneumatology: The Holy Spirit in Ecumenical, International, and Contextual Perspective*. Grand Rapids: Baker Academic.

————. 2009. *The Spirit in the World: Emerging Pentecostal Theologies in Global Contexts.* Grand Rapids: W. B. Eerdmans.

Kaufman, Gordon D. 2004. *In the Beginning: Creativity.* Minneapolis: Augsburg Fortress.

Kauffman, Stuart A. 1993. *The Origins of Order.* New York: Oxford University Press.

————. 2008. *Reinventing the Sacred.* New York: Basic Books.

Keller, Catherine. 2003. *Face of the Deep: A Theology of Becoming.* New York: Routledge.

————. 2008. *On the Mystery.* Minneapolis: Fortress Press.

Kidwell, Sue, ed. 2001. *A Native American Theology.* Maryknoll, NY: Orbis Books.

Kim, Grace Ji-Sun. 2009. "In Search of a Pneumatology: Chi and Spirit." *Feminist Theology* 18(1): 117–36.

————. 2011. *The Holy Spirit, Chi, and the Other.* New York: Palgrave Macmillan.

Kim, Kirsteen. 2006. "Indian Contribution to Contemporary Mission Pneumatology." *Transformation: International Journal of Holistic Mission Studies.* 23(1): 30–36.

————. 2007. *The Holy Spirit in the World.* Maryknoll, NY: Orbis Books.

King, Joan C. 2004. *Cellular Wisdom.* Berkeley, CA: Celestial Arts.

Kirwen, Michael C. 1994. *The Missionary and the Diviner.* Maryknoll, NY: Orbis Books.

Kovel, Joel. 1991. *History and Spirit.* Boston: Beacon Press.

Kripal, Jeffrey John. 2001. *Roads of Excess, Palaces of Wisdom: Eroticism and Reflexivity in the Study of Mysticism.* Chicago: University of Chicago Press.

Krumpos, R. D. 2011. *The Greatest Achievement in Life: Five Traditions of Mysticism.* eBook: www.supranational.org

LaCugna, Catherine. 1991. *God for Us: The Trinity and Christian Life.* New York: Harper.

Lampe, G. W. H. 1977. *God as Spirit.* Oxford: Clarendon Press.

Lane, Nick. 2009. *Life Ascending.* London: Profile Books.

Laszlo, Erwin. 1998. *The Whispering Pond: A Personal Guide to the Emerging Vision of Science.* Rockport, MA: Element Books.

————. 2004. *Science and the Akashic Field.* Rochester, VT: Inner Traditions.

Leakey, Richard, and Roger Lewin. 1996. *The Sixth Extinction.* London: Weidenfeld & Nicolson.

Lewis-Williams, D. J. 2002. *The Mind in the Cave.* London: Thames & Hudson.

Lipton, Bruce. 2005. *The Biology of Belief.* Santa Rosa, CA: Elite Books.

Lombardo, Thomas. 2006. *The Evolution of Future Consciousness.* Bloomington, IN: AuthorHouse.

Lonergan, Bernard. 1957. *Insight: A Study of Human Understanding.* Vol. 3 of *The Collected Works of Bernard Lonergan.* Toronto: University of Toronto Press.

Marcuse, Herbert. 1964. *One-Dimensional Man.* London: Routledge.

Marshall, Michael. 2011. "Dawn of the Living." *New Scientist* 211 (August 11): 33–35.

Mayson, Cedric. 2010. *Why Africa Matters.* Maryknoll, NY: Orbis Books.

Mbiti, John. 1991. *Introduction to African Religion.* Oxford: Heinemann.

McFadyen, Alistair. 1990. *The Call to Personhood.* Cambridge: Cambridge University Press.

McFague, Sallie. 1987. *Models of God.* Philadelphia: Fortress.

———. 1993. *The Body of God: An Ecological Theology.* Minneapolis: Augsburg Press.

Midgley, Mary. 2010. *The Solitary Self.* Durham, UK: Acumen.

Miller, Donald, and Tetsunao Yamamori. 2007. *Global Pentecostalism.* Berkeley: University of California Press.

Moltmann, Jürgen. 1981. *The Trinity and the Kingdom.* New York: Harper & Row.

———. 1985. *God in Creation.* New York: Harper & Row.

———. 1992. *The Spirit of Life: A Universal Affirmation.* Minneapolis: Fortress .

Moon, Young Bin. 2010. "God as a Communicative System Sui Generis: Beyond the Psychic, Social, Process Models of the Trinity." *Zygon* 45(1): 105–26.

Moore, Thomas. 1992. *Care for the Soul.* New York: HarperCollins

———. 1994. *Soulmates.* New York: HarperCollins.

Morgan, Lewis H. 1962 [1851]. *The League of the Iroquois.* New York: Citadel.

Morowitz, Harold J. 2002. *The Emergence of Everything.* New York: Oxford University Press.

Muller-Fahrenholz, Geiko. 1995. *God's Spirit: Transforming a World in Crisis.* New York: Continuum.

Murphy, Nancey. 1997. *Reconciling Theology and Science: A Radical Reformation Perspective.* Telford, PA: Pandora Press.

Murray, Robert. 2006. "The Holy Spirit as Mother." In *Symbols of Church and Kingdom,* 312–20. New York: T. & T. Clark.

Neville, Robert C. 1991. *Behind the Masks of God.* Albany: State University of New York Press.

Oladipo, Caleb Oluremi. 1996. *The Development of the Doctrine of the Holy Spirit in the Yoruba (African) Indigenous Christian Movement.* New York: Peter Lang.

O'Murchu, Diarmuid. 2002. *Evolutionary Faith.* Maryknoll, NY: Orbis Books.

———. 2008. *Ancestral Grace: Meeting God in Our Human Story.* Maryknoll, NY: Orbis Books.

———. 2010. *Adult Faith.* Maryknoll, NY: Orbis Books.

Orr, Katherine. 2005. *Beautiful Heart, Beautiful Spirit: Shing-ling-mei Wudang Qigong.* Kaneohe, HI: DragonGate Publishing.

Pagels, Heinz. 1981. *The Cosmic Code.* New York: Simon & Schuster.

Panikkar, Raimundo. 2004. *Christophany: The Fullness of Man.* Maryknoll, NY: Orbis Books.

Pannenberg, Wolfhart. 1976. *Theology and the Philosophy of Science.* Louisville, KY: Westminster Press.

———. 1988. "The Doctrine of Creation and Modern Science." *Zygon* 23(1): 3–21.

Peacock, Arthur. 2001. *Paths from Science toward God.* London: Oneworld Publications.

Phan, Peter. 2004. *Being Religious Interreligiously: Asian Perspectives on Interfaith Dialogue.* Maryknoll, NY: Orbis Books.

Pinnock, Clark H. 1996. *Flame of Love.* Downers Grove, IL: IVP Academic.

Primack, Joel, and Nancy Abrams. 2006. *The View from the Center of the Universe.* New York: Riverhead Books.

Rahner, Karl. 1975. *Theological Investigations*, Vol. 13. London: Darton, Longman & Todd.

———. 1978. *Foundations of Christian Faith.* New York: Seabury Press.

Rambo, Shelly. 2010. *Spirit and Trauma: A Theology of Remaining.* Louisville, KY: Westminster John Knox Press.

Reid, Duncan. 1997. *Energies of the Spirit.* Atlanta: Scholars Press.

Reid-Bowen, Paul. 2007. *Goddess as Nature.* Burlington, VT: Ashgate Books.

Rifkin, Jeremy. 2009. *The Empathic Civilization.* Cambridge: Polity Press.

Robinette, Brian D. 2011. "The Difference Nothing Makes: Creatio ex Nihilo, Resurrection and Divine Gravity." *Theological Studies* 72(3): 525–57.

Rolston, Holmes, III. 2006. "Generating Life on Earth: Five Looming Questions." In *The Evolution of Rationality*, ed. F. LeRon Schults, 195–223. Grand Rapids: Eerdmans.

Rosen, Robert. 2005. *Life Itself: A Comprehensive Inquiry into the Nature, Origin, and Fabrication of Life.* New York: Columbia University Press.

Roughgarden, Joan. 2009. *The Genial Gene.* San Francisco: University of California Press.

Ruse, Michael. 1986. *Taking Darwin Seriously.* Oxford: Blackwell.

Rynne, Terrence. 2008. *Gandhi and Jesus.* Maryknoll, NY: Orbis Books.

Saunders, Nicholas. 2003. *Divine Action and Modern Science.* Cambridge: Cambridge University Press.

Schaab, Gloria. 2007. *The Creative Suffering of the Triune God*. New York: Oxford University Press.

Simmons, Ernest L. 2006. "Quantum Perichoresis: Quantum Field Theory and the Trinity." *Theology and Science* 4(2): 137–50.

Smith, Adrian B. 2008. *God, Energy and the Field*. Winchester, UK: O Books.

Smith, James, and Amos Yong. 2010. *Science and the Spirit: A Pentecostal Engagement with the Sciences*. Bloomington: Indiana University Press.

Smolin, Lee. 1997. *The Life of the Cosmos*. Oxford: Oxford University Press.

Spretnak, Charlene. 1991. *States of Grace*. San Francisco: Harper San Francisco.

Steinhardt, Paul. 2011. "The Inflation Debate." *Scientific American* 304, no. 4: 18–25.

———, and Neil Turok. 2007. *Endless Universe*. New York: Doubleday.

Stewart, John. 2000. *Evolution's Arrow: The Direction of Evolution and the Future of Humanity*. Canberra: Chapman Press.

Swimme, Brian. 1996. *The Hidden Heart of the Cosmos*. Maryknoll, NY: Orbis Books.

———, and Thomas Berry. 1992. *The Universe Story*. San Francisco: Harper.

Taylor, John V. 1972. *The Go-Between God*. London: SCM Press.

Taylor, Steve. 2005. *The Fall*. Winchester, UK: O Books.

Teilhard de Chardin, Pierre. 1969. *Human Energy*. London: Collins.

———. 1970. *Activation of Energy*. London: Collins.

Ter Haar, Gerrie. 2009. *How God Became African*. Philadelphia: University of Pennsylvania Press.

Tinker, George E. 2004. *Spirit and Resistance: Political Theology and American Indian*. Minneapolis: Fortress Press.

Ulanowicz, Robert. 2009. *A Third Window: Natural Life beyond Newton and Darwin*. West Conshohocken, PA: Templeton Press.

Van Lommel, Pim. 2010. *Consciousness beyond Life*. New York: HarperCollins.

Verdral, Vlatko. 2011. "Living in a Quantum World." *Scientific American* 304, no. 6: 20–25.

Vigil, Jose Maria, ed. 2010. *Toward a Planetary Theology*. Montreal: Dunamis Publishers.

Vondey, Wolfgang. 2009. "The Holy Spirit in the Physical Universe." *Theological Studies* 70(1): 3–36.

———. 2010. "Does God Have a Place in the Universe? Physics and the Quest for the Holy Spirit." In Smith and Yong 2010, 75–91.

Wallace, Marc. 2002. *Fragments of the Spirit*. Harrisburg, PA: Trinity Press International.

————. 2005. *Finding God in the Singing River.* Minneapolis: Fortress Press.

Ward, Keith. 2000. *Religion and Community.* Oxford: Oxford University Press.

Welker, Michael. 1994. *God the Spirit.* Minneapolis: Fortress Press.

————, ed. 1999. *The Work of the Spirit.* Grand Rapids: Eerdmans.

Wheeler, John A. 1990. "Information, Physics, Quantum: The Search for Links." In *Complexity, Entropy, and the Physics of Information,* ed. W. Zurek, 1–28. Redwood City, CA: Addison-Wesley.

Whitehead, A. N. 1960. *Religion in the Making.* New York: Meridian Books.

Wilber, Ken. 1984. *Quantum Questions: Mystical Writings of the World's Great Physicists.* Boulder, CO: Shambhala Publications.

Wiles, Maurice.1982. *Faith and the Mystery of God.* London: Continuum (Trinity Press International).

Wilson, E. O. 1993. *The Biophilia Hypothesis.* Shearwater Books.

Wink, Walter. 2002. *The Human Being: Jesus and the Enigma of the Son of Man.* Minneapolis: Fortress.

Winter, Miriam Therese. 2009. *Paradoxology: Spirituality in a Quantum Universe.* Maryknoll, NY: Orbis Books.

Yong, Amos. 2005. *The Spirit Poured Out on All Flesh.* Grand Rapids: Baker Academic.

————, ed. 2009. *The Spirit Renews the Face of the Earth.* Eugene, OR: Pickwick Publications.

Young Lee, Jung. 1996. *The Trinity in Asian Perspective.* Nashville: Abingdon Press.

Zizioulas, John. 1985. *Being as Communion.* New York: St. Vladimir's Seminary Press.

Index

Aborigines, spirituality of, 93–95
Adeney, Miriam, 179, 180
Advaita, 163
Africa/Africans
  belief systems of, 105–13
    and connection with natural
    world, 100, 101
    Christian influence on, 113, 114,
    115, 116, 117
    and human origins, 99, 102
    Islamic influence on, 113, 114
agape, and divine communication, 56
Ahimsa, 122
Akasha, 33, 122
Akashic field, 33
Altner, Gunter, 49
altruism, 75
alusi, 110
Amen, 132
Anapanasati Sutta (mindfulness of
  breathing), 124
ancestor worship, 104
ancestral spirits, 107, 110, 111, 112,
  113, 129, 130
angakkuq, 90
animism, African, 103, 104
anthropology, transcendental, 82,
  152, 153
Appasamy, A. J., 123
Aristotle, 26, 76, 189, 191
Arrhenius, Svante, 66
Asia
  and human origins, 120
  indigenous religions/spirituality
  of, 119, 120, 130–33
  religions of, 121–26
  religious environment, 119, 120
Assagioli, Roberto, 188

Assemblies of God, 174
atomic world, 32
Aum, 132
aura, 46
autopoiesis, 48, 49, 56, 79, 80, 187
Azusa Street Revival, 172, 173, 205

Bakongo, belief system of, 111
baptism, in Holy Spirit, 176
Barrow, John, on origins of life, 65
Barth, Karl, 141
befriending, 166
belonging, 191
Bemba, belief system of, 111, 112
Bergmann, Sigurd, 137, 196, 204
Berry, Thomas, 55, 79, 80, 100, 101,
  187, 188, 192
Betcher, Sharon V., 98
big bang, 19, 20, 39
biophilia, 75
birthing, as creation, 149, 150
Blackfoot People, religion of, 93
Boff, Leonardo, 80, 198
bomohs, 133
Bracken, Joseph, 52, 135
Brahma, 122
Brahman, 122
brain, and mind, 17, 18
brane, 37
Buddhism, 123, 124
  and the Spirit, 124
Burns, Charlene, 75
Bwembya, 112

cells, and memory, 32, 83
CERN. See European Organization
  for Nuclear Research
chaos, and spirit, 29

Chenchiah, P., 123
Chettiar, V. Chakkari, 123
Chi, 45, 110, 117, 120, 127, 128, 129, 216n11
Chief Seattle, on web of life, 96
Chopra, Deepak, 32, 83
Chown, Marcus, 18
Chukwu, 110
Church of God in Christ, 174
church, and work of the Holy Spirit, 141, 142, 143
Clayton, Philip, 11, 39, 40, 138, 154, 187
cocreating/cocreation, 45, 56, 65, 97, 100, 102, 138, 149, 150, 151, 168, 185, 192, 193, 206
collective unconscious, 212
Comblin, José, 86, 87
communion, 75, 80, 187, 188
compassion, 184
condor, in Inca tradition, 91
Confucianism/Confucius, 128, 129
Congar, Yves, 142
consciousness
    and Akashic field, 33, 34
    and creativity, 38, 39
    and Holy Spirit, 33, 34
cosmic background radiation, 18
Cox, Harvey, 180
creatio ex nihilo, 22, 24, 28, 39, 150
creatio ex profundis, 25, 28, 30, 39, 40, 150
creation
    anthropocentric priority of, 22, 23, 59, 6 5, 71
    and the big bang, 20
    community of, 75–84
    by dismemberment of primo dial being, 22, 23
    erotic Spirit in, 155–69, 186
    and Genesis, 23, 24
    and the Great Spirit, 198, 199
    and pneumatological theology of, 83
    and primacy of Spirit, 65
    as primary revelation, 12–15; of God, 55
    Spirit at work in, 162
    spirit energy in, 130, 198
    by splitting or ordering of primordial unity, 23

supernatural in, 57–60
    wisdom of, 11, 12
creation-and-destruction, paradox of, 81, 165, 213n2
creation myths, 22–26, 89, 90, 109
creativity, 24, 38, 39, 149, 150
    divine, 13, 14, 38, 39
Cunningham, David, 191

dabhar, 43, 44, 45
dance, and creation, 36
Davidson, John, 35, 36, 39, 63
Davies, Paul, 21, 26, 68, 73
Deamer, David, 72
Deleuze, Gilles, 79
Delio, Ilia, 149
Demallie, Raymond J., 88
Diadochos of Photiki, 144
differentiation, 79, 187
discernment, 21, 213–14n4
DNA, 66, 83, 185, 217n16
Dowd, Michael, 19, 26
dread, and God and the universe, 29
Dreamtime/Dreaming, 94, 95, 97
dualism, 9
Dunn, James G. D., 146
Dupuis, Jacques, 147
Durga, 132
Duve, Christian de, 63, 65

earth, as center of universe, 23
earth diver creation, 22
ecotheology, 158
Edwards, Denis, 137, 139, 142, 148, 151, 158, 162, 187, 195
Einstein, Albert, 3, 29, 76, 77, 78
Eliade, Mircea, and myths of origin, 22, 23
Eliot, T. S., 5, 15
emergence myths, 22
emptiness, fecund, 63
energy, 32–35, 198
energy, and Holy Spirit, 4, 143, 144, 198
    divine, 144
    home of, in humans, 45
    scientific understanding of, 45, 46, 47
ensoulment, 104
entanglement, 77, 78, 79, 80
entrainment, 79

epiclesis, 202
epigenetics, 49
Epstein, Mark, 119
eros, God/Spirit and, 155–69
erotic
    and creativity, 157, 158, 186
    and divinity, 159, 160
Eucharist, and Spirit, 202, 203
European Organization for Nuclear
    Research (CERN), 21, 28, 161,
    215
evolution, 9, 68, 69, 185, 203
experience, 5, 6

Faber, Roland, 24, 25, 52, 155, 157,
    158
Faraday, Michael, 51
field theory, 46, 51
flatness problem, 19
Four Directions, 93
foursquare gospel, 175
Fox, Everett, 24
Fox, Matthew, 168, 169
Fox, Patricia, 191
Fox, Sidney, 66, 67
fractals, 36
Frazer, James, 103
friendship, as relation with Holy
    Spirit, 151, 166
future, lure of, and the Spirit, 203, 204

Gaia hypothesis, 70, 71
Gates, Larry, 211
Genesis, and creation, 23, 24, 29
genial gene, 184
Gilbert, Paul, 184
glossolalia. See tongues, speaking in/
    interpreting
God
    as anthropocentric projection, 26
    in creation, 57–60
    as creativity, 58
    idea of, in Stephen Hawking, 26
    mind of, 27
    philosophical speculation about, 14
God/gods, and creation, 26
Gould, Jay, 69
Gould, Stephen J., 75
Great Chain of Being, 73
Great Earth Mother, 95, 96, 123,
    130, 131, 132, 133, 141, 149,
150, 154, 157, 158, 159, 161,
    167, 206
Great Mystery, 27, 88, 93
Great Spirit
    Aboriginal wisdom of, 85–98
    in African religions, 116, 117
    in Asian indigenous religions, 130,
        131, 200
    Brahman as, 122, 123
    and Chinese belief, 126, 127
    and created order, 83
    and *creatio ex profundis*, 39
    and creation, 26, 30, 40, 198, 199
    and Divine Life, 10, 11
    foundational beliefs about, 85–86
    groundedness in, 98
    in Hopi belief, 89, 90
    indigenous understanding of, 4,
        11, 12, 30, 55, 84, 85–98, 124,
        157, 197, 198, 200
    and Jainism, 121
    and life, 73
    as life force, 86, 157, 158, 186,
        200
    and lived experience, 86
    in Native American spirituality,
        97–98
    and origins of life, 64
    and the real, 124
Gregersen, Niels Henrik, 50
Gregory of Nazianzus, 196, 204
Gregory of Sinai, 144
Gregory Palamas, 144
Gribbin, John, 61

Haight, Roger, 146, 147
Harvey, Graham, 103
Hathaway, Mark, 80, 198
Haught, John F., 203
Ha-wen-ne-yu, 88
Hawking, Stephen, 21, 26, 27,
Hawking-Turok Instanton Theory, 20
Heffner, Philip, on humans as
    co-creators, 40
Hegel, G. F. W., 11
hiddenness, divine, 56
Higgs, Peter, 33
Higgs field, 33, 215n7
Hildegard of Bingen, 141
Hinduism, 122, 123
Hodgson, Peter C., 12, 59, 190

holistic analysis, 8
Holy Spirit
  and befriending, 166
  Christian idea of, 12, 13
  in Christian theology, 137–54
  and creation, 22, 39, 40
  and energy, 4, 198
  hiddenness of, 56
  and Hindu *Shakti*, 132
  indwelling of, 138, 139
  in Islam, 125, 126
  as mother figure, 151
  as Paraclete, 167–69
  new pneumatology of, 138–40
  and passion, 198
  and Pentecostals, 178
  and self-organization, 49
  and *Shakti*, 123
  and Sophia Wisdom, 150, 151,
    158
  and spirit, 198
  universal activity of, 155, 156
  See also Great Spirit, Spirit/spirit
Homo erectus, 120
Homo floresiensis, 120
Homo sapiens, 93, 120
Hopi, belief system of, 89, 90
horizon problem, 19
Hoyle, Fred, 66
human beings
  and capacity to relate, 185
  origins of, 23
  as transpersonal, 188, 189, 190,
    191
  and the web of life, 184, 185
Human Genome Project, 49
Huygens, Christian, 79

Ibo (Igbo), belief system of, 110,
    116, 117
illusion, and nonduality, 164
immune system, 50
impermanence, 124
Inca, religion of, 91, 92
Incarnation, 102, 152, 211, 220
indigenous experience, 8
individualism, 183, 184
infinite open universe, 20
inflation
  and the big bang, 19, 20, 39,
    213n3

eternal, 20
information, and origins of life, 64,
    68, 69
intelligence, human, 11, 12, 13
intelligent design, 38, 50, 165,
    215–16n9
interconnectedness, theory of, 72
interdependence, 75, 76
interiority, 79, 80, 187, 188
Inuit, and Great Spirit, 90
Iroquois, and Great Spirit, 88
Islam, 125, 126

Jainism, 121, 122
James, William, 188
Jesus
  and creation, 152, 153
  as divine and human, 152, 153
  as empowered by the Spirit, 201
John (Gospel author), on Jesus and
    the Spirit, 201
John of Damascus, spiritual view of
    energy of, 45
Johnson, Elizabeth, 43, 97, 123, 140,
    141, 148, 151, 158
Joseph, P. V., 123
Jung, Carl, and the Holy Spirit, 132,
    188, 211, 212

k'u, 92
Kaggen, 108
Kali, 132
Kalu, Ogbu U., 177
kami, 128
Karkkainen, Veli–Matti, 171, 176,
    206
Kauffman, Stuart A., 58, 64
Kaufman, Gordon D., 14, 24, 58
Keller, Catherine, 25, 28, 39, 40,
    150, 154, 155, 187
khora, 24, 25, 150
ki, 45, 127. See also chi
Kikuyu, belief system of, 107, 108
Kim, Grace Ji-Sun, 45
Kim, Kirsteen, 59, 147
Knitter, Paul F., 119
Kripal, Jeffrey John, 160

LaCugna, Catherine, on the Trinity,
    140, 141, 191
Lampe, G. W. H., 146

Lane, Nick, 67
Large Hadron Collider, 21
Lash, Nicholas, 141
Laszlo, Ervin, 31, 33
Lee, Young, 131
Lenshina, Alice, 112
levitating super-turtle, 73
life
  age of, 65
  as cosmic process, 71–72
  and developing complexity, 68, 69
  features of, 68
  human, and the cosmic-
    planetary story, 12
  and information, 68, 69
  and knowledge, 69, 70
  origins of, 63–74
  from the seabed, 67
  as system, 70–71
  and what it does, 68, 69
  and wisdom, 69, 70
life elements, core, 67
life force, 6, 11, 13, 14, 24, 26, 37,
    39, 40, 45, 50, 55, 56, 68, 73,
    84, 86, 88, 92, 93, 112, 127,
    141, 142, 158, 161, 162, 167,
    186, 196, 197, 200, 209
Lipton, Bruce, 49
Logos, 22, 145, 158
Logos Christology, 145
Logos-Sophia, and creation, 25, 158
Lonergan, Bernard, methodology of,
    5–7
Long, Charles H., 22, 23
Lovelock, James, 70

Maasai, belief system of, 105, 106
Macquarrie, John, 141
Malinke (Mandinka), belief system
    of, 112, 113
Maori, religious beliefs of, 130, 131
Marcuse, Herbert, 7, 189, 199
Maslow, Abraham, 188
Maturana, Humberto, 48
Maximos the Confessor, 144
Maya, 132
  traditional religion of, 92, 93
McFague, Sallie, 141, 148, 166
meditation, 124
memory, and cells, 32
Middle Spirit, 44, 72, 166

Midgley, Mary, 48, 49, 199
Miller-Urey experiment, 66
mind, and ultimacy, 27, 28
mindfulness, 123, 124
Moltmann, Jürgen, 43, 51, 75, 138,
    139, 156, 165, 196
Moon, Young Bin, 56
Moore, Thomas, 183
Morgan, Lewis H., 88
Morowitz, Harold J., 71
Morris, Simon Conway, on life, 64
M-theory, 37
Muller-Fahrenholz, Geiko, 44
multiverse, 20, 21, 61, 149
Murphy, Nancey, 54
Murphy, Roland, 158
myths of origin. *See* creation myths

Native Americans, and Great Spirit,
    87–93
natural selection, 69
natural world, African connection
    with, 100, 101
nature spirits, 111
Navajo
  and relationality of all living
    things, 90, 91
  religion of, 90, 91
Nesteruk, Alexei, 31
Neville, Robert C., 11
Newton, Isaac, 52, 53
Ngai, 105, 106, 107
nganga (healers), 111
Niitsítapi (Original People), 93
Nikhilananda, Swami, 132
nkisi (fetishes), 111
Nkulunkulu, 106
nondualism, philosophy/spirituality
    of, 163, 164
nonduality, Spirit of, 163–66
nothing, as something, 35, 36
nyama, 112, 113
nyamakalaw, 112
Nzambe, 111

Odal, Crace, 131
Odinani, 110
Oglala Lakota (Sioux), and Great
    Spirit, 88, 89
Old Man, 93
Olodumare, 109

one-dimensional man, 7, 189, 199
original blessing, 100
Originating Source, 11
orisha, 109
Osage, pantheistic religion of, 92
Otto, Rudolf, on the numinous, 14

Pacha Mama (earth mother), 91
Pacha Tata (earth father), 91
panentheism, 11, 39, 55, 87, 198
Pannenberg, Wolfhart, 51, 156, 157
Panikkar, Raimundo, on Jesus and
    the Spirit, 201, 202
Panspermia, 66
Paraclete, 142, 167–69
patriarchy, 9, 54, 55, 81, 114, 116,
    150, 157
    and creation, 25, 26
Paul, Saint
  on Jesus and the Spirit, 201
    theology of the Spirit in, 209,
    210
Pentecost, in Africa, 102, 103, 117
Pentecostal Church of God, 174
Pentecostal movement, 171–81, 205,
    206, 221n33
Pentecostal World Conference, 174
Pentecostalism
  in Africa, 117
  as symbolic of Spirit energy, 179,
    180, 181
Pentecostals
  and church origins, 174, 175
  and Holy Spirit, 178
  impact on conventional
    churches, 177–79
  as social and political force, 178,
    179
Penzias, Arno, 18
personalism, 135, 187, 188
personhood, and the Spirit, 199
peyote religion, 92
Philo of Alexandria, 145
Planck, Max, 37, 38, 39
Plato, 24, 25, 76, 150
pneuma, 44, 127
Polkinghorne, John, 54
Pollard, William, 54
Prana, 45
predator–prey phenomenon, 72
primordial–soup theory, 66, 67

primordial spirit power, 29, 116
profundity, 28, 29. See also creatio
    ex profundis
puma, in Inca tradition, 91

qabuvil, 92
Qi. See Chi
qigong, 127
quantum-based divine action, 54, 55
quantum theory, 76, 77
    and role of Holy Spirit, 53, 54, 55
quantum vacuum zero–point energy,
    33

Rahner, Karl, 82, 152, 153
raison d'être, theological, 50–57
Ramakrishna, Sri, 132
Rambo, Shelly, 44, 52, 72, 81, 164,
    166, 168, 171
Rangi, 130
Ratzinger, Josef, 145, 146
real, as relational, 76
reason, 9
Reid-Bowen, Paul, 159, 161, 162
relationality, 7
    and divinity, 141
    and the Trinity, 4, 81
    of all living things, 90, 91
    theological implications of, 80, 81
    See also communion, relationship,
      web of life
relationships
    and creatures, 75–84
    vibrational, 78–80
religion
    and cosmic origins, 22–26
    and science, 5, 13, 31
reproduction, human, and erotic lure
    of the Spirit, 186
revivals, 172, 173
Rogers, Carl, 188
Rolston, Holmes, on origins of life,
    64
Rosen, Robert, 71
Roughgarden, Joan, 184
ruach, 44, 45, 216n10
ruach elohim, 44, 186, 187, 216
Ruse, Michael, 69
Russell, Letty, 141
Russell, Robert J., 54

San bushmen, 108, 109
 and ancestral spirits, 108
Satipatthana Sutta (attending to
 mindfulness), 124
satyāgraha, 80, 81, 166, 217
Saunders, Nicholas, 54
Schaab, Gloria L., 58, 59
Schrödinger, Erwin, 77
Schüssler Fiorenza, Elisabeth, 123,
 151, 158
science
 and divine truth, 21
 and the mystical, 26, 27, 28
 and religion, 53, 54, 55
 and Spirit, 51, 156, 157
scripture, literal interpretation of,
 175, 176
selfish gene, 49
self-organization
 and energy, 48–50
 and Holy Spirit, 49
sexuality, 186
Seymour, William J., 172, 173
Shakti, 132
 and Holy Spirit, 123
shamanism, 90
 and Great Spirit, 133–35
shamans, 108, 109, 133, 134
Sharon Bible School, 174
Shinto, 128
Shiva, 122
Simmons, Ernest L., 56
singularity, 149
snake, in Inca tradition, 91
Sophia tradition, 158
Sophia Wisdom
 and creation, 158, 159, 162
 and Spirit, 158
Sotuknang, 90
Spider Woman/Spider Grandmother,
 90
Spirit/spirit
 Absolute, 11
 and Africa, 99–117
 in African religion, 100–2, 114
 biocentric, 162, 163
 and church, 142
 and creation, 29
 Eastern/Orthodox view of, 143,
 144
 and entanglement, 80

erotic, female metaphors for, 158
 and erotic creation, 161–63
 as erotic force, 157–59, 186
 and Eucharist, 202, 203
 as force that energizes all of
 creation, 51, 52, 198. *See also*
 life force
 gifts of, 60, 61
 as Great Mother, 157
 and person, 186
 personal presence of, 187
 and personhood, 199
 and relationality, 84, 190
 role in Trinity, 200, 201
 transpersonal, 192, 193
 at work in created universe, 53,
 156
Spirit Christology, 144–47
Spirit energy, 44, 45, 198. *See also*
 energy
Spirit force, 52, 107. *See also* life
 force
Spirit of life, 72–73
Spirit power, 112, 113
spirits
 African, 105–13
 in Shinto, 128
spiritualism/spiritualists, and the
 Great Spirit, 207, 208
spirituality
 Chinese, 126, 127
 Eastern, Western view of, 135
 indigenous African, 114, 115
 of Native Americans, 96–98
 Polynesian, 130, 131
 and religion, 9
spiritus, 44
Spretnak, Charlene, 98
string theory, 78
 and creation, 36, 37
strings, vibrational, 35–37
Sun Tzu, 127
surplus of meaning, 164
Swimme, Brian, 34, 35, 79, 80, 187,
 188
synesthesia, 200
systems, relational theory of, 71

T'ien, 129
Tahiti Taa-roa, 130
Taoism, 129, 130

tapu, 131
Tawa (Sun Spirit), 99
Taylor, John V., 1, 3, 44, 50, 51, 84, 160
Teilhard de Chardin, Pierre, 59, 72, 73, 152, 206
Ten Commandments, of indigenous Americans, 96
thealogy/theology, 161, 162
theory of everything (TOE), 73
Thomas Aquinas, on creation, 12
Tillich, Paul, 146
tongues, speaking in/interpreting, 173, 175
transpersonal, 6, 13, 15, 39, 53, 55, 56, 60, 86, 103, 130, 135, 149, 188, 189, 190, 191, 192, 195, 200, 210, 222
Trinity, 3, 4, 13, 81, 137, 138, 139, 140, 141, 186, 191
  Asian Christian theologians on, 147, 148, 149, 200
  Eastern/Orthodox view of, 143, 144
  reenvisioning of, 153, 154
Turok, Neil, on infinite open universe, 20
Tylor, Edward, and animism in Africa, 103

Ulanowicz, Robert, 71
Ungambikula, 94
United Pentecostal Church, 174
unity and diversity, and Great Spirit, 6
universe
  age of, 9
  evolutionary, 9
  origins of, 18, 19, 20, 21
  and primordial sacredness, 192
  Spirit at work in, 156

vacuum
  creative, 31–42
  energetic, 32–35

Van Lommel, Pim, 33, 34, 39, 188
Varela, Francisco, 48, 49
Verdral, Vlatko, 77
Vishnu, 122
von Rad, Gerhard, 187
Vondey, Wolfgang,, 206

Waal, Frans de, 75
Wakan Tanka, 88
Wa-kon-tah, 92
Wallace, Marc I., 59, 104, 148, 162, 163, 165, 166
Ward, Keith, 54
web of life, 108, 184, 185
Westermann, Claus, 187
Wheeler, John A., 33, 64
Whitehead, A. N., 24
Wilber, Ken, 55, 73, 149, 188
wild, Spirit of, 159–61
Wiles, Maurice, 146
William, Daniel Day, 183
Wilson, E. O., 75
Wilson, Robert, 18
Winter, Miriam Therese, 60, 63, 77
wisdom
  human and divine, 9, 13
  of indigeneous peoples, 10, 197, 198
  multidisciplinary, 8
witchcraft, 112, 115
Witten, Edward, 37
Wittgenstein, Ludwig, 195
Word of God, 43, 132

Yellow Emperor, 127
Yong, Amos, 83, 178, 179, 180, 181, 186, 187, 206
Yoruba, belief system of, 109, 116, 117

zero-point energy, 32, 33
Zizioulas, John D., 75, 141, 142, 191
Zulu, belief system of, 106, 107